Death with Dignity

The Case for Legalizing Physician-Assisted Dying and Euthanasia

COLLECTION MANAGEMENT

Death with Dignity

The Case for Legalizing Physician-Assisted Dying and Euthanasia

Robert Orfali

Mill City Press
Minneapolis

Copyright © 2011 by Robert Orfali, LLC
www.DeathWithDignityBook.com

Mill City Press, Inc.

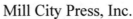

Minneapolis, MN 55401
Tel. 612-455-2294
www.millcitypublishing.com

Library of Congress Cataloging-in-Publication data

Orfali, Robert.
Includes bibliographical references.
1. Death—United States. 2. End-of-life—United States. 3. Terminal illness—United States. 4. Palliative care and hospice—United States. 5. Euthanasia—United States. 6. Physician-assisted dying—United States. I. Title.
First Edition 2011

ISBN-13: 978-1-936780-18-1
LCCN: 2011923739

Cover design by Jayne Cloutier

Printed in the United States of America

179.7

In Memory of My Soulmate
Jeri Edwards Orfali
September 5, 1952 - June 19, 2009

An extraordinary woman radiant in beauty and aloha.
I wrote this book to help pass "Jeri's Bill"

Table of Contents

Table of Contents

Introduction

"People don't want to do this underground or covertly, with hushed tones, with great risks to themselves and their loved ones. They want to have their physician involved. They want hospice care involved. They want their family there without shame or risk."

—Barbara Coombs, CEO, Compassion & Choices[1]

As Dr. Ira Byock so eloquently reminds us, "We are, each one of us, at every moment, a heartbeat away from death." Most of us prefer to avoid thinking about our death. If we happen to think about it, we tend to imagine a quick, painless death—a sudden heart attack, accident, or a Hollywood-style instant death: Poof! Gone! Unfortunately, the diseases that once killed us swiftly (pneumonia, influenza, cholera, infections, and massive heart attacks) have been replaced by the Big Six—heart disease, cancer, stroke, lung disease, diabetes, and Alzheimer's. Typically, these diseases are chronic, long-term, and degenerative. Dying in the age of chronic disease is an extremely complicated process that involves a lot of anguish, pain, and suffering. The lucky few will go suddenly. But the remaining 80% will not leave life the way they would have liked to: "at home and without needless suffering."[2]

Most of us will die in small steps. We'll find ourselves navigating through a labyrinth of confusing end-of-life choices. We will spend our last days (often years) in sterilized torture chambers—hospitals, nursing homes, and even hospices. The terminally ill needlessly

---

[1] Robbie Brown, "Arrests Draw New Attention to Assisted Suicide," *New York Times*, March 10, 2009.

[2] Stephen P. Kiernan, *Last Rights: Rescuing the End of Life System From the Medical System* (St. Martin's Press, 2007).

endure torture at the end of their lives. Did I say *torture*? Yes, let's call it by its name. In this case, both the torturers and the tortured are us. Our archaic laws prevent our doctors from assisting us with our death when we voluntarily request it. In most states, we haven't repealed these laws yet. Consequently, there is no one to blame but ourselves. We have put legal shackles on the people who can help us die with dignity.

We have the technology that enables us to avoid this needless suffering. We have the control switch that can end it all, on request. It's called *euthanasia*, which in Greek means "an easy and gentle death." It's the technology we use to lovingly end a pet's painful life. We make the choice of euthanasia (or painless death) for them. However, no one can, nor should, make that choice for us. It must be *voluntary euthanasia*—we would have to voluntarily request the prescription when we are terminally ill. As an added precaution, we would self-administer it. This type of euthanasia is called *assisted dying*. If we legalize it, as we have in Oregon and Washington, doctors will simply add it to their arsenal of end-of-life care. Compared to the current options, this would be, by far, the most humane, dignified, and painless final exit. As a society, we would have legalized death with dignity. It would become another end-of-life choice—another way to go. Having that choice does not necessarily mean that we would exercise it. Think of it as insurance—it buys us peace of mind. It's there if we need it. We can always choose to die the old way; most of us will.

What's Taking So Long?

So why isn't euthanasia legal? Suicide, of course, is not against the law in the United States and most advanced countries. *Assisted suicide*, however, is not legal. To do assisted dying right, it would have to be integrated into the practice of medicine. We need the help of doctors, nurses, and hospices to make it all work seamlessly. According to the U.S. Supreme Court, the decision to legalize euthanasia must be done at the state level. Every state must have this discussion and then put it to a vote. Some states—for example, Oregon—have had this discussion and lifted the prohibition. In the 2006 landmark case *Gonzalez v. Oregon,* the U.S. Supreme Court reaffirmed its position, by a 6-3 decision, in support of Oregon.

For most states, however, the goal remains elusive—very close, but no cigar. According to polls, the U.S. public is strongly in favor of euthanasia. For example, in a 2003 poll in Hawaii, where I live, the public was 71% in favor with 20% opposed. Yet, the *Death with Dignity* bill continues to fail year after year. The last time, our legislators failed to pass it by a two-vote margin.

So why does the majority not prevail? The answer is that the 20% opposed are strongly-motivated, well-financed, and highly-organized. On the other hand, the 71% who are pro-euthanasia are almost leaderless. Most of us prefer to avoid the topic of death: who wants to get up on a sunny Hawaiian day and go lobby the legislators for a better death? We have other things to do with our lives. There are exceptions. I was able to identify three groups who at various times have put some energy into the assisted-dying cause:

- ***Physicians, but not all.*** When it comes to assisted dying, the medical establishment is a house divided. In 2006, the *American Medical Women's Association (AMWA)* adopted a policy in support of Aid in Dying. In 2008, the *American Medical Students' Association* adopted a policy reiterating and broadening its support of Aid in Dying. However, the *AMA* hierarchy remains firmly against it, even though there is strong support among its members. Physicians are taught to fight disease till the very end. Consequently, they don't do death well. But, times are changing. The new field of palliative medicine is about end-of-life care and pain management. It has helped reduce some of the terminal torture, especially when coupled with hospice care. In addition, there is a vast underground of doctors who quietly (and illegally) help their patients die. It's all very secretive. Sometimes, they go public. The most famous example is

Dr. Jack Kevorkian, whose flamboyant mercy killings ignited a national debate on euthanasia.

- *People who are terminally ill.* Some may get involved because they know death is coming. Typically, they are fighting their own disease and have little energy to give to the general cause of euthanasia. Instead, they attend self-deliverance conferences hoping to obtain information about do-it-yourself dying. What pills? How many? How do I take them? They also need names of compassionate doctors who will write prescriptions to help them die.

- *Family members who navigated a loved one through death.* These are typically people who witnessed the agony and suffering of the last days and feel that more could have been done for the dying. They now better understand the system and know its shortcomings. Their lives in the aftermath have taken a new direction, and they are determined to help others (and themselves) find a better way of dying. Some form or join advocacy groups for assisted dying. For example, Derek Humphry founded the *National Hemlock Society* after helping his fatally-ill wife, Jean, die. In his words, "She asked me to help her end her life."[3] In 1991, he self-published *Final Exit*, which sold over half a million copies and remained on the *New York Times* bestseller list for 18 weeks. It's an instruction manual for do-it-yourself euthanasia. In 2005, *Hemlock* merged with another organization to become *Compassion & Choices*, which is now the largest U.S. advocacy group for patients' rights at the end of life.

As you can see, this is a mixed bag of organizations and accidental activists. Many of the activists are not in it for the long run. They simply want to inform the public and then get on with their lives. Their opponents, however, are in it for the long run.

So, Why Did I Write This Book?

I belong to the third group. I decided to do something after I helped navigate my soulmate, Jeri, through the maze that led to her natural

---

[3] Derek Humphry, *Final Exit* (Carol Publishing, 1991).

death from ovarian cancer. I described the experience and process in my book *Grieving a Soulmate*. To net it out, I was traumatized by Jeri's death process and it had a big impact on my grieving. The scenes from the last days kept haunting me. Consequently, I spent a long time trying to understand what had happened. Could we have done better? Did Jeri needlessly suffer? Did I let her down? Ironically, Jeri had the perfect hospice death—she died relatively quickly from a blood clot. But I was still haunted by the 16 hours of "torture" she endured at the end of her life.

Jeri was a strong proponent of active euthanasia, but that's not how she died: it wasn't a legal option in the state of Hawaii. During my grieving, I constantly ruminated over her hospice death and tried to compare it with the assisted-dying alternative. I came to the conclusion that those 16 hours of needless torture could have been avoided had euthanasia been a choice for her. I also concluded that hospice gave Jeri the best possible death under the circumstances. And for that, I will always be grateful.

Like all terminal patients, Jeri ought to have been allowed to decide how she wanted to die. She was not given the opportunity to make that choice. Consequently, I wrote this book to help make it a choice for others. It's my tribute to Jeri. As I said, Jeri had a very soft landing. Many won't be that lucky. Their torture may extend over weeks and months. I pity them and their survivors. We must give everyone the choice to avoid this final torture if they so desire.

This book may be short, but it's packed with information. I only use Jeri's personal narrative to illustrate some of the key decision points. This book is not about Jeri. It's about euthanasia and why it must be legalized. Specifically, I advocate the legalization of physician-assisted dying modeled after Oregon's *Death with Dignity Act*. My contribution to the effort is to help inform the public by making the book freely available in all e-book forms—including Kindle, iPad, iPhone, Nook, Android, and Sony. So just tell your friends to download it into their readers. You can't beat "free." Send them an e-mail with the links.

Hopefully, this will make the book go viral and disseminate the information widely. Most of the proceeds from the print version will go towards advertising the book; all profits will go to charity.

Who Is This Book For?

We will all die; so this book is for everyone. We all have a vested interest in understanding our choices at the end. This book teaches you how to navigate the maze we call "end of life." You'll become a more informed consumer. Most importantly, it tells you how you can effect some of these choices. With a very small amount of effort, you can considerably reduce the angst, suffering and anxiety that most of us will experience at the end. A vote, a few e-mails and phone calls, can bring about change and help reduce your own suffering and that of your loved ones. Read this book, get informed, and then inform others.

Finally, I want to reiterate that supporting the right to choose does not imply that you will pick euthanasia at the end. It's like being pro-choice on abortion without needing one. For most people, euthanasia is never a first choice. If all goes well, a natural death always seems preferable. But having that choice provides insurance for the dying. It gives them a sense of being in control of their death, which can greatly reduce their terminal anxiety. It also provides an exit option when all else fails.

How This Book Is Organized

I tried to keep the chapters focused and packed with information. Each chapter covers an issue in depth and some may be quite long. Here's the plan:

- *Chapter 1* sets the tone. It gives you a feel for the despair, confusion, and emotional chaos that surround death. I introduce the strongest of these dilemmas: mercy killings. Then I contrast this chaotic environment with the civilized death which our pets are offered. I introduce the terminology and technology of modern-day euthanasia. I go over the different flavors of euthanasia—including active, passive, slow, voluntary, involuntary, and physician-assisted dying. I decipher the confusing terminology and discuss some of the moral and legal issues. Finally, I present the results of opinion polls to give you a feel for how society at large views euthanasia.

- *Chapter 2* explains the logic, as well as the lure, of euthanasia. First, I go over what it means to have that choice. Then, I explain why Jeri wanted that option. Next, I recount the dilemma she faced in a state where assisted dying is not a legal option. Again, the discussion is not about Jeri. However, she was a professional problem solver during her life and she subscribed to the principle, "My life, my death, my choice." So, it's enlightening to follow her decision process when she faced her terminal prognosis. She contemplated that decision with a lot of clarity and documented some of it. I use Jeri as a case study to help you understand the anguish which the terminally ill face. Their terminal anxiety is shared by their caregivers and loved ones. I will tell you how Jeri's decision could have affected me in a very dramatic way. Yes, caregivers can turn into mercy killers out of deep love. It's a very emotional time filled with sadness, fear, and angst. I try to deconstruct the decisions that take place during that emotional pressure cooker and present them as objectively as possible.

- *Chapter 3* is about how we die today without the assisted dying option. I explain how to navigate the end-of-life maze in hospital ICUs and hospices. I cover the advances in palliative care, hospice, and pain management. I tell you how to avoid the worst type of end-of-life torture—death in the ICU. Then, I provide the best-case scenario for hospice and palliative care, using Jeri's death as an example. Finally, I tell you what's missing and why the system "as is" has reached its limits. I suggest a quick fix. However, the real solution is to add physician-assisted dying to the palliative-care repertoire. I go over the advantages and synergy that this added choice provides.

- *Chapter 4* is about where we are today and how we got here. I trace the major milestones of the modern end-of-life choice movement— the court decisions, senate bills, parliamentary laws, and country and state battles. In the U.S., physician-assisted dying for the terminally ill is now legal in the states of Oregon, Washington, and Montana. In Europe, various forms of euthanasia are legal in Switzerland, the Netherlands, Belgium, and Luxembourg. The passive and slow versions of euthanasia are now legal and widely accepted in most advanced countries. They've become part of the standard medical practice.

- *Chapter 5* is about euthanasia as it is practiced in the real world. I cover the lessons learned from three decades of experience in the Netherlands. Then, I analyze 12 years of data from the state of Oregon's experiment with physician-assisted dying. The Oregonians have created a fine-tuned system that maximizes the dying patient's autonomy, while providing maximum safeguards with minimal bureaucracy. In many ways, Oregon may have discovered the perfect system of palliative care; it's Yankee ingenuity at its best.

- *Chapters 6 and 7* are about euthanasia's detractors and their concerns. This is not a traditional "left versus right" issue. Today, the main groups that are aligned against the passing of euthanasia bills are: the Catholic church, the pro-life movement, and *Not Dead Yet* (an advocacy group for the disabled). In 2010, they were joined by the populist *They're Trying to Kill Granny* movement. The issue is also a cause for concern for some civil libertarians, physicians, and hospice workers. The arguments against euthanasia fall into three broad categories: 1) the sanctity of life must be preserved, 2) the slippery slopes must be prevented, and 3) the medical system can alleviate end-of-life pain. I'll address each of these concerns in great detail. I'll provide points and counterpoints and let you be the final judge.

- *Chapter 8* is a call to action to make physician-assisted dying legal. I start the chapter with a review of the "euthanasia underground" and its implications for society. Baby boomers are very Internet-savvy. Consequently, when their time comes, they'll know where to find the necessary pills, exit bags, and helium tanks. Necessity is the mother of invention; it's just a matter of time before a budding entrepreneur starts marketing a single-pill solution—an *exit pill* that is both legal and widely available. So, we will have a free market solution to fulfill this missing option. The implications are self-evident. One way or another, the assisted-dying option will become widely available. Will it be underground? Or, will it be legally available as a palliative-care option with safeguards? We must decide. I end the chapter with an interview with the politician who is spearheading the legalization movement in Hawaii—house majority leader Blake Oshiro. We go over the bill that he is proposing and the safeguards it contains. I also quiz him on what it will take to pass this bill. Maybe, Hawaii will become the fourth state to legalize physician-assisted dying for the terminally ill.

The bottom line is that there is no real lobby for the terminally ill. Instead, there's a grass-roots movement that is both altruistic and selfish. It's altruistic because we want to help our loved ones die better. It's selfish because we are also helping ourselves die better. Let's face it—we're all going to die someday. In the words of the late Elizabeth Edwards, "The days of our lives, for all of us, are numbered." It follows that we all have a vested interest in understanding and effecting the workings of an end-of-life system that controls how we die. This book is my modest contribution towards a better understanding of that system.

Personal note: *What qualifies me to write this book? In my previous life, I specialized in complex, distributed software systems. I learned how to deconstruct complexity and come up with better solutions. Jeri and I teamed up with Dan Harkey to coauthor books that helped a new generation of programmers understand the esoteric technology of collaborative software on large computer networks. Our books were written in an easy style to help guide these programmers and demystify the complexity of these systems. The books became bestsellers; we sold over a million copies. In this book, I use these same analytical skills to* *unravel and demystify the most complex system I've ever encountered: our end-of-life system. I will describe how we die in America today. You'll get the good, the bad, and the ugly. I hope to make a modest contribution by explaining how to eradicate some of the "ugly" and cut down on the suffering.*

I also wrote a book on grieving that deals with the same issue from a survivor's perspective. With these two contributions behind me, I now hope to get out of the death business until my time comes. There's just so much of this stuff one can take. On the other hand, this was my window to write these two books; I was writing while under the influence of the deep emotions that accompanied the death of my soulmate. I was able to look at the system from a different perspective, another angle. Hopefully, it well help guide you or your loved ones through the end-of-life maze.

Chapter 1

Father to Son: "Please, Kill Me"

"It could be that Americans struggle with death because they have made nearly everything else in their lives subject to reason, systemization, and control—from the timing of conception and manner of birth onward. Only death remains outside the corral, the wild horse that will not be tamed."

—*Stephen Kiernan*[1]

Dying in the modern world is hard; death itself is the easy part—it's the release from dying. In this chapter, I first give you a feel for the profound range of emotions that the end-of-life can trigger. Often, it's a heart-breaking tragedy of ordinary people. I explain how euthanasia could be a possible solution for these tragic end-of-life situations. For some, it can be the antidote to the dreadful suffering and isolation of a slow death. For others, it can be a form of insurance in case all else fails.

As you would expect, "euthanasia" is a loaded term. The topic is highly controversial: people have been grappling with it for ages. The current debate over euthanasia straddles multiple disciplines—including ethics, law, public policy, medicine, philosophy, and the existential meaning of life and death. Consequently, the terminology can be daunting; there is code to decipher and euphemisms to unravel. Also, there's a lot of historical baggage to untangle.

---

[1] Stephen P. Kiernan, *Last Rights: Rescuing the End of Life System From the Medical System* (St. Martin's Press, 2007).

After clarifying the terminology, it becomes easier to introduce the technology and explain "who does what to whom." I'll end the chapter with the results of opinion polls. They should give you a feel for where we stand on this issue as a society, including doctors, patients, and voters.

Keith Olbermann: "My Father Asked Me to Kill Him"

My first story takes place in *New York Presbyterian,* one of the top ten medical centers in the U.S. The date is February 19, 2010. Six months earlier, Theodore Olbermann, an 80-year-old architect, was admitted to the hospital to have his colon removed. The operation was a success. However, major complications ensued after the surgery. Theodore was suffering from pneumonia, kidney failure, liver failure, and many infections. He was on feeding tubes, dialysis, respirators, and antibiotic drips.

That day, like almost every day, Theodore was visited by his son Keith (MSNBC's well-known news anchor and political commentator). After recording his shows, Keith would head for his father's bedside and read to him. On the evening of February 19, Keith went into his father's hospital room and found him "thrashing his head back and forth" and mouthing the word "Help!" This is what transpired next:

> *Dad:* Stop this. Stop, stop, stop...
> *Keith:* Do you want me to stop all of this? Do you know what happens?
> *Dad:* Yes.
> *Keith:* What, you want me to smother you with a pillow?
> *Dad:* Yes, kill me.
> *Keith:* Obviously, I'm not going to do that...
> *Dad:* Help, help, help...

As his father's health-care proxy, Keith was able to request that Theodore be sedated. Luckily, the doctors agreed to do it. Theodore Olbermann died peacefully on March 13, 2010. May he rest in peace.

In the days that followed, Keith went on the air to reflect upon the end-of-life drama he had just witnessed. He explained to his viewers: "The paradoxical truth is that the people who desperately try to save your life sometimes manage to only (or also) torture you.... There was now terrifying torture. My father needed it to stop." Then, Keith asked: "What are your options when dad says 'Kill me'? Or, what are your options when dad is in a coma and can't tell you a damn thing?"

Unlike the rest of us, Keith had access to a pulpit from which he was able to broadcast the end-of-life dilemma he faced. He was able to eloquently articulate a drama that millions of us silently face at the end of life—when we are slowly dying, or when we helplessly watch our loved ones die. If you get a chance, watch the entire video of the broadcast—it's an eye-opener.[2]

The Unlikely Flare-Gun Killer

The next story takes place in the state of Hawaii, on the island of Oahu's windward side. Robert Yagi and his wife Leatrice, both 71, had lived a quiet, retired life in the tiny, rain-forest community of Olomana at the base of the Koolau Mountains. By all accounts, Robert Yagi was a loving and caring husband. He was described as "pleasant and quiet." According to neighbor Francis Calleon, the Yagis had lived in the community for more than three decades and he had never seen them argue. He added that the couple "often went places together."[3]

In mid-2009, Leatrice became terminally ill and Robert took care of her. In October of that year, Leatrice was admitted to the nearby Castle Hospital Medical Center, which is about a five-minute walk from the Yagis' home. According to a police affidavit, Robert "was seen daily in her room, tending to her needs and keeping her company." Here's what happened next.

---

[2] http://www.msnbc.msn.com/id/3036677/vp/35572842#35572842.

[3] Mary Vorsino, "Motive in Shooting Not Clear," *Honolulu Advertiser,* December 10, 2009.

Thursday, December 10, 2009 (at 6:10 p.m.): Robert burst into Leatrice's hospital room and shot her with a plastic flare gun loaded with a shotgun shell.[4] According to Castle officials, Leatrice suffered minor injuries in the shooting but no other patients or staff were "endangered by the perpetrator." Police believed Robert wanted to kill himself after shooting his wife. They arrested him for attempted second-degree murder. Robert had no prior criminal history. Consequently, he was released on $150,000 bail and banned from returning to the hospital. Court documents say that Robert Yagi "may have wanted to end the life of 71-year-old Leatrice Yagi because she's suffering from a terminal illness."

Sunday, December 13, 2009: Honolulu police found Robert Yagi dead in his Olomana home. He had apparently committed suicide by hanging. Leatrice recovered from her gunshot wound. Five months later, she died from her disease after being re-admitted to the hospital.

The Yagis' tragedy resulted in an incredible outpouring of emotion in the state of Hawaii. It seemed as if the whole state was mourning with the family. Thousands of letters to the Honolulu papers were posted online. The majority were from young people who viewed Robert Yagi as a lover—not a killer. He was a compassionate hero who tried to kill his wife because he loved her. He tried to end her agony (and his) with a mercy killing, followed by suicide. The Yagis' tragedy renewed the debate over Hawaii's *Death with Dignity* bill modeled after Oregon's.

Note on how the press covered the event: *Initially, the press alluded to some crazy old man who tried to kill his wife by breaking into Castle Hospital. Later, the compassionate angle of the story began to appear. On December 10, the "Honolulu Advertiser" published an article that focused on "caregiver stress." I was a caregiver for ten years, so I understand caregiver stress. In my opinion, Robert Yagi was not driven*

---

[4] Note: Press and police reports say it was a flare gun with shotgun shells. However, I heard it could have been a shotgun with flares inside. In any case, the gun malfunctioned.

to desperation by the stress of caregiving. At the time of the shooting, Castle Hospital was providing the bulk of Leatrice's caregiving, not her husband. What probably drove him to desperation was the unbearable agony of watching his beloved wife suffer in her hospital bed. He tried to end her agony. The day after Robert's suicide, the story finally got the proper treatment in the press. On December 14, the "Honolulu Advertiser" ran an in-depth article that focused on the debate over physician-assisted dying in Hawaii.[5]

What Can Be Done?

Both of these stories took place in modern American hospitals. Unfortunately, even with the best of care, death remains the "wild horse that will not be tamed." However, there is absolutely no reason for these tragedies to occur at the end of life. It's cruel and unusual punishment for both the patients and their families.

So what happened to the ancient Greek idea of euthanasia, *the easy and gentle death*? In ancient Greece and Rome, citizens were entitled to a good death to end the suffering of a terminal illness. To that end, the city magistrates of Athens kept a supply of poison to help the dying "drink the Hemlock."[6] Despite the Hippocratic Oath, it was very common for physicians to end the lives of dying patients with their consent. The physicians either handed their dying patients the poison for which they asked or administered it themselves, at the patient's request.[7]

Fast-forward to the present. This book is about restoring that ancient practice. If our dying loved ones voluntarily request it, they must be

---

[5] Tim Sakahara, "Husband's Suicide Resurrects Right to Die Debate," *KGMB HawaiiNewsNow*, December 14, 2009.

[6] Michael Manning, *Euthanasia and Physician-Assisted Suicide* (Paulist Press, 1998).

[7] Ron Hamel, Editor, *Choosing Death: Active Euthanasia, Religion and the Public Debate* (Trinity Press, 1991).

given the option of drinking "the Hemlock." The modern-day lethal drug of choice is called *Nembutal*; it's far gentler than what the ancient Greeks used.[8]

In the sections that follow, I will briefly introduce the terminology and technology of modern-day euthanasia. At this point, we just need a working understanding of what this is all about. We will get into the fine-print and details as the book progresses.

Passive Euthanasia: How Many of Us Die

In modern society, euthanasia has come to mean a death free of anxiety and pain, with some kind of physician assistance. It's a deliberate act (or omission) that results in hastening a patient's death to spare suffering. Surprise! Many of us actually die from euthanasia today in America's hospitals. It's called *passive euthanasia*; it does not involve lethal medication. Instead, doctors terminate a dying patient's life by withholding or withdrawing medical treatment. For example, a feeding tube is removed, a dialysis machine is stopped, or a respirator is disconnected. Often, they let death happen by not resuscitating a patient. It's all legal and voluntary. Doctors act according to a patient's living will or advance directive.

What makes passive euthanasia legal? It's legal because you never ask to have life terminated. Instead, you're asking for the life support to be terminated. You are not asking for help to commit suicide. Instead, you are simply invoking your right to refuse treatment—including life support. You then die because nature takes its course. Of course, everyone knows that the removal of life support results in certain death. But, it's "don't ask, don't tell." Also, never call it euthanasia. It's against the law. Instead, you must either call it "letting die" or "allowing to die." The physicians are not helping you commit suicide. Instead, you are firing them. You no longer need their services. So they're removing their life-support equipment and going home. And

---

[8] The hemlock poison is from the plant *Conium Maculatum*—a poisonous member of the parsley family. By today's standards, it's not a particularly good poison.

they're "letting you" slowly waste away. You will then die from either the progressing disease, suffocation, or dehydration. The death will be recorded as being both legal and natural.

But, let me delve into this a little more deeply. Consider the case where the removal of a respirator is accompanied by sedation, at the request of the patient. The result is certain death. Why? Normally, you are "weaned off" the respirator a little at a time to give the body a chance to learn to breathe on its own again. However, should a patient request it, the physician is allowed to administer sedatives to relieve the terrifying panic and sense of suffocation that results from disconnecting the respirator. But, the sedatives also suppress the breathing and prevent the relearning. The result is certain death. Is this killing or letting die? I'll let you decide. In any case, this is a perfectly legal way to die; it is humane and morally accepted by most.

Note on Terri Schiavo: *In 2005, the Terri Schiavo case reinvigorated those who are opposed to the removal of any type of life support. The highly-visible protest against the removal of Terri's feeding tube was spearheaded by the pro-life movement, previously known for its anti-abortion activism. You can protect yourself from this type of interference through a living will. Yes, there are some who are ready to turn the clock back on any advances in palliative care.[9] I guess they want us to suffer at the end.*

Slow Euthanasia: How the Lucky Ones Die

You may have heard the term *slow euthanasia*.[10] Typically, it's associated with the use of *terminal sedation*—a very common practice in hospices. The terminal patient is sedated into unconsciousness to

---

[9] Lewis Cohen, *No Good Deed: A Story of Medicine, Murder Accusations, and the Debate over How We Die* (Harper, 2010).

[10] Anemona Hartocollis, "Hard Choice for a Comfortable Death: Sedation," *New York Times*, December 28, 2009.

relieve the pain. Artificial hydration and nutrition are withheld because they may cause adverse effects, such as pulmonary edema (i.e., water in the lungs). Then death is slowly caused by whichever comes first: 1) the progressing disease taking its course, 2) respiratory failure caused by the ramping up of sedative drugs, 3) pneumonia, 4) kidney failure, or 5) starvation and dehydration.

Today, this practice is medically-accepted and legal. In the words of Supreme Court Justice Sandra Day O'Connor: "There is general agreement that a patient who is suffering from a terminal illness and who is experiencing great pain has no legal barriers to obtaining medication, from qualified physicians, to alleviate that suffering, even to the point of causing unconsciousness and hastening death."[11]

The argument Justice O'Connor used is called the *doctrine of double effect*, which means that an action can have two effects, one intended and the other foreseen but not desired.[12] In this context, it means that hastening death is okay as long as it's not the physician's primary *intent*. The primary intent of terminal sedation is the relief of pain— death is just collateral damage. In this case, it seems we're not to be held accountable for the secondary effects of our actions. Also, you must never call this practice euthanasia or even terminal sedation. The politically correct term is *palliative sedation.*

In states that do not support voluntary euthanasia, palliative sedation is the most compassionate way to die. It's the only way to control unbearable pain. With enough sedation, the dying are finally put into a state of deep unconsciousness. We're told that they do not suffer when they're in that state. Eventually, they'll die, but "not too quickly." The process is not easy on the families. However, it's not as traumatic as watching a loved one die in an intensive care unit. I'll have a lot more to say about palliative sedation in Chapter 3.

---

[11] U.S. Supreme Court, *Washington v. Gluksberg* (1997).

[12] The doctrine has its roots in medieval Catholic theology, especially in the thought of Thomas Aquinas.

Involuntary Euthanasia: How Our Pets Die

Involuntary euthanasia is how our pets die in America today. As a society, we are incredibly compassionate when it comes to our dying pets. We will not let them suffer at the end of their lives. Period. So, how do we do it? We euthanize our pets rather than watch them slowly die in pain. Of course, our pets don't have a say in this—it's involuntary.

Involuntary euthanasia must *never* be legalized for humans. Why? It has too much potential for abuse. For example, shortly after they came to power, the Nazis set out to engineer a "better" race by euthanizing their "undesirables"—the handicapped, the insane, and then the elderly. Much of this happened under the supervision of German doctors. The exterminations were medicalized. Of course, we're not Nazis. Our pets are very precious and we lovingly "put them to sleep."

There's much we can learn from the technology that provides this gentle death to our pets. Dr. Ronald S. Weiner ("Dr. Ron") is a long-time veterinarian from Los Gatos, California. I'll let him explain the process:

> *Robert:* Thank you for taking my questions. How long have you been a vet?
> *Dr. Ron:* A little over 35 years.
> *Robert:* How many pets have you euthanized?
> *Dr. Ron:* Around 4,000.
> *Robert:* What type of pets?
> *Dr. Ron:* Cats and dogs.
> *Robert:* Can you briefly describe the process?
> *Dr. Ron:* First, I place a catheter IV on the pet to insure a smooth injection. Then, I use a syringe to inject a highly-concentrated *pentobarbital* solution. Often, Valium is given before the injection.
> *Robert:* What happens next?
> *Dr. Ron:* The pet lapses into coma within a few seconds as the drug causes marked respiratory depression and ultimately stops the heart

for a peaceful death. This usually occurs within one or two minutes. The heart just stops.

Robert: Do pets experience any pain?

Dr. Ron: I do not believe they feel any pain at all. It's all very humane.

Robert: How far back does this practice go?

Dr. Ron: I'd say over a century.

Yes, our pets have it good at the end—the medical technique that puts them to sleep is top-notch. Apparently, it also works well on humans. The Australian euthanasia doctor Philip Nitschke writes, "My experience in those days of legal voluntary euthanasia taught me that the drug pentobarbital (commonly known as *Nembutal*) provides the most peaceful death imaginable. And it never fails."[13] He is writing about his experience in 1996, when the Northern Territory of Australia led the world to become the first place where it was lawful for a terminally-ill patient to request medical assistance to die.

Voluntary Euthanasia: How Some Would Like to Die

Why can't we extend the same loving mercy to terminally-ill human beings? Why can't we grant ourselves the right to die with dignity? Unlike our pets, we have the mental capacity to *voluntarily* choose when to die and how to die. Voluntary choice, when coupled with a painless technique, gives us total control over how we die and when we die; it's the ultimate death with dignity. Yes, we can do better than our pets. Unfortunately, our pets have it better now when it comes to the technology of dying.

There are exceptions. The terminally ill in Switzerland, Belgium, the Netherlands, and the states of Oregon, Montana, and Washington have access to this technology: Nembutal is on the approved list of drugs that doctors can legally prescribe to the terminally ill. In these countries and U.S. states, terminally-ill humans can experience an

---

[13] Philip Nitschke and Fiona Stewart, *The Peaceful Pill Handbook* (Exit International US, 2009).

"easy and gentle" death if they request it. *Voluntary euthanasia* is an explicit request for a physician to help you die. The help can come in one of two ways:

- *Self-administered.* In this case, you're asking for a prescription of Nembutal or some other barbiturate to take your own life. The physician writes you a prescription and then you're on your own. You take your own life when you're ready. This guarantees that it's voluntary. In the U.S., proponents of this method call it *physician-assisted dying* or simply *assisted dying;* opponents use the terms *physician-assisted suicide* or simply *euthanasia.*

- *Physician-administered.* In this case, the physician will inject a lethal dose when you request it. This method requires that the physician play a more active role; it may be useful for people who can't self-administer. This approach is called *voluntary active euthanasia (VAE)* by its proponents. Its opponents call it *euthanasia.*

The European euthanasia movement supports both methods. In contrast, the U.S. movement only supports the first method, which is now legal in the states of Oregon, Washington, and Montana.

Note on terminology: Like the rest of the U.S. movement, I am only in favor of the first method (see Chapter 2). In this book, I interchangeably call it voluntary euthanasia, assisted dying, or just "the Nembutal." This lets me deal explicitly with the anti-euthanasia arguments in terms that can be understood. Like the ancient Greeks, I believe euthanasia is a noble word; it's time to reclaim this word from those who malign it. Again, I want to make it very clear that this book only condones voluntary euthanasia for the terminally ill. The dying person must make the choice: no one else can. Bottom line: I am in support of a voluntary, easy, and gentle death that is assisted by a physician in the form of a legal prescription for Nembutal. My model is the state of Oregon's "Death with Dignity" Act.

What the Polls Say

Over the years, national polls have consistently shown the U.S. public to be largely in favor of physician-assisted dying. This includes the majority of patients, physicians, and voters. Here are some examples:

- *Gallup polls* consistently indicate that Americans overwhelmingly support euthanasia. They were asked the question: "When a person has a disease that cannot be cured, do you think doctors should be allowed by law to end the patient's life by some painless means if the patient and his family request it?" In the 2007 poll, 71% were in favor while 27% were opposed.

- A 2002 *Harris poll* found that 2-1 majorities continued to support rights to both euthanasia and physician-assisted suicide. 61% favored the implementation of Oregon's *Death with Dignity Act* in their own states.[14]

- An April 2005 *Harris poll* found that two-thirds of the public would like their states to allow aid in dying as is currently allowed in Oregon. A 70% majority was in favor of a law that would "allow doctors to comply with the wishes of a dying patient in severe distress who asks to have his or her life ended."

- A 2005 national survey conducted by the *Institute for Religious and Social Studies* found that 57% of the 1088 doctors polled believe it is ethical for a physician to assist a competent, dying patient to hasten death.[15]

- A 2010 national survey of 10,000 U.S. physicians conducted by *Medscape* found that 59.3% of respondents agreed that "physician-assisted suicide should be allowed in some cases."[16]

---

[14] Humphrey Taylor, Harris Interactive, *2-1 Majorities Continue to Support Rights to Both Euthanasia and Doctor-Assisted Suicide*, January 9, 2002.

[15] Louis Finkelstein, Institute for Religious and Social Studies, *Physician-Assisted Suicide Survey* (February, 2005).

[16] http://www.medscape.com/viewarticle/731485.

- In 2006, a California poll conducted by the *Field Research Corp.* showed that support for physician-assisted dying transcended party lines and religious affiliations. Californians were asked: "If you yourself were terminally ill and were expected to die within six months, would you want your doctor to be able to assist you in dying if you requested it?" The "yes" replies were as follows: 62% of all adults, 76% of Democrats, 51% of Republicans, 62% of Independents, 56% of Protestants, 54% of Catholics, 46% of born-again Christians, 65% of Latinos, and 70% of non-Hispanic Whites.[17]

These polls show that, as a society, we are ready for changes in the law to better reflect the public's values and needs. There is no need to hide behind arcane, medieval sophistries like "the double effect." The public seems more than ready for an open discussion about dying options.

The Bottom Line: Whose Death Is It Anyway?

For most of us, dying will not be "easy and gentle." In ancient Greece and Rome, voluntary euthanasia was used to achieve a good death. As a society, we already practice some form of euthanasia without openly acknowledging it. Without terminal sedation (i.e., slow euthanasia), death from the chronic diseases that are now killing us would be unbearable. The cessation of life support (i.e., passive euthanasia) is another advance that makes modern dying more tolerable. There is still torture in our hospices and hospitals, but without these palliative practices it could be much worse.

Voluntary euthanasia provides another option in the continuum of palliative care choices that are becoming available to us. In later chapters, I will use empirical data to demonstrate that these approaches are complementary and synergistic. Together, they provide better end-of-life care. I will also argue that there is no moral difference between

---

[17] Mervin Field and Mark DiCamillo, "The Field Poll: Continued Support for Doctor-Assisted Suicide," (March, 2006).

a physician's assistance in dying by: 1) prescribing the Nembutal, 2) removing life support, or 3) activating terminal sedation without nutrition or hydration. It's all the same.

Philosophically, this debate is about our right, when terminally ill, to choose how to die. It's about the right to control how much we have to suffer and when and how we die. It's about having some control over our dying process in a system that can aggressively prolong life with invasive technology. Luckily, we also have the technology that allows us to experience "a gentle death" on our own terms, rather than by medically set terms. In his famous essay *On Liberty*, John Stuart Mill argues strongly for our right to self-determination. He writes, "Over himself, over his own body and mind, the individual is sovereign.... He is the person most interested in his own well-being."[18] These words were written over a century ago.

Opponents argue that assisted dying is not self-determination because it requires the help of a physician. Instead, it's a *joint action* by both the patient and physician. In other words, we don't have the autonomy to act on our own—we need the prescription. If you think about it, physicians are just the gatekeepers to the Nembutal—they write prescriptions for barbiturates. Our laws granted them a monopoly over controlled medications by way of these prescriptions. Hypothetically, a change in law could allow terminal patients to pick up their Nembutal directly from city hall, just like in ancient Athens. The Nembutal is a one-size-fits-all prescription; it doesn't require a physician's dosing expertise or help to administer.

In most states, a prohibition law against physician-assisted dying is restricting our right to self-determination; the prohibition prevents dying patients from doing what's best for themselves without hurting others. In this case, the prohibition is of no benefit to society at large. So, we must remove the prohibition and legalize the Nembutal for those who are dying. For each state, it comes down to a vote. For states that carry the vote, the polls seem to indicate that the majority of

---

[18] John Stuart Mill, *Three Essays* (Oxford University Press, 1978).

physicians are willing to prescribe the Nembutal and help us through the dying process. They will not abandon us at the end.

The twelve-year old Oregon experiment provides solid evidence that assisted dying works in the real world. Oregon supplies a proven legal framework that we can emulate throughout the United States. It also serves as our lab for the technology and the safeguards, which are both first-rate. The system in Oregon has consistently demonstrated that it is capable of providing an "easy and gentle" death without abuses. Based on opinion polls, society seems ready to have the Nembutal option added to our end-of-life choices.

I'll close this chapter with a quote from medical ethicist Dr. Jonathan Moreno: "Euthanasia, and especially physician-assisted suicide, appears as the ultimate post-modern demand for dignity in an era of technologically-mediated death."[19]

---

[19] Jonathan D. Moreno, Editor, *Arguing Euthanasia* (Simon and Schuster, 1995).

Chapter 2

My Life, My Death, My Choice

"I don't want to achieve immortality through my work. I want to achieve it through not dying."

—*Woody Allen*

Physician-assisted dying for the terminally ill is a very simple concept. It means that at the end you should be able to ask your physician to prescribe a lethal dose of medicine, preferably in liquid form that you could easily mix with a drink when the time comes. You self-administer the medication by swallowing your drink. If you're no longer able to swallow, you self-inject the medicine through a catheter or feeding tube. Ideally, a nurse would be present to provide advice and moral support. It's really that simple. However, the devil is in the details—legal, moral, societal, and practical—when it comes to the issues that surround euthanasia.

In this chapter, I deal with euthanasia from a dying patient's perspective. I try to answer the following questions: What's the thought process at the end? How do you choose "how" to die? What's the logic? What are the tradeoffs? Can you get around legal barriers in states that don't support assisted dying? What are the risks? What are the implications? How much assistance will you need?

How do I answer these questions from a dying patient's perspective? The short answer is: from the experience of my late wife, Jeri. She provides the perfect case study. In her previous life as a Silicon Valley executive with high-tech startups, Jeri was known for her laser-sharp analytical skills. She knew how to make complex decisions and deal with uncertainty. (Her graduate degree was in general systems theory.) Jeri left behind a trail that explains some of her thinking when she faced death. Also, she was very open with me when we broached the topic. Why? Because I was very sick at the time. So, it wasn't clear who was going to die first. Everything was on the table. It was a discussion among dying peers.

In this chapter I will focus on Jeri's decision process when it came to her choice of dying. I cover this topic for the first time here. I'll give you just a bit of narrative and then get down to the issues. You can read the details of Jeri's death in my book *Grieving a Soulmate*.

Jeri Receives Her Final Notice

Jeri was 47 when she was diagnosed with ovarian cancer in 1999. For the next nine years, she kept the cancer in check with back-to-back chemotherapy regimens. She was lucky to live in Hawaii. She became a surfer at age 50 and even won a trophy in her age group. The surfing and the ocean kept her fit during her chemo years. They helped her rebound after each chemo session. Her cancer never went into remission. However, it was microscopic and well-contained within the abdomen.

We received the first piece of bad news in late March 2008, about 15 months before Jeri's death. A routine CAT scan revealed that the cancer had spread outside the abdomen and some of it was now in her lungs. This was very bad news. The good news was that the cancer's spread did not seem to affect Jeri's quality of life. On the outside, she looked fine. She would say, "Look, I'm very healthy except for a small problem—cancer." She continued her chemo regimens, followed by good surfing days. Of course, Jeri had just received her official death sentence.

She Had a Dream: Dying, Jeri's Way

In April 2008, I became very sick. For a time, it looked like I would die first. In a reversal of roles, Jeri became my caregiver. As I lay in bed one day, I noticed that she was doing a lot of research on death and dying. I was not very lucid, but I felt the topic was highly relevant. So, I called her over and she sat next to me on the bed. What followed was the most extraordinary conversation. Here's my best recollection of what was said that day:

Robert: You're doing a lot of reading on dying. What are your thoughts?

Jeri: I'm not afraid of death. I'm afraid of dying in pain. I really don't want to needlessly suffer at the end.

Robert: What are you discovering? Do you have a plan?

Jeri: I don't have a plan, yet. But I have a dream...

Robert: A dream?

Jeri: Yes, a dream. It's about how I'd like to die.

Robert: I'm all ears.

Jeri: In my dream, we rent a beautiful oceanside suite at the Moana overlooking my surfing spot. We sit on the lanai and enjoy watching the surfers. There's a big swell and they're taking some great rides. Later, our closest friends join us for a nice bottle of wine. We talk story and reminisce. We laugh a lot. At sunset, I say goodbye to everyone and have one more toast to the good life. Then, I drink my final cocktail...

Robert: Your final cocktail?

Jeri: Yes. It will be mixed with something that will put me to sleep forever. I'll pour a vial into my drink. Don't wake me until I die...

The conversation ended suddenly. Jeri and I were both in tears. I hugged her tightly and wouldn't let go. It was all very emotional. I couldn't imagine life without Jeri. She had to reassure me that she wouldn't die for a while. She laughed and said, "Don't worry, Babe. I plan to catch a lot more waves before I die." Jeri wanted to savor every good moment she had left on this earth. She wanted to surf and continue to live as long as possible. In her words, "Until my life becomes more bad than good." Having seen her take chemo all those years, I knew she could absorb quite a bit of "bad." She was exceptionally brave.

At this point, Jeri was in the planning stages. She was trying to formulate a working plan for how she wanted to die. Once she had a plan, she would shelve it until she was ready. Maybe, she wouldn't ever need it. It was just preparatory work. Jeri loved to choreograph things in advance. In this case, she wanted her forthcoming death to be a happy event which she could fully imagine. She wanted it to be a celebration of her good life. Her death would be a reflection of the way she had lived. She wanted to control the process of death as much as possible. She did not want uncontrolled suffering and pain. That was *her* dream! We all have our dreams of how we want to go. And, we all want some level of control over our death. That's why many of us have an advance directive.

Note on Jeri's dream: *During my grieving, I spent a long time thinking about Jeri's dream. I came to the conclusion that it had been very therapeutic. It helped her cope with the death sentence she had just received. Her answer was to subsume her death by orchestrating it. She was going to set the narrative for her death as she had done for her life—she would provide the ending. In other words, Jeri was not going to let death define her. Instead, she was going to define death. This is the ultimate form of existential self-empowerment. It's also a very rational coping strategy. Think about it. How would you react if you were handed a death sentence? Jeri's answer was to take it on. She was a tough surfer chick who had spent years fighting ovarian cancer. She was not going to abdicate control at the very end. She would die on her own terms—Jeri's way.*

Do-It-Yourself Dying With Help From the Internet

Jeri was a top-notch researcher and planner. The question was whether she could turn her dream into a working solution. She had a big obstacle to overcome: euthanasia was not a legal option in Hawaii. At first, that didn't seem to bother her. After spending a few hours on the

Internet, she found almost everything she needed to execute her plan, including:

- *Brand name lethal drugs and their dosages.* She was able to locate two well-known drugs which in combination could do the job. However, the required dosages were huge. In total, she would need to swallow 180 pills. Why so many? That's what it takes to get a lethal dosage using ordinary drugs. Jeri did not like to swallow pills. With further research, she discovered how to blend them into an applesauce drink that would ease their digestion.

- *Prescriptions from online pharmacies.* These were easy to procure on the Internet. Her drugs could be shipped overnight by several online pharmacies.

- *Method of administration.* The information is all over the Internet. She had to go on a liquid diet a few days before the event. Then, she would take some anti-nausea tablets a few hours before ingesting the pills. The idea was to not throw up. Of course, the solid pills would have to be ground and dissolved in some liquid before intake. She would have under five minutes, the median time to unconsciousness, to swallow the pills.

It looked like Jeri had all the pieces. However, something appeared to be missing. She said, "It's not that easy. I'm still working on it."

Her Letter to *Compassion & Choices*

A few days later, Jeri was still searching for answers. She had made several calls to *Compassion & Choices* in Oregon, who assigned her a case worker (or counselor). Here's an unedited version of a letter Jeri sent to her case worker on May 7, 2008:

Dear Helen,

Thank you for taking the time the other day to discuss with me my situation and your services. I appreciate your help very much. As I told you, I was diagnosed with Ovarian Cancer Stage 3C in December of 1999. I have been on chemotherapy most of the time since then. I have been lucky. The chemotherapy has allowed me to have a high quality of life while holding the cancer at bay. My cancer has not affected me much so far (although the chemotherapy certainly has). I have been able to carve out a beautiful life around the treatments.

However, two months ago my cancer count (CA-125) began to rise sharply. And a CT-Scan showed that the cancer had spread from the lymph nodes in my abdomen to my lungs and upper lymph system. I am continuing to try different chemotherapies to stop the disease progression (and get more of those great quality days). However, I also want to begin to prepare for the case that we cannot stop it. To this end, I have completed my will, and advance directive. Given your recommendation, I have begun to look into hospice care alternatives—to be ready for the time I will need them.

My goal is to have as many quality days as possible. I have experienced days under chemotherapy when I would rather have been dead. I hung on because I knew the pain would be over within days. But there may come a time when I will see that the pain won't be over—that the pain medications won't work. I do not want to live in that state knowing that there is no chance for it to improve. I have had a great life (which I still want as much of as possible), but then I want to have a good death with dignity. Therefore, I am seeking your help in obtaining information on options to hasten my death. Can you please send me this information? Thank you again for your invaluable service.

Sincerely,
Jeri

This beautiful letter clearly documents Jeri's wishes for the end of her life. She wrote these words, about 13 months before she died, when she was totally lucid. However, I was totally confused. What did Jeri need from *Compassion & Choices* that she did not already have? She had the pills, the dosage, and the method. It all looked very doable. What was missing from her plan?

Help, I Need Somebody

I finally asked Jeri, "What do you need from these people? Why are you writing to them?" She was a bit teary-eyed and didn't respond right away. There seemed to be a lot going on in her mind. Eventually, we had this very informative conversation:

Robert: What, exactly, is missing from your plan?

Jeri: I need someone on standby when I take the pills. I'm hoping that they provide that service.

Robert: Why do you need to have these people on standby? I'll always be by your side. You just swallow that stuff and it's over. Right?

Jeri: Wrong. The statistics I was able to find, mostly from the AIDS community, show that one out of three attempts had botched. Those who failed ended up in intensive care. I don't want to end up there. I need someone who will assist me to finish the job in case I throw up the stuff. I don't want to wake up in a psychiatric ward or in an intensive care unit.

Robert: What? You want someone to put a pillow over your head to finish you off?

Jeri: Yes, exactly. It's typically a plastic bag. And, I don't want you doing it. You're my lover. You'll never be able to do it. You don't have it in you. Besides, you're non-violent. I can't and won't depend on you to kill me. You absolutely don't have my permission to do it.

Robert: Baby, these people can't do it either. You know it's against the law. It won't happen. All they can do is hold your hand. No one is going to kill you.

Jeri: You're right. I told you that I didn't have all the answers.

Robert: What about that stuff they use in Oregon? They say it's 100% effective.

Jeri: You mean Nembutal. I couldn't find it on the Internet. Believe me, I searched everywhere. We'd have to go to Mexico to find it, and we wouldn't be able to bring it back through customs. It's illegal. The stuff I located is inferior. It requires a plastic bag to finish the job, but the bag may come loose. I'll need assistance if that happens. Like I said, I haven't found a clean solution yet.

Robert: Why don't you ask Dr. Terada for a prescription?

Jeri: No way! I would never put him in that situation. It would incriminate him. Do you want him to lose his license? He's a great oncologist. He's helped me fight my cancer all these years. Other women with cancer desperately need him. I'll never ask him to do anything illegal.

Robert: Sorry! I wasn't thinking. You're absolutely right. Have you considered other ways of going?

Jeri: Like shooting myself? No, I won't do anything violent. I want to die peacefully—by going into deep sleep. The pills are my only option. I just need to make it all work.

Obviously, Jeri was in a bind. She didn't have access to the best technology—meaning Nembutal. Consequently, she would need some form of assistance in dying, mostly for backup. Of course, *Compassion & Care* did not provide that service. Jeri's plan was not going to work. She needed the help of a physician who would write her a prescription for Nembutal as they do in Oregon. But this was not a legal option in Hawaii. So, for the first time in her life, "can-do Jeri" did not have a solution.

When Lovers Become Killers

Jeri's plan hit a brick wall because there was a possibility that it would have required a *mercy killing*. In contrast to legalized assisted dying, self-deliverance does not involve a physician. Typically, assistance in dying is performed, out of love and compassion, by a close family member. In the eyes of the law, mercy killing is murder. More often than not, the charge is downgraded to first-degree manslaughter which implies a lack of intent to kill. At the end of the day, most mercy killers are acquitted by sympathetic jurors and judges. The few who are found guilty receive light sentences.

So, is mercy killing a crime or a moral duty? Are the killers criminals or saints? Is the killing self-serving or altruistic? Does law of family trump law of state? Is there a flaw in the law or in juries' moral sense? There are many more such questions. Our society does not have the answers, which explains the ambivalence. The lenient verdicts are a moral dodge, an easy way out. Moral clarity dictates that if mercy killing goes unpunished, then it must be legalized. The law is flawed: the people's moral sense is not.

Mercy killing is precisely what legalized physician-assisted dying was designed to avoid. The orderly transaction between doctor and patient is meant to eliminate the need for desperate killing which is in clear violation of the law. Tranquil lethal dosing replaces very personal and sometimes gory methods of killing, such as strangulations, suffocations, and shootings. Instead of a non-regulated desperate act, legalized euthanasia is a well-regulated professional transaction. The idea is to prevent the tragedy of killing for love, which is an incredibly devastating, life-shattering act of desperation.

Prison is the least of their problems for family members who receive a cry for help from loved ones who want to die. This dreaded cry brings about a horrible, no-win dilemma. If they assist in their loved one's suicide or death, they will probably end up grieving forever; if they refuse, they are likely to suffer from both endless grief and guilt for not helping. To break out of this predicament, some will kill their loved ones and then take their own lives. The press calls it "murder-suicide." Jeri was seeking outside help because she did not want me to face this horrible dilemma. I was lucky that she was such a careful planner.

Killing Yourself While You Still Can

The timing of a do-it-yourself death is critical. Without access to a liquid vial of Nembutal, it becomes crucial for the terminally ill to kill themselves while they are still able to self-administer the pills and *before* they are unable to swallow. The technology dictates the timing. In this case, the underground pill technology is sub-optimal compared to the legal prescriptions of Nembutal. Consequently, many of these suicides are premature. People die while they still have some good life left in them.

Too-early self-deliverance can be very hard on the survivors. They may grieve for that extra time they could have had with their loved ones. During Jeri's last days, I savored every remaining microsecond I had with her on this earth; it was beyond precious. I would gladly trade the rest of my life for one more day with Jeri. I had thirty wonderful years with her, but every moment counts when you're grieving; you always want more.

You Waited Too Long

Conversely, there are those who wait too long. They want to extract every moment they can out of life. Jeri could have ended up in this category. She wanted to live as long as possible. Even at the very end, she was able to enjoy some of life's little pleasures. Typically, people will choose to live as long as they retain their dignity and the pain is still manageable. The danger is that they can hit a point of no return when self-deliverance is no longer an option. For example, this can happen when they are no longer able to swallow pills or self-administer the medication.

Not Too Early and Not Too Late

For Jeri the right time to die was not too early and not too late. She also wanted her death to be quick, peaceful, and surrounded by love. In an ultimate act of self-determination, she wanted to choose both the venue and the optimum time for her death. Finally, she wanted to die in a state of deep sleep. To paraphrase Woody Allen, "She wasn't afraid to die. She just wanted to be sound asleep when it happened."

Unfortunately, it's very difficult to achieve this ideal goal with underground euthanasia. First, you do not have access to the best technology, liquid Nembutal. Second, it's very hard to pick the optimal time without the proper support system. I'll have a lot more to say about this later.

Unnecessary Anxiety and Stress

As a terminally-ill person, Jeri ought to have been allowed to control her death. She should have had the right to choose the best way to go. Every feasible option should have been on the table. Unlike most people, Jeri had choreographed how she wanted to go, but she was never given that option. It was not legal. She also discovered that the underground approach to self-deliverance is not easy: there are too many legal blocks, too many things can go wrong, and the timing is seldom right. Even a top-notch planner like Jeri couldn't figure it out.

Without a plan, Jeri felt very exposed. She was afraid of what was to come. She was anxious about her forthcoming death at a time when she should have been enjoying every precious moment that she had left on this earth. As her caregiver, I felt the same anxiety. I was terrified that she would needlessly suffer at the end. It was all very stressful. Both of us would have felt much better had there been a legal exit path to fall back on, if all else failed. So, the lack of a fall-back plan affects more than just the aesthetics of dying. It's also a source of deep anxiety.

How Much Physician Assistance?

This question is the major dividing line between the American and European approaches to legalized physician-assisted dying. In the Netherlands, it is legal for either a physician or the dying patient to administer terminal medication. In contrast, Oregon's *Death with Dignity Act* requires that the dying self-administer the medication and no one else. Why? Because it provides the ultimate assurance that the act is voluntary.

From a dying person's perspective, there are two instances where a physician's assistance may be further required: 1) in the highly unlikely event self-administration fails (Oregon's failure rates are almost zero); 2) if the dying person chooses to live longer than he or she can self-administer and then needs assistance.

From a moral perspective, there is no difference between a physician helping someone die by prescribing the lethal medicine versus administering it. It's all the same. We have the same kind of situation when removing life support: we rely on advance directives to ensure the will of the patient, even though someone else pulls the plug.

In this book, I advocate whatever is best for dying patients. The trade-off they face is a few more days of living versus an iron-clad guarantee that their assisted death is *voluntary*. When I first started writing this book I was in favor of a few more days. Consequently, I was leaning towards the European model. Later, I changed my mind after long discussions with the Oregon people. They convinced me that direct physician intervention was not necessary. Jeri could have had her two extra days and still terminated her own life.[1]

What made me change my mind? The short answer: liquid Nembutal. Jeri would have been able to swallow it almost to the very end. If she had reached the point where she couldn't swallow it, she could have self-administered the liquid by way of a catheter. (It is perfectly legal for a nurse to insert a catheter for hydration purposes.) What if Jeri was unable to self-administer? Then, she wouldn't have been able to have the Nembutal. On the other hand, being in that bad a shape would have made her a candidate for terminal sedation—a legally available option from hospices.

It appears that the people in Oregon have the answers. Their technology provides maximum safeguards through self-administration and maximum flexibility for timing one's death. In addition, the dying can ask to have a physician present for support, advice, and standard comfort care. For example, attending physicians can clear an airway in the case of regurgitation or administer medication to relieve pain. In 2009, the state reported that a physician or health-care provider was present in 87% of the cases at the time of ingestion. In the remaining

---

[1] Roland Halpern of *Compassion & Choices* spent a lot of time and effort educating me. He was very patient.

cases, the patient, for whatever reason, did not want to have a doctor or health-care provider present.[2]

Lessons Learned

Self-deliverance is very difficult in states where assisted dying is not a legal option. Yes, it can be done but there's also a lot that can go wrong. So reader beware. If you're in this situation, you may want to carefully consider the hospice alternative before attempting the do-it-yourself approach. Jeri's predicament clearly illustrates why assisted dying must be legalized. It's that missing insurance that she really wanted.

Here are the benefits that legalized assisted dying, Oregon style, provides in this situation:

- *Greatly reduces terminal anxiety and angst*. Knowing that you have access to legalized assisted dying gives you peace of mind. It's an insurance policy. You know that you can always pull the plug if things are really bad. You are able to stop worrying prematurely about the pain and agony that the disease might cause in its final stages. It helps lessen your angst during this anticipatory period.

- *Eliminates a major source of mercy killings.* There is no need for family members to kill their terminal loved ones who are in pain. The act is now firmly in the hands of the dying person with guidance from the medical team. The family can now breathe a sigh of relief. Family members can attend to the needs of their loved ones at the end without fear that they will be asked to commit murder.

- *Eliminates a major source of murder-suicides.* By eliminating the murder half, legalized assisted dying also eliminates the suicide that follows. In a strange way, assisted dying may help preserve life.

- *Eliminates the need for clandestine pills.* Legalized assisted dying eliminates the need for dangerous do-it-yourself solutions. Instead of

---

[2] Oregon Department of Human Services, *Twelfth Annual Report on Oregon's Death with Dignity Act* (March, 2010).

the "not-so-lethal" underground pills, you will have access to Nembutal. This means there will be no more botched suicide attempts that require plastic bags over the head to finish the job.

- *Eliminates the need to incriminate helpful physicians.* Legalized assisted dying eliminates the need for a euthanasia underground. There's no need to shop for sympathetic physicians who illegally prescribe lethal drugs. It's now all out in the open.

- *Lets you operate within the medical system.* With legalized assisted dying, you're not on your own any longer. The medical establishment can help you with all the death-related issues. Your final drugs will come from a reputable pharmacy. The dosage, determined by doctors, will be based on the best medical knowledge. Your designated caregiver can pick up the prescription. You'll have access to nurses and doctors. In Oregon, doctors and nurses are often present at the time of death. It's all very familiar, comforting and legitimate. You're actively involved in all the decision-making that surrounds your death. At the very end, you can decide to die without leaving your bed.

- *Provides death with dignity.* Assisted dying lets you decide how much function and dignity you want left when you die. You can wait until everything shuts down, or you can go sooner. You get to determine when enough is enough.

- *Makes the terminally ill feel they're in control.* At the end, you gradually start to lose control over every function. You feel totally helpless. You're at the mercy of the disease, your caregivers, and the system. The assisted dying option puts you back in control. It would have made Jeri feel that she had total control over the most important decision—her dying. The remote control switch would have been in her hands; she could have chosen to click or not to click. Note: Research from Oregon shows that the primary motivation for physician-assisted dying is the desire for control.

- *Provides a peaceful and restful death.* The technology of euthanasia allows you to die painlessly, in deep sleep. It's what most of us envision as an ideal death. There's no need for a violent act of self-destruction. You don't have to blow your brains out, hang yourself with a noose, jump off a cliff, or smother yourself with a plastic bag. You simply fall asleep and never wake up.

- *Allows the terminally ill to choose the optimum time to die.* Legalized assisted dying gives you full control over the exact timing of your death. You can decide when enough is enough. This eliminates the timing problem Jeri faced, "Not too early and not too late." It's important that the choice of the time of death be made by the person who is dying. Typically, the family encourages their loved ones to hold on: we want to enjoy them as long as we can. However, unless you're into sadism, there's nothing enjoyable about watching a loved one being tortured by a disease in its final stages. It's important to let them know that it's okay to go. The decision of when to go is now in their hands. Note: Jeri had a vision of how she wanted to die, but she could have delayed her death as long as she wanted. There was no set date. Also, she didn't have to go that way. All the choices would be hers to make, up to the very last second. And, she could always change her mind.

- *Makes it possible to visualize one's death.* Imagining your death can be very empowering and highly therapeutic. For example, Jeri's dream had a very calming effect on her. She could visualize her forthcoming death and see something beautiful ahead. She imagined death as a celebration of her life. It became an event she could look forward to—like a wedding or anniversary. She imagined that her death would be peaceful, in a beautiful setting, surrounded by love and friends. It was a powerful visualization that helped her cope. She was able to look death in the face without fear. Legalized assisted dying makes it possible to envision such beautiful, calming, and self-empowering deaths.

- *Allows the terminal to focus on the more important issues.* During the last days of her life, Jeri should not have had to mull over the technology of dying. Instead, she should have spent every waking moment enjoying what was left of her life and looking back at what it was all about. Legalized assisted dying would have given her that option.

- *Eliminates a major source of grief.* In *Grieving a Soulmate* I explain that "the last days" have a huge impact on the grieving that follows. A "good death" leaves behind loved ones in peace. In contrast, a tortuous and painful death is the stuff of nightmares. During grieving, these final scenes are constantly being replayed and ruminated over. They are the source of lava-hot grieving pains called *grief bursts*. The survivors feel guilt for not having stopped the suffering. They feel helpless for not having been able to help their loved ones when the disease spread. The scenes from the last days can haunt them. When it comes to memories, these last few days can overshadow an entire lifetime of good living. You see your loved one through the prism of these last few days. Consequently, a good death with a proper goodbye is equally important to the survivors.

- *Provides an iron-clad guarantee that it is voluntary.* The Oregon model does not require a physician to administer a lethal injection. Jeri could have done it all through self-administration. This provides maximum protection against abuse.

- *Provides safeguards that benefit the patient.* States that support assisted dying require that physicians inform the patients about all other treatment options available to them before they prescribe the Nembutal. Mostly, they want to make sure you understand that other avenues may be available. In other words, they want you to be an informed consumer. Typically, two doctors will go over your concerns about pain management, the process of dying, and the loss of control. If you're overly anxious or depressed, they can send you to a psychiatrist for a trial run of anti-depressants. In Oregon, they'll point you to a hospice palliative-care specialist who can further explain your options for managing pain and dealing with disability as the disease progresses. Even if she had the Nembutal, Jeri would have used hospice as long as she could keep the pain under control.

Disability wasn't her biggest worry. She knew that she could fully depend on me with additional help from her girlfriends and home-care assistants. She was going to postpone that final goodbye as long as she could. Jeri made informed decisions. You should note that the role of the physicians is to provide patients with information to help them make these kinds of decisions; it's informed consent. Doctors, hospices, psychiatrists, and family members may have their own biases, values, or agenda. So buyer beware! Remember, it's your life. Only you can make this final decision; no coercion is allowed.

This type of "good death" is definitely within reach in places where physician-assisted dying is legal. This option is now available in the states of Oregon, Washington, and Montana. The next chapter is about hospice and palliative care, our current best options in states where the prohibition against assisted dying is still in effect.

Chapter 3

The Way of Hospice and Palliative Care

"These days, swift catastrophic illness is the exception; for most people, death comes only after a long medical struggle with an incurable condition—advanced cancer, progressive organ failure (usually the heart, kidney, or liver), or the multiple debilities of very old age. In all such cases, death is certain, but the timing isn't. So everyone struggles with this uncertainty—with how, and when, to accept that the battle is lost. As for last words, they hardly seem to exist anymore. Technology sustains our organs until we are well past the point of awareness and coherence.... In the past few decades, medical science has rendered obsolete centuries of experience, tradition, and language about our mortality, and created a new difficulty for mankind: how to die."

—Dr. Atul Gawande[1]

Nothing had prepared me for Jeri's final days: I was completely taken by surprise. Everything happened very fast and it seemed that all I could do was react. After almost ten years of caregiving, I thought nothing could surprise me; I would just deal with each crisis as it presented itself. I was wrong. The last days are very different and extremely demanding. Why was I so unprepared after all these years? The short answer is that there is no step-by-step guide for how to deal with death by cancer—or death from any chronic disease, for that

---

[1] Atul Gawande, "Letting Go: What Should Medicine Do When It Can't Save Your Life?," *The New Yorker*, August 2, 2010.

matter. I had to grope my way across this strange landscape we call the "end of life" while weighed down by the extreme anguish of seeing my partner go. The only real guidance I had received was from Jeri, who had given me a very clear directive: "Please, make sure I do not suffer at the end. I don't want pain."

In this long chapter, I will explain why modern medicine does not do end-of-life well, especially in the era of slow dying. Consequently, the majority of us will end up suffering. We will experience the "bad death." However, there are sizable pockets within the current system where a relatively "good death" can be had. Think of it as a parallel end-of-life system. With some skillful navigation and lots of luck, you may discover the system of hospice and palliative care. Hopefully, you'll discover it soon enough to reap the benefits. Hospice is more than just "a place to die." It's an end-of-life philosophy. I can tell you from first-hand experience that the end-of-life care Jeri received in that system surpassed my wildest expectations.

To help you understand the system of hospice and palliative care, I will briefly go over Jeri's last days and the decisions that we faced along the way. The key to a "good death" is to make the transition from the medical system into the parallel end-of-life system and do it soon enough. I will cover the lessons we learned in the process of giving Jeri her good death. You'll be getting a guided tour of America's current end-of-life system. I'll tell you what works, what doesn't work, and who does what to whom and when. This is the information I wish I had when I was helping Jeri navigate through her dying process.

As good as they are, hospice and palliative care do not provide all the answers. There are many gotchas. This parallel system is not for everyone. It shouldn't come as a surprise that I'm not particularly fond of terminal sedation; I will explain why the Nembutal does a better job and should be added to the current palliative mix. Furthermore, we need the Nembutal option when all else fails. If I was terminally ill, hospice and palliative care would be my first choice. However, I would also want a legally-acquired vial of Nembutal in my pocket, just in case. I will end this long chapter by making the case that hospice and the Nembutal can be synergistic: we need both.

Slow Dying: Fighting Till the End

Until recently, the dying process was brief, sudden, and unexpected. Life-threatening diseases—such as infections, difficult childbirth, pneumonia, or heart attacks—would kill within days. Adults lived into their sixties. Today, we live much longer. We die from chronic diseases that progress over years. The quote from Dr. Atul Gawande describes the predicament of slow dying. Typically, it involves a long medical struggle with an incurable condition.

The trajectory of a modern death is slow decline, periodic crises, continuous medical interventions, and then death. This is complicated by the fact that modern medicine has the technology to sustain us past the point of awareness. So it's hard to know when we're actively dying. For doctors and their patients, death signifies defeat. It means losing in the war against the disease. Patients are encouraged to think positively, never lose hope, and fight to the very end. Here's a short description of how these wars play out against our most common chronic illnesses:

- *Cancer*. About one-quarter of Americans will die from cancer. Typically, the fight against cancer starts with a de-bulking operation. Next, there are the endless chemo cycles, radiations, and last-ditch clinical trials. There are visits to the emergency room to deal with chemo side effects. Later, there are hospital stays to deal with the pain caused by the cancer in its final stages. Finally, there's a period of rapid decline; death comes relatively quickly.

- *Heart disease.* This is the leading cause of deaths in the United States and is a major cause of disability. About every 25 seconds an American will have a coronary event, and about one every minute will die from one. This disease once killed people quickly. Now, most of us will live a long time with diseases of the heart and the circulatory system. There's a ton of technology that can be thrown into the fight against heart disease. The list includes stents, bypass surgery, defibrillators, valve replacements, transplants, medications, and so on. Each technological intervention has its side effects. Initially, people feel okay on an average day but suffer shortness of breath with physical exertion. Over time the condition worsens and reduces activity to a minimum. In the final stages of heart failure, emergency room visits grow more frequent. Life support medications temporarily improve the pumping of a failing heart. At the end, there are numerous hospital stays to relieve shortness of breath. Sometimes, weeks are spent in rehab facilities. Patients can appear to be near-death one day and then do better the next. Usually, death will be sudden when it happens.

- *Lung disease.* These are diseases like emphysema, pulmonary fibrosis, and chronic bronchitis. They are marked by intense periods of shortness of breath that require hospitalizations. As the disease progresses, the frequency of hospital visits increases. Towards the end, there could be several hospital visits a month as the lungs start to steadily decline. Treatments include the use of round-the-clock inhalers, bronchodilators, and oxygen. Various medications are administered to clear the airways, reduce anxiety, and to fight infections and inflammations. Eventually, patients are put on mechanical ventilators and kept sedated in intensive care units (ICUs). An incision may be made in the throat to insert a breathing tube. Some patients may be released to nursing homes with semi-portable ventilators.[2]

- *Kidney failure.* Many people have progressively diminished kidney function as they age. The two kidneys can also be damaged by diseases such as diabetes, heart complications, and severe infections. This damage results in an accumulation of toxins in the blood that would normally be cleansed by the kidneys and then eliminated

---

[2] David Feldman and Andrew Lasher, *The End-of-Life Handbook* (New Harbinger, 2007).

through urination. A few lucky patients will receive kidney transplants. The rest will require dialysis treatment to mechanically remove the toxins from the blood. Typically, this treatment is received three times a week and keeps patients alive for years. While prolonging life, dialysis does little to halt the progression of diabetes that may have caused the kidney failure. Often the treatment causes infections in the bloodstream, which may require hospital stays. Of course, diabetes can cause other serious complications that may require amputations and other treatments. Death by withholding dialysis treatment can be relatively peaceful and quick—usually, patients die within seven to ten days. They'll require palliative treatment to ease the transition. In the United States, about 20,000 people each year choose to terminate dialysis and accept death.[3]

- **Brain failure.** This includes Alzheimer's, vascular dementia (small strokes), and Parkinson's disease. In 2010, 5.3 million Americans of all ages suffered from Alzheimer's.[4] It's a very difficult disease for caregivers. As the disease progresses, patients are unable to recognize their loved ones or make decisions. In the final stages, they forget how to use their muscles and are bed-bound.[5] They have trouble eating, swallowing, and breathing. Most end up in nursing homes. Repeated hospital stays may be needed to treat low blood pressure, infections, aspiration pneumonia, and shortness of breath. Eventually, the patient may end up in the ICU on life support attached to ventilators, antibiotic drips, heart monitors, and feeding and hydration tubes.

Modern medicine is a superb fighting machine designed to combat these chronic illnesses. The fight begins with our 911 emergency

---

[3] Lewis Cohen, *No Good Deed: A Story of Medicine, Murder Accusations, and the Debate over How We Die* (Harper, 2010).

[4] Alzheimer's Association, "2010 Alzheimer's Disease Facts and Figures," *Alzheimer's & Dementia* (Vol. 6, 2010).

[5] Joanne Lynn and Joan Harrold, *Handbook for Mortals* (Oxford University Press, 1999).

response systems, hospital emergency rooms, and ICUs. Our physicians are highly-trained specialists with access to sophisticated technology, such as CT and MRI scans, surgical robots, mechanical ventilators, dialysis machines, high-precision radiation, artificial hearts, biotech, and so on. The physicians are trained to win against the disease, and their job is to keep us alive for as long as possible. They have succeeded and we now live into our eighties.

Most of Us Die in Hospitals

The modern medical fighting machine was designed to keep us alive, not to help us die. Death is seen as an "inadequately treated disease"— a failure of modern medicine. Hospitals are not in the business of nursing the chronically ill. They're not set up to provide end-of-life care. Typically, you are admitted for a specific condition. You are then released as soon as you get treated. In Jeri's case, she was admitted and released several times during her last two months—mostly, to deal with her shifting pain. Patients with chronic illnesses are often rescued from the brink of death by high-tech interventions in the ICU. It's a constant roller coaster with recovery, followed by decline, followed by slight improvement. You can never tell when the next visit to the ICU may be the final one.

Note: I believe that most insurance companies require that you be released from a hospital after treatment is completed. You just can't say, "I think I'm going to die sometime, and I'd like to spend my remaining days in the hospital." Of course, they'll take you in if you need prolonged acute care. In this case, you may end up dying in the hospital's ICU, intubated with all sorts of life-support equipment.

According to U.S. government statistics, about 50% of all patients with chronic illness die in hospitals; another 25% die in nursing homes. (Note: In 2008, 22% of patients who died in nursing homes were also enrolled in hospice.) Most of these hospital deaths are unplanned. Hospitals may provide comfort care when they think a patient has just hours or days left to live.

Nursing homes provide comfort care but very little treatment. They refuse to take responsibility for end-of-life care. Like everyone else, they dial 911 when a patient needs serious medical attention. Typically, the ICU then stabilizes the patient's condition and sends him or her back to the nursing home. This may occur several times before a fragile and exhausted patient dies.[6] This revolving door between the nursing homes and the ICUs makes it hard to foresee where people in these situations will end up dying.

ICUs and Nursing Homes: The "Bad Deaths"

Dying in a hospital ICU is probably the most brutal type of death in America today. Why? Because ICUs are aggressive, life-saving, high-tech machines. Even for patients with less than a 5% chance of survival, the presence of the life-sustaining technology creates a moral imperative to use it for last-ditch interventions. Instead of dying gently, patients will end up going through a torture process. The torture progressively escalates as the condition worsens—first a ventilator, then feeding tubes, followed by an incision in the chest (a *thoracotomy*) to manipulate the lungs, esophagus, or heart, and the list goes on. If a heart stops beating, a surgeon may have less than a few minutes to rip through the skin, crack open the patient's chest, and then manually massage the organ to force circulation—there's no time for anesthesia. Yes, modern medicine can be aggressive. Here's a description of such a death as witnessed by ICU nurses:

> "Sally was 52 years old when she was admitted to our ICU with empyema and severe congestive heart failure. We knew Sally and her family well, including her husband and two teenage children. Sally had spent two months in our unit with viral cardiomyopathy and pneumonia. During her second admission, her team of physicians, including cardiologists, pulmonologists, infectious disease specialists, and cardiothoracic surgeons, agreed that the

---

[6] George D. Lundberg, *Severed Trust: Why American Medicine Hasn't Been Fixed* (Basic Books, 2000).

chance of successfully treating the empyema without a thoracotomy was small. Furthermore, the physicians agreed that extubation after surgery would be unlikely. Unfortunately, Sally did not respond to antibiotic therapy, underwent a thoracotomy, and returned to the unit intubated....

As time went by, Sally began to write 'let me die' and to tug at her endotracheal tube. As they restrained and sedated Sally, the nursing staff, caught between the multiple physicians and Sally's family members, felt increasing emotional turmoil. Although Sally's family had witnessed her inconceivable deterioration, they were unable to initiate discussions about death and dying and saw no alternatives to her present situation. Although the nurses developed a close relationship with the family, nursing staff were uncomfortable initiating discussions about treatment options. Finally, a new consulting pulmonologist began the discussion of withdrawing life-support treatment. The family responded with relief, and Sally died several months after her admission."[7]

Watching their loved ones die in the ICU can be very hard on families. Typically, they don't understand all the complicating factors or the goals of the treatment. The environment is extremely high-tech and disorienting. Families just want the suffering to end. They just want to take their loved ones home like they did during previous ICU interventions. This time, it's different. Their loved ones won't make it.

The Modern Torture Chambers

Most patients have not had direct discussions with their loved ones about death and dying. For example, Sally did not have an advance directive. However, even if she had explicitly specified *no intubation* in a directive, it would have been a difficult decision for the family to enforce. For example, what would you do if your loved one in an ICU cried: "Help! I can't breathe. I'm suffocating"? Many health-care

---

[7] P. Miller et al., "End-of-Life Caring in Intensive Care Unit: A Challenge for Nurses," *American Journal of Critical Care* (Vol. 10, 2001).

proxies would probably override the directive and request that their loved one be put on a respirator. Unfortunately, it's a slippery slope from then on. One intervention leads to the next. The system has its own dynamic, which you just set in motion.

For the next days and weeks you're likely to watch your loved one being tortured in front of you. The torture chamber is postmodern with bright lights, loud noises, and high-tech equipment everywhere. You'll hardly be able to touch your loved one who is buried in tubes and surrounded by machines. The tubes in the mouth make it impossible to speak. Many will have their arms tied to the side of the bed to prevent them from pulling away the tubes to free themselves. Often, they'll be communicating through their eyes and pleading with you to let them die (or help them die).

Notice that the torture chamber at the end of life is the same facility that kept the chronically ill alive all those years—remember all those interventions. It's part of that superb system that has extended our average lifespan by twenty years. What went wrong? Unfortunately, near the end, our body starts to experience multiple failures as it starts to shut down. The ICU people will, of course, rise to the challenge, as they've always done. They have the equipment and technology to keep almost any organ going. When an organ begins to fail, they respond by attaching a new machine to keep the dying body going. Pretty soon the dying person is totally intubated. There's a machine or intervention for each failed organ. So, the person can be kept artificially alive for weeks and months. Annually, around 540,000 Americans die using ICU services.[8] As many as 50% of those dying patients receive care that is beyond their wishes during these last days.[9]

The SUPPORT investigation of 9,000 patients dying in hospitals is the most comprehensive study of its kind ever undertaken. The findings

---

[8] D. C. Angus et al., "Use of Intensive Care at the End of Life in the United States: An Epidemiologic Study," *Critical Care Medicine* (Vol. 32, 2004).

[9] G. M. Rocker et al., "End-of-life issues in the ICU: A Need for Acute Palliative Care," *Journal of Palliative Care Supplement* (October, 2000).

were very disturbing. Here's some of what they revealed about dying in U.S. hospitals: 38% of patients who died spent ten or more days in an ICU; more than 50% of patients who died had moderate to severe pain during the last five days of life; more than 50% of the patients were conscious prior to death; many suffered from shortness of breath; most struggled with severe side-effects such as intense fatigue, confusion, nausea, constipation, skin sores, dry mouth, and itchy skin; only 47% of the physicians knew what their patients' desires for end-of-life care were; only 46% were aware of their patients' do-not-resuscitate (DNR) orders; and 46% of DNR orders were written within two days of death.[10]

If you ask me, dying in an ICU is a high-tech nightmare. Watching a loved one die there will make grieving very painful. As Virginia Morris puts it:

"The people who are dying are typically distanced, both physically and emotionally, from loved ones, who can't hurdle the physical intrusions of the hospital, and who often don't have any idea how to help or what to do. They feel powerless and frightened in the face of death. They don't know how to offer their love, to say their good-byes, or to provide solace to a loved one who is dying in such a way."[11]

Between hospitals and nursing homes, the situation has become so dire that in 2003 the *National Association of Attorneys General*, an organization of the fifty states' top law-enforcement officials, declared end-of-life patient care the top consumer-protection issue in the country.[12]

---

[10] The SUPPORT principal investigators, "A controlled trial to improve care for seriously ill hospitalized patients: the Study to Understand Prognoses and Preferences for Outcomes and Risks of Treatments (SUPPORT)," *JAMA* (Vol. 274, 1995). Also check the follow-up articles.

[11] Virginia Morris, *Talking About Death* (Algonquin Books, 2004).

[12] Stephen P. Kiernan, *Last Rights: Rescuing the End of Life System From the Medical System* (St. Martin's Press, 2007).

Hospice: Another Way to Die

At this point, you're probably screaming, "Where's the Nembutal?" Hold on! There's another way to die in America. You may still need the Nembutal, but let's first explore the alternative. In 2008, approximately 38% of all U.S. deaths were under the care of a hospice program.[13] Here's where these people died: 40.7% at home; 22% in a nursing home facility; 21% in a hospice in-patient facility; 6.1% in an assisted-living facility; and 10.1% in an acute-care hospital not operated by the hospice team.

The bad news is that 35.8% were in the hospice program for less than a week before they died. Typically, this means they did not get the full benefits of hospice care. For example, some could have been sent to hospice to die after a prolonged ICU stay. Also, there's another 10.1% who were sent back to the ICU to die. Consequently, only 20% of the dying in America are getting a proper hospice death. The good news is that the hospice movement is spreading out—it's now in nursing homes, prisons, and assisted-care residences. It's also good news that one in five Americans will probably experience a relatively "good death." One in ten may even die in their own home surrounded by family and friends.

So, what makes a hospice death good? The short answer: It's better than the alternative. When it comes to dying, "good" is relative. Hospice death is low-tech, holistic, and family-friendly; it's based on comfort care rather than constant medical interventions. It takes place in a residential setting instead of in a hospital. It focuses on pain management instead of treating the disease. Mostly, it's a more natural and comfortable way to die.

Origins of Hospice and Palliative Care

The modern hospice movement originated in England in 1967, when Dame Cicely Saunders founded *St. Christopher's* to provide palliative

---

[13] National Hospice and Palliative Care Organization, *Facts and Figures: Hospice Care in America* (October, 2009).

care and pain management for the dying. Her program included psychological, spiritual, social, and bereavement services for the dying and their families. Her goal was to create a future in which "no one dies alone or in pain."[14] She emphasized that family must be involved in the caregiving to ensure that the dying "live fully until they die." The central medical philosophy of hospice is: "We do not prolong life artificially or hasten the dying process unnaturally." Dame Saunders was actively opposed to euthanasia. However, she was a big fan of liquid morphine, which she felt the patient did not need "to earn."

In 1974, Florence Wald, a nursing dean at Yale who worked with Dame Saunders, opened the first U.S. hospice unit in Connecticut. In 1983, Congress approved Medicare payment for hospice care, but only after curative care is stopped—you can't have both. By 2008, the number of U.S. hospices grew to 4,850. Hospices are now located in all 50 states. According to the *National Hospice and Palliative Care Organization*, "The majority of U.S. hospices are independent, freestanding agencies. The remaining are either part of a hospital system, home-health agency, or nursing home. Hospices range in size from small all-volunteer agencies that care for fewer than 50 patients per year to large, national corporate chains that care for thousands of patients each day. In 2008, 76.7% of hospices had fewer than 500 total admissions."

Dame Saunders' early emphasis on "both the sophisticated science of our treatments and the art of our caring" became the basis for modern *palliative medicine*. In 1997, the World Health Organization defined palliative care as: "The active total care of patients whose disease is not responsive to curative treatment." In September 2006, palliative medicine became a recognized medical subspecialty in the U.S. It now has its own fellowships, hospital departments, and medical school courses. Its practitioners provide pain management, symptom control, and counseling for people with advanced disease. Non-hospice palliative care is offered simultaneously with life-prolonging and

---

[14] Constance E. Putnam, *Hospice or Hemlock?* (Praeger, 2002).

curative therapies in hospitals. These programs are now available in more than 80% of U.S. hospitals with more than 300 beds.[15] Palliative care and hospice work in tandem. You can think of hospice as intensive palliative care for people who have stopped curative treatments of their disease. There are an estimated 13,000 hospice and palliative care programs in the world.[16]

Hospice and palliative care have changed the paradigm on how we die. Yet, this new paradigm is not very well understood by either the public or the doctors. Some think that hospice implies "giving up." Others have a vague idea that "it's where you go to die and it's a good thing." However, we rarely understand hospice's deep implications on how we die. Most importantly, we don't know how or when to ask for hospice care. So, many of us end up dying in the ICU instead. Some will discover hospice—but not soon enough.

The So-Called "Death Panels"

Most of us prefer to avoid the topic of death. We live in a death-denying culture. However, denial can have some serious ramifications. Closing our eyes and letting the system follow its course could easily land us intubated in an ICU at the end of our lives. To prevent this outcome, we need to protect ourselves and understand our choices. And, we need to think about it while we still can. Typically, it means having several *conversations* about death and dying. This is especially important for the chronically ill. It could make the difference between having a relatively "good death" and a very "bad death." It's the difference between dying in the ICU versus dying under the care of hospice.

Ironically, some politicians called these conversations *death panels,* and they campaigned against having them funded by Medicare. It

---

[15] Amy S. Kelley, et al., "Palliative Care—A Shifting Paradigm," *New England Journal of Medicine* (Vol. 363, 2010).

[16] William H. Colby, *Unplugged: Reclaiming Our Right to Die in America* (Amacom, 2006).

seems that they do not want us to have any control over how we die. It seems that even discussing the topic is taboo.

Most doctors would also prefer not to discuss the topic. Why? It's very emotional and complicated. To do it justice would require hours of discussions with the patient. Doctors are trained to heal, not to discuss death. They are taught to fight the disease with everything in their arsenal. No surrender. So they would rather initiate another treatment than deal with the existential issue of dying. Continuing the treatments also protects doctors against malpractice lawsuits.

Luckily, this is an area where palliative-care specialists can be of great help.[17] Even though insurance does not pay for these consultations, we must have these discussions to understand what our options are. In the next sections, I will tell you about three death-related conversations you must initiate: How do I protect myself? When do I stop fighting? Where will I die? The first conversation is straightforward and practical. The next two are blurrier; I will use Jeri's conversations to demonstrate the issues. In states where physician-assisted dying is legal, you can have one more conversation: How will I die? Sadly, it was not an option for Jeri. In Chapter 5, I cover this missing but very important conversation.

First Conversation: How Do I Protect Myself?

This is a conversation you must have immediately. Remember the family tug-of-war over poor Terri Schiavo. You can easily protect yourself from these types of situations by providing an *advance directive* consisting of two documents. You'll need a *Living Will* that specifies the type of life-support care you would want in various situations. For example, "if I become terminally ill or injured" or "if I become permanently unconscious." Because you can't anticipate every situation, you'll also need a *Durable Power of Attorney for Health Care*. This document lets you appoint your *health-care proxy*—the

---

[17] Timothy Quill, *Caring for Patients at the End of Life* (Oxford University Press, 2001).

person who will make health-care decisions for you.[18] Be sure to pick a proxy you can trust to navigate the health-care system on your behalf.

Remember, it is a pretty complicated terrain out there: death can be quite chaotic. For example, you may have specified "no intubation," but what if you need a ventilator for a short time? This is where your choice of proxy becomes important. It's also a good idea to write a *goodbye letter* that provides additional guidance to your proxy. For instance, you could write, "Don't continue treatments if there is no hope of recovery to my normal lifestyle." You can then specify what "normal" means for you. The letter can also include your instructions on cremation or burial and the memorial service. Bottom line: Make sure your proxy knows the system well and understands your wishes.

Some states support the use of a directive known as a POLST form, short for *Physician Orders for Life-Sustaining Treatment.* A health-care professional completes the form after having a conversation with you to understand your wishes and goals of care. Both you and a doctor must sign the POLST form in order for it to be valid. The POLST complements your advance directive and is not intended to replace that document. You should insist on completing a POLST upon admission to any medical facility. It ensures that the physician has read and understood your directives and choice of health-care proxy.

At the end, your physician may issue a *Do Not Resuscitate (DNR)* order. Typically, this medical order is kept in your hospital charts. You'll also need an *at-home DNR* to keep paramedics from resuscitating you in case someone calls 911. Yes, you must do everything you can to protect yourself from the system.

Additionally, learning more about death won't kill you. Most of us go out of our way to avoid the topic of death and especially its details. As a result, we're totally unprepared when end-of-life confronts us. We're

---

[18] Every state has its own versions. *The National Hospice and Palliative Care Organization* (www.caringinfo.org/stateaddownload) has all 50 state forms available for free download.

all going to die, so the least we can do is spend a few hours learning about death. The knowledge will make us better navigators and more informed consumers when the time arrives. I tell my friends that they should all read *Talking About Death* by Virginia Morris. Check the resources at the end of this book for additional reading.

Second Conversation: When Do I Stop Fighting?

Eventually, there comes a point where the disease has progressed and it's time to stop the fight and prepare for the next phase—dying. Yes, you must manage your death just like you managed your disease. To do this, you must step back, change course, and redirect your energy. Now is the time to deal with death.[19] Of course, this is easier said than done. When is it really over? Who will make the decision? Who will initiate the discussion?

As I said earlier, each chronic disease has its own trajectory. Each patient is different. The active phase of dying, the body's shutting down, is well understood—I cover this in detail in *Grieving a Soulmate*. What we don't understand well is when to stop the treatment because it's not working any longer. Doctors want to maintain hope, and they always seem to have one more trick up their sleeves. Patients want to live, and so they side with their doctors. However, the danger is ending up dying in an ICU during one more intervention. So how do you change the course?

I will use Jeri as a case study to show what's involved in these conversations. I lifted the material from *Grieving a Soulmate.* If you're interested, you can read the details in that book. Jeri was an incredible chemo warrior. She had fought the disease nonstop for almost ten years. In the previous chapter, we went over how she handled the news that her cancer had spread—about 15 months before her death. She spent the next ten months trying out different chemos and surfing. However, the chemos seemed to be getting less and less effective. We

---

[19] It may be a good time to read Elizabeth Kübler-Ross, *On Death and Dying* (MacMillan, 1969).

could tell that the cancer was spreading from the rising CA-125 counts. We stopped counting when the cancer marker rose to 547—the norm is below 35. Outwardly, Jeri was still doing fine. These were very good months for her. She learned how to "walk" on her surfboard. She even managed to get me through my operation and other health-related issues. We took turns caregiving. It was a very sweet time.

No More Chemo

By February 2009, Jeri had exhausted all chemos. After more than nine years, none seemed to work. The cancer had become chemo-resistant. Dr. Terada told us, "I didn't think I'd ever run out of chemos." A new CAT scan revealed that the cancer had spread extensively. She had a new tumor on her bladder, and the ones in the lungs had become bigger. It looked like the end was near. Of course, no one could tell by looking at Jeri. She was beautiful and strong. Her friend Kathy would say, "She's a force of nature." Outwardly, Jeri looked like a surfer—an athlete. Inside, the cancer was ravaging her.

No more chemo. I was stunned. I felt that same sinking feeling I had when I first learned of Jeri's cancer. I heard myself asking Dr. Terada, "Does this mean we should start hospice now?" He was taken aback by the question. He reflected for a second and then answered, "No, not yet. You can go talk to them if you like, but it's not time yet. If you're in hospice, we can't do further treatments like radiation. We may need to radiate to manage the pain."

In contrast to the rest of us, Jeri had a big smile on her face. On the way to the car she told me, "Now that chemo is over, I can just surf every day until I die." It seemed like a great plan. I was all for it, but I still didn't have a clue about what would happen next and when. I didn't want to share my fears with Jeri. Instead, I replied, "Yes, keep surfing." Jeri did spend the next two months surfing.

I always thought that Jeri's death process would start with a failed organ. After the latest CAT scan, I expected either the bladder or a lung to go first. Instead, the first thing to fail was a limb. In mid-April, two months before her death, her right leg started to hurt. A week later, she was out swimming when the leg pain jumped through the roof. I had to rescue her out of the ocean. It was her last swim. She could hardly walk to the shore. My friend Mike helped me get her back home in a taxi. The next day, she was in a wheelchair. This was the first of a series of heartbreaks. Dr. Terada responded by prescribing Vicodin— her first narcotic painkiller. He also started Jeri on radiation. The hope was that it would shrink the tumors enough to diminish the pain. Perhaps, she would even regain the use of her leg and surf again. We had high hopes.

The Vicodin kept the pain under control for about a week. During that time, Jeri could move around in her wheelchair and go places. But it didn't last long. The pain baseline started to shift upwards again as the cancer spread. The growing tumors were pushing on nerves and causing more pain. Within three weeks she was taking the equivalent of 100 Vicodins per day in the form of Oxycontin, Fentanyl, and Methadone.

How Much Time Does She Have to Live?

Eventually, Jeri ended up in the hospital for pain management. She was treated by a world-class team of palliative-care specialists headed by Dr. Daniel Fischberg. Conveniently, Jeri's radiation treatment was also in the same hospital. So all the doctors she needed were under the same hospital roof. Again, the hope was that this dream team would find the right combination of treatments to get Jeri back in the surf lineup. This time, it didn't work.

About a month before Jeri died, I found enough courage to ask Dr. Terada the dreaded question, "How much time does Jeri have left?" He gave me the straight answer, "Well, I don't exactly know, but it's less than six months." Jeri was on the bed listening very attentively. When he left the room, she said, "Thank you for asking the question. I needed to know. It makes me feel better." In contrast, I felt like I had just been stabbed in the heart. I had to ask her, "Why does knowing this make you feel any better?" She answered, "Now I know what to expect." I was very sad.

Third Conversation: Where Do I Die?

With less than six months to live, Jeri became a candidate for hospice care. Dr. Terada signed a paper that allowed representatives from hospice to talk to us in the hospital. Because of where we lived, the choice narrowed to a single hospice, St. Francis. Tracy, the palliative-care counselor, encouraged us to take the hospice route. She wanted Jeri to be released from the hospital to the hospice. I was not convinced. Here's my best recollection of the exchange that took place that day:

Tracy: Hospices do a much better job than hospitals for end-of-life care. All the surveys show that.

Robert: I'm not convinced. I know, for a fact, that in this hospital you can keep Jeri's pain under control. We could just stay here until she dies. Her insurance covers 365 days of hospital stays. We have Dr. Terada and Dr. Fischberg here. Why would we go anywhere else?

Tracy: Hospices provide excellent pain management. Dr. Terada will still be Jeri's primary physician. In addition, they have their own doctors. Jeri will be much more comfortable there. Probably the most important thing is that they can also help you take care of her at home. She can be at home instead of in a hospital. Besides, you can always return to this hospital if things don't work out. All it takes is one signature.

Robert: But she won't have access to all the hospital equipment. What if she needs an EKG or blood transfusion?

Tracy: Yes, it's a different philosophy. Jeri can always come back to the hospital if she needs special treatment. You should talk to the hospice representatives directly and hear what they have to say. I can arrange for an interview tomorrow.

Tracy's most compelling argument was that I could have Jeri back home. The hospice people would provide round-the-clock support for pain management, which I felt we really needed to make it work from home. Later, I turned to Jeri and asked, "Where do you want to be?

The choices are: hospital, hospice facility, or home." She had a very clear-headed answer, "Let's first talk to the hospice people and see what they have to say."

The next day we got a visit from the hospice representative. We wasted no time getting down to the issues that concerned us. Again, this is my best recollection of what was said that day:

Jeri: I don't want to die in pain. When I need it, will you give me enough pain medicine to make me fully unconscious? How do I know that with a name like St. Francis you just won't end up sprinkling me with holy water and giving me last rites, instead of inducing a coma?

Hospice representative: You'll just have to trust your doctors to do what's right for you. Dr. Terada will still be there with you. We also have our own doctors who'll be managing your pain at all times.

Jeri: So how would we manage the pain at home? What happens if I get breakthrough pain that suddenly gets out of control in the middle of the night? How do we get the pain meds?

Hospice representative: We provide all your pain meds free of charge. Unlike regular doctors, our doctors can fax pain-medication prescriptions directly to a 24-hour pharmacy where you can pick them up. Our volunteers can also pick up the meds and bring them to you.

Robert: What happens at the brink of death when things start to break down all at once? If it really gets bad, can you guarantee her a room in the hospice facility?

Hospice representative: We'll always guarantee her a room when she gets into the active death process. We set aside a number of rooms for these type of situations. Just don't call 911.

Jeri: So, how will you determine that I'm actively dying?

Hospice representative: We will assign you a registered nurse (an RN) who will track your progress. Your RN will be visiting you at home on a regular basis—three times a week, or more if you need it. We also have an RN on duty at all times. Just call us when you need help.

Jeri: What other services do you provide at home?

Hospice representative: We'll provide—free of charge—all the equipment you'll need for home care. The list includes hospital beds, bathroom chairs, oxygen tanks, commodes, bronchodilators, bedside tables, and so on. We don't provide the actual home care. Your caregiver, Robert, will take care of you. Of course, he may need to hire help. I'll provide you with a list of agencies that specialize in home care. If Robert needs relief, you can stay in our facility—provided we have space. It will cost you $300 per day.... We're fully booked right now. Would you like me to put you on our waiting list? You can stay in the hospital until a room frees up.

Jeri: Yes, please put me on the waiting list. But Robert and I will need to research this some more before we sign up.

The meeting was very informative. Now Jeri wanted me to visit the hospice facility and report back to her. The next morning, my friend Spinner and I drove up the Pali highway to visit the hospice facility. The landscape was stunning—green forests and steep cliffs with waterfalls, as far as the eye could see. I got off at Queen Emma's summer palace. The hospice was in a beautiful mansion that stood right across from the palace gardens. Inside, the place was immaculate. There was a nice courtyard with tables and chairs. The rooms were superb and the staff seemed very friendly. It felt like we were at a bed-and-breakfast in the Napa Valley wine country. Spinner liked it, too. She said, "Jeri is going to love this place. It's so pretty."

I went back to the hospital to report to Jeri on what we had just seen. I had also talked to many people who said the hospice was really excellent. The ratings were, unequivocally, good. Here's my best recollection of the conversation I had with Jeri that day concerning hospice:

Robert: Where do we go from here? What are your thoughts?

Jeri: I like this hospice stuff. Perhaps, that's the way to go.

Robert: But I want you at home. Of course, I don't want you to suffer. Your comfort should always come first.

Jeri: It will take a lot of effort to take care of me at home. Why do you want to put yourself through that ordeal?

Robert: Because I love you. I'm really happy to be able to do this for you. I'm glad you saved my life last year, so that I can be here for you today. Last week, you told me you wanted to die near the ocean, looking at Diamond Head. The hospice is in the mountains. Of course, it's beautiful there, too. If I could provide you with the same care, would you prefer to be at home?

Jeri: Yes, I would prefer to be at home. Listen, I have a plan that may work. What I want to do next is to get released to the hospice facility. I can spend a few days there and get to know the doctors and nurses. I also want to see if this hospice stuff works. In the meantime, you can get the apartment ready for me. I'm sure the hospice people will tell you what you'll need for home care. It's part of what they do. You can take me home when you're ready.

Robert: Yep, it's a very good plan. Let's make it happen.

The next day, Jeri was released from the hospital to the hospice. It was on May 28, three weeks before she died. There were many tears as she said goodbye to the team that had taken her this far, but she was excited about going to the hospice. I wheeled her to the car, and we took the short drive up the hill to the hospice. For the next six days, this was her new home. It certainly beat the hospital room.

Jeri really loved the hospice facility and staff. The nurses were exceptionally good. She also liked and trusted her new hospice doctor. From her bed, Jeri could see emerald-green mountains. But, most of the time, she was not in bed. Instead, she was in her wheelchair exploring the grounds and visiting with her friends. She felt very alive. Unfortunately, the people in the adjoining rooms were all in the process of dying. Sometimes, Jeri could hear sounds of death. In the mornings, she was the only patient who could enjoy breakfast on the outside patio, overlooking the mountains.

Jeri felt very alive in a facility for the dying. This turned out to be a good thing because she got to meet the people who would later help her die. They all got to know her before she was on the brink of death. A few days later she told me, "I don't belong here, yet. Take me home." I was ready. With help from friends, I had turned our small apartment into a hospice suite.

Hospice: Not for Everyone

Hospice care certainly beats sudden and repeated trips to the emergency room, followed by lengthy hospital stays. However, to be eligible for hospice care, a doctor must declare that a person has no more than six months to live. Doctors can predict cancer deaths with some confidence. It's much harder to predict deaths from other chronic diseases.

Unlike hospitals, round-the-clock home care is not covered by insurance for patients who are in the hospice system. Home care for the dying requires an enormous amount of effort and time. It takes a team effort, a village. Caregiving for the actively dying can be incredibly complicated and expensive. For example, Registered Nurses (RNs) typically charge $50 per hour. In some cases, you may need round-the-clock RN support. Do the math to see if your finances can handle it.

Warning: Long-term care could easily be the wild card that wipes you out financially. You should consider buying long-term care insurance while you still can. If you don't have a caregiver, you may consider moving into a nursing home to obtain round-the-clock care. Again, this can be very expensive without long-term care insurance. Luckily, the poor are covered through Medicaid.

Pain Management: A Critical Issue

Pain management is a delicate and tortuous balancing act. It may take a lot of tweaking to get it right. "Enough" narcotics is whatever works to alleviate your pain. Hopefully, you'll remain lucid to have a life. Narcotics can be safely administered for months—or even years— before death. Don't worry: you won't turn into a drug addict, even if the doses seem terrifically high. At the end of life, there should be no maximum amounts set on pain relief. It's also important to use enough medication to prevent break-through pain. The medication must always stay ahead of the pain.

Note: All these medications have side effects—such as constipation, nausea, delirium, somnolence, lack of awareness, and respiratory failure—which must be managed. Also, don't underestimate the effort it takes to acquire narcotic-based meds. Be sure to fill the prescriptions before you leave the hospital. Always factor in the lag time needed to contact doctors and to obtain "permissions" for pain medications. Sometimes, your proxy can also be your pain advocate. Managing pain can be grueling even in hospitals; it's much easier in a hospice setting. Hospice and palliative care departments are particularly adept at end-of-life pain management.

Some of the extreme pain conditions—for example, nerve and neuropathic pain—may require high-tech procedures, such as the insertion of *epidural catheters* which deliver the narcotic directly to the spine. Typically, the hospice does not provide such procedures. You may want to have these done at the hospital before you sign up for hospice. In addition, *morphine pumps* are an added expense for most hospices. Consequently, they won't provide one unless you ask for it. In the final days, these pumps are needed to provide a steady supply of narcotic into the bloodstream. Make sure your proxy knows all of this.

Often, there will be unbearable suffering when the disease progresses to its terminal stages. Along with regular pain, there is a slew of "distressing symptoms." For example, the vast majority of patients with advanced cancer will have difficulty breathing.[20] At the end, they may appear to be gasping for air—they may feel like they're

---

[20] Suresh K. Reddy et al., "Characteristics and Correlates of Dyspnea in Patients with Advanced Cancer," *Journal of Palliative Medicine* (Vol. 12, 2009).

suffocating. This terrifying condition, called *dyspnea*, can sometimes be alleviated with oxygen, tranquilizers, and opiates such as the ones used for pain. Opiates tend to expand the arteries in the lungs, easing the passage of air. Often terminal sedation may be required to fully alleviate the condition.

In 1990, Dr. Vittorio Ventafridda, one the world's leading pain specialists, shocked the profession when he reported that 50% of his patients with advanced cancer had to be sedated into unconsciousness to relieve their pain. He reported that half of the "unbearable suffering" was caused by pain and the other half by shortness of breath.[21] To learn more about the experience of end-of-life pain, I recommend you read Marilyn Webb's book *The Good Death*—most of the information in it is still relevant.[22]

Palliative Sedation: Can You Depend on It?

Without euthanasia, the only way to control unbearable suffering today is through sedation to the point of unconsciousness—or *terminal sedation*. Patients are given a combination of narcotics, barbiturates, and anesthetics to induce coma. Death comes slowly from either the progressing disease, pneumonia, or starvation if artificial nutrition (and hydration) is withheld.

The hospice movement can claim that all pain can be managed because hospices have access to terminal sedation, which they call *palliative sedation*. They can reassure the dying that even their most distressing physical symptoms can be relieved. Of course, the administration of palliative sedation is just a way to put you to sleep forever. Typically, artificial hydration and nutrition are also withheld to prevent edema in the lungs. When that step is combined with palliative sedation, the person is put into a deep sleep and then allowed to die slowly.

---

[21] Vittorio Ventafridda et al., "Symptom Preference and Control During Cancer Patients' Last Days of Life," *Journal of Palliative Care* (Vol. 6, 1990).

[22] Marilyn Webb, *The Good Death* (Bantam Books, 1997).

Not all hospices use palliative sedation. According to the *National Hospice and Palliative Care Organization (NHPCO)*, its use on terminally-ill patients "ranges between 1% and 52%." This is a huge spread. It means that some hospices won't alleviate the excruciating pain at the end, while others use the technique on 52% of their patients.

On May 5, 2010, the NHPCO Ethics Committee issued a position statement on the use of palliative sedation.[23] Their position is that palliative sedation is appropriate "for the small number of imminently dying patients whose suffering is intolerable and refractory." They define *imminently dying* to mean "a prognosis of death within 14 days." *Refractory suffering* is "suffering that cannot be controlled despite aggressive efforts to identify tolerable therapy that does not compromise consciousness." As for a *small number*, it's somewhere between 1% and 52% of dying patients, but they consider "the upper end of the range as problematic." Finally, they want the treatment to be *titrated*, which means the level of sedation must be slowly increased to a level that is effective.

I find the NHPCO position to be extremely disturbing. If followed, it will result in a lot of unnecessary suffering. In my view, hospices must initiate palliative sedation *as soon* as the pain cannot be controlled by other means. Remember, Dame Saunders' vision was to deal with death in the most comfortable and caring way possible—letting people die in excruciating pain is *not* comfort care.

Also, physicians have no way of determining "14 days from death"— especially in low-tech hospice settings with no access to CAT scans and other sophisticated imaging and monitoring equipment. Why 14 days? What's so magical about that number? The NHPCO's answer: This is how long it takes to die when hydration is withheld.

---

[23] Timothy W. Kirk et al., "NHPCO Position Statement and Commentary on the Use of Palliative Sedation in Imminently Dying Terminally Ill Patients," *Journal of Pain and Symptom Management* (May, 2010).

Oh boy! I'll have a lot more to say about the serious ramifications of this "ethics directive." It's definitely a step in the wrong direction. Let's not give up on the Nembutal.

Hospice: Yes, There Is Unbearable Pain

Palliative medicine claims that, in theory, it should be able to control 95% of pain among those who are terminally ill. Even in this best-case scenario, more than 100,000 people will die in the U.S. each year experiencing unbearable pain. In practice, the numbers are much higher. Maybe that 95% pain-free number can be achieved, at *Memorial Sloan-Kettering's Cancer Center*, by Dr. Kathleen Foley and her team, which includes the world's leading pain specialists. Unfortunately, these numbers are not being seen at the nation's hospices which provide palliative care for the masses. Even with liquid morphine and palliative sedation, the record is dismal.

Among hospice patients who were asked about their pain level one week before death, 5% to 35% rated their pain as "severe" or "unbearable." An additional 25% reported their shortness of breath to be "unbearable."[24] This does not include other symptoms such as open wounds, pressure sores, confusion, vomiting, and emotional pain. The NHPCO's new conservative guidelines will only make this bad situation worse. Of course, hospice is much better than the ICU alternative, where 50% die in pain.

Jeri's Good Death, Hospice Style

Back to Jeri's story. Two weeks before she died, Jeri was back home overlooking the ocean and Diamond Head. She was so happy to be back. For the next ten days, she experienced a textbook-perfect hospice way of dying. The days were filled with fun and laughter. Her "girlfriends" turned this time into one big celebration. "We're going to bring Jeri to the ocean," became their battle cry. They were joined by

---

[24] Timothy Quill and Margaret Battin, Editors, *Physician-Assisted Dying: The Case for Palliative Care and Patient Choice* (Johns Hopkins University Press, 2004).

Nicole, our home-hospice RN. And, they enlisted the help of some very muscular Waikiki beach boys, who vowed they would carry Jeri into the ocean and then tow her to the surf lineup.

Everyone laughed and joked a lot. Jeri was slowing down, but she didn't seem to miss a beat. She was the heart of the party. She would soon tire, though, and take a short nap. This is when we planned the outing of the day. For example, we organized shopping trips to buy her new clothes. She would try them on with three of us helping her in the changing room. Several times, we took her out to dinner at some of her favorite restaurants. Jeri enjoyed her outings. She would put on makeup and get all dressed up for the occasion. Even though it made her tired, she was always ready to go.

Watching Surfers From the Moana

Eight days before Jeri died, I rented an ocean-front room at the Moana Surfrider for a 10-day stay. It was right on the beach directly overlooking her favorite surfing spot. For the next five days, the hotel room became our outing destination. We would leave home for the Moana each day at noon and return later in the evening. It was only a five-minute drive, but it took much preparation.

From the lanai of her hotel room, Jeri had a perfect view of what turned out to be the biggest swell of the year. She would wave at her surfer friends. In one gag, the girlfriends decided to bring the ocean to Jeri. So they showed up one day with a big container of ocean water with sand at the bottom. Jeri could then immerse her feet in ocean water while looking at the waves outside.

In the evenings, we would all eat dinner in the room overlooking the ocean. Jeri liked the celebration of life that these feasts represented— the sharing of good food with good friends. Even though she couldn't eat much, Jeri would sit in her wheelchair at the head of the table. Her attention would alternate between the waves outside and her friends inside. She had a say in all that was happening around her. She seemed keenly aware, but she would also withdraw inside her mind for short spells. Later, when I grieved, I kept asking myself: "What was she thinking then?" Now, I think I know the answer: She was starting to withdraw from life to prepare for death.

Gasping For Air

Towards the end of the tenth day of Jeri's home-hospice stay, everything began to unravel. The day started out okay; we took Jeri for her normal outing to the Moana. The surf was up, the girlfriends showed up, and it was a good day. However, that night, Jeri began to actively die. I did everything I could to help her through the night. The next morning, Nicole called to say she was on her way. She walked into our apartment at 8 a.m., accompanied by the hospice doctor. They were followed by the girlfriends. Thirty minutes later, the medical supply people showed up with oxygen tanks. Jeri made a face when she saw them. She turned to her friend Deborah and asked, "Does this mean I'm being grounded?"

For the rest of the day, Jeri seemed to be okay as long as she inhaled her oxygen. She didn't seem to care for the oxygen nozzle on her nose. She kept pulling it away, which sent her gasping for air. The girlfriends thought she was getting hot flashes, so they would turn up the fan.

That night was really bad. Every half hour, Jeri would sit up, pull away the oxygen nozzle, and then gasp for air. I would respond by soothing her and then gently putting the nozzle back on her nose. This went on all night long. Several times, I called the hospice for advice, but they had none. I was tempted to call 911 to have Jeri put on a respirator, but this was not what she wanted. She definitely did not want to end up on life support in a hospital. So I just held her hand and calmed her down to help her get through another night.

The next morning Nicole called to say she was on her way. But I now faced a new problem: Jeri couldn't swallow her pain pills. Luckily, we had some liquid morphine from a previous treatment. So I gave her morphine, with Nicole's permission. But, we had an even more serious problem. After listening to Jeri's lungs through her stethoscope, Nicole had a very worried look. She said, "I think her lung may have collapsed. She's going to die today. We must take her back to the hospice facility, now." I was totally stunned. All I could mutter was, "But, she wants to die at home." Nicole just said, "Robert, she's going to be much better off in our facility. You must do what's best for Jeri. I have a room waiting for her. Our transporters are on their way." All I could say was, "OK, but if she gets better I want her back home."

"I Want to Go Home"

One hour later, Jeri was back in a hospice bed. The doctor had prescribed a heavy dose of liquid morphine. Jeri had a very hard time swallowing, so I requested that they put her on a morphine pump. Unfortunately, the pump didn't arrive until early the next morning. Jeri's girlfriend Kathy volunteered to pick it up herself. The doctor had to intervene to have the delivery of the pump expedited by courier.

Later that Tuesday, Jeri briefly came out of her semi-coma. She pointed her finger at me and then gave me a very loving smile. My heart melted. She also beamed when she recognized the girlfriends. Then she asked, "Where am I?" When she finally realized that she was back at the hospice, she pulled away her sheets and said, "I want to go home. I want to go home." I felt terrible. I had let her down. All I could say was, "Baby, please trust me. You're better off here." Luckily, the girlfriends were able to distract her and they talked about something else.

The Death Rattle

The girlfriends and I kept the vigil going around the clock. Jeri woke up once and gave me her most beautiful smile. I gave her a very wet kiss. I noticed her lips were dry, so I kept moistening them with kisses. I was holding her hands when she said, "I'm so tired. I need to rest." These would be her last words. She then fell into deep coma for the next two days. Jeri seemed to be at rest, at last. But on the evening just before she died, she began to make loud gurgling sounds as she breathed. I was terrified. I called the nurses. They tried to clear her throat, but the sounds didn't stop. The gurgling continued for the next two hours. The nurses kept reassuring me that she was not in pain. I still wanted them to do something. Later, I was to find out that this was the infamous "death rattle." Jeri died a few hours later. Her heart just stopped beating. Goodbye my love.

Hospice: Superb, but Suboptimal

Jeri experienced the perfect hospice death. She was not alone when she died and death came relatively quickly. Later, a nurse told me she may have died rapidly from a blood clot that penetrated the lungs. In any case, she had a very soft landing. The big surprise was how well hospice worked. Yes, it's a radical departure from the ICU. The system focuses on total care for the dying and the people who are with them at the end. Hospice is not just "a place to go to die." Hospice is a set of beliefs—a new philosophy for health care. It works exactly as Dame Saunders envisioned it: "As long as a person continues to live, a great deal can be done." However, the system also has a major flaw. Here are my observations:

- *Hospice people understand dying and are the perfect guides.* Without a doubt, the hospice team that took care of Jeri really understood death and dying—they were pros in a death-denying society. Over the years, hospices have accumulated a tremendous knowledge-base on dying. They've become society's repository of information about end-of-life—a very valuable service for those of us who have no familiarity with death. Most importantly, the hospice people also understand the emotional needs of the dying. I watched them talk softly to the dying and treat them like people till the very end. They were gentle, compassionate, and caring. They even helped me with my grief after Jeri died.

- *Hospice helped Jeri die in a non-clinical setting.* Jeri fully experienced the hospice way of dying. She received the best comfort care. Initially, the pain management technology was top-notch and it kept her relatively comfortable. Jeri was able to enjoy most of her remaining days at home surrounded by loved ones. She was able to visit places and say her goodbyes to the world. There was much attention to detail that made all this possible. For example, the hospice home nurse would tweak the pain medicines almost daily to allow Jeri to go on her outings. The nurse even tried to provide a beach wheelchair to take Jeri to the ocean. The last days are made up of many small gifts. There is a lot of life at the end—mostly in pursuit of these small gifts and joys. Hospice is about "allowing a dying person to live their last moments."

- *Hospice enabled Jeri's loved ones to help her die.* Helping Jeri die was a profound and loving experience for us. It was, by far, the most tender and loving caregiving moments I had ever experienced with Jeri. I was so much in love with her at the end. It's impossible to imagine two people being more intimate and close. It's incredibly sad to see your lover go, but it's also a powerful bonding experience. It is the culmination of your love. The experience was also profound for the girlfriends and their husbands. Thanks to hospice, Jeri was back at home with us. Home and the Moana were so much better than being at the hospital. Despite her deteriorating situation, Jeri was able to enjoy life's little pleasures and make the most of them. We knew that she would only be with us for a short time, so we wanted to savor every moment. We were able to shower Jeri with love to alleviate her angst. Hospice facilitates this type of bonding by providing a family-friendly setting. It's a very special privilege to help a loved one die well; hospice enables us to exercise this privilege.

- *Hospice's weak link, palliative sedation, is suboptimal.* It works, but it's crude. Compared to the Nembutal alternative, it results in a lot of unnecessary suffering. In *Grieving a Soulmate* I calculated that if euthanasia had been an option, Jeri would have avoided the suffering of Monday night and Tuesday morning—a total of 16 hours. Jeri did not experience the best possible death for her situation, but she came very close. We were just 16 hours off the ideal time. When it comes to grieving, 16 hours of witnessing unnecessary suffering can haunt you for a very long time. You remember every second and replay every scene over and over again. I wrote this book because of these

16 hours. Jeri wanted to die in her own way. She had a dream. Unfortunately, that option was not legal in Hawaii when she died. We gave her the best possible death under the circumstances. She was lucky to have palliative sedation as her second-best option.

Personal note: Am I expecting too much? Some of you may be thinking that Jeri had a wonderful death, compared to most people. In the bigger scheme, 16 hours of pain and suffering does not appear to be much. Why make it such a big deal? The answer: It is a big deal. Here's something to chew on. Just imagine that your house is invaded by a gang of sadists. They tie you up, gag you, but leave your eyes uncovered so that you can watch. Over the next 16 hours, you helplessly watch while they torture your loved one to death. How would you feel? Yes, it's a big deal. The disease was the invader and I stood by helplessly watching Jeri suffer. Given that she was a strong proponent of euthanasia, she ended up suffering needlessly during those 16 hours. She even said, "I waited too long." To calibrate you, Jeri was incredibly tough. This opinion was shared by all her doctors, including the palliative pain specialist. Those four words meant that her pain had reached unbearable levels—a lot more than most people could stand. It was torture. Jeri was needlessly tortured because of the prohibition against the Nembutal. I wrote this book because of those four words: "I waited too long." They haunted me during my grieving.

Hospice: The Report Card

The good news is that we have a superb end-of-life system, that almost works. The hospice system needs some serious tweaking, but we're lucky to have it. It's the polar opposite of the ICU alternative. So, in America today we can have the best of deaths or the worst of deaths. We can have hospice or we can have intubation. We can have comfort care and pain control, or we can have last-ditch heroic interventions. In the next section, I will explain how Nembutal can make hospice an even better experience. I will also present a modest proposal for improving hospice without the Nembutal.

Hospice and the Nembutal: The Case for Synergy

Here's an interesting statistic: In 2009, 91.5% of Oregon's terminally-ill patients who took the Nembutal route were also enrolled in hospice at the time of death; 98.3% died at home.[25] Why did these people choose the Nembutal while they were under hospice care? Clearly, something was lacking. Yes, hospice is a wonderful system. I will explain that it can be even better if the Nembutal is added to its palliative repertoire. It would be one more comfort option available to hospice patients at the very end. They could benefit from the hospice way of dying and also have the Nembutal if they request it. There's a case to be made for synergy.

Nembutal or Palliative Sedation: The Ethics

Before I start explaining what the Nembutal brings to the table, let me quickly address the ethics of Nembutal vs. palliative sedation. As you know from Chapter 1, death from palliative sedation, even when accompanied by voluntary starvation and dehydration, is totally legal in the United States. In June 2008, the *American Medical Association (AMA)* endorsed the practice at its annual meeting. Palliative sedation is morally and ethically accepted—even by the Catholic church. As the 2009 directive of the *National Conference of Catholic Bishops* explicitly states: "It is not euthanasia to give a dying person sedatives and analgesics for the alleviation of pain, even though they may deprive the patient of use of reason, or shorten his life." This wide acceptance is based on two principles: 1) the main *intent* of terminal sedation is the relief of pain, which is a good thing (i.e., the principle of *double-effect*); and 2) the voluntary withholding of nutrition is based on the patient's right to refuse treatment (i.e., the right of *self-determination*).

Interestingly, that same reasoning can be applied to the Nembutal approach. Harvard professor of medical ethics Dr. Dan Brock makes a

---

[25] Oregon Department of Human Services, *"Twelfth Annual Report on Oregon's Death with Dignity Act,"* (March, 2010).

very convincing case to that effect.[26] The Nembutal approach involves two separate acts by two parties: the physician and the patient. Dr. Brock argues that the physician can justly claim that the Nembutal prescription's main intent is to relieve the patient's *anxiety about dying*. Because of the great advances in palliative care, the physician can truthfully claim that he or she does not expect or intend that the patient use the Nembutal to die.

The patient is told that no one needs to die in pain—the system says "trust us." Consequently, the patient can claim that the primary intention is not to use the Nembutal but just to have it as a form of backup insurance. If all else fails, the patient will take the Nembutal to relieve the pain—death is just a side effect. *Warning*: Like morphine, too much Nembutal can cause death.[27]

According to the time-honored principle of the double effect, the Nembutal option is ethically and morally justified. As you know from Chapter 1, I am not a fan of the double effect doctrine. I only use it here to put Nembutal on par with palliative sedation from an ethics perspective. It may give ethicists something to ponder, while we move on to the more practical issues. I'll have a lot more to say about the ethics and safeguards in later chapters.

Nembutal or Palliative Sedation: Which Is Better?

By now, it should be clear that hospice provides a compassionate way to die. However, I have a lot of misgivings about palliative sedation. The biggest advantage of palliative sedation is that it is legal and available today. Another advantage is that it does not require you to take your own life, a big plus for most people. However, the method has some very serious shortcomings, when compared to the Nembutal

---

[26] Timothy Quill and Margaret Battin, Editors, *Physician-Assisted Dying: The Case for Palliative Care and Patient Choice* (Johns Hopkins University Press, 2004).

[27] Sidney Wanzer and Joseph Glenmullen, *To Die Well* (Da Capo Press, 2007).

alternative (i.e., the Oregon approach). Here are the advantages of Nembutal over palliative sedation:

- *Provides optimal timing.* You get to control the right time to go. Pain is very subjective, and only you can determine what constitutes "unbearable pain." You take the Nembutal at the point when hospice cannot control the pain by any other means. Your pain relief is immediate. You don't have to deal with the NHPCO's edict of "waiting until 14 days before death." You don't have to deal with their "titration" or go-slow edict. Even in cases where the doctors approve the palliative sedation, you don't have to suffer "16 hours" of torture while waiting for the morphine pumps to be connected. These long response-times translate into unnecessary torture. The torture must be made to end within minutes—not hours, days, and months. The Nembutal response-time is guaranteed to be within minutes.

- *Guarantees relief in an unpredictable system.* The Nembutal is your guaranteed delivery method for relieving unbearable pain. It protects you from the whims of hospices that do not provide palliative sedation. It protects you from being tortured in an ICU. You have peace of mind. You carry your delivery-from-pain mechanism with you at all times. You are not at the whim of a capricious and unpredictable system. Even with hospices, there's no way to tell in advance whether they will use palliative sedation even if you need it. The NHPCO numbers indicate that there's a huge disparity among hospices in the use of palliative sedation. With usage numbers ranging between 1% to 52%, obtaining palliative sedation in a hospice becomes pure luck of the draw. You'll need the Nembutal option to protect yourself from the vagaries of the system. Hopefully, you'll never have to use it.

- *Guarantees that it's voluntary.* Palliative sedation happens as part of the treatment. The act can be carried out without an explicit discussion with an alert patient. Yes, it's hard to think clearly when you're in pain. There may be a consultation with the family before the sedation is applied, but it uses a lot of code. Why? Because it can't be explicitly said that the patient is being killed. In contrast, the Nembutal approach lets you take your own life. There is no possibility of abuse. There is no code to decipher. By taking your own life, you are ensuring that you sincerely and independently opt for death. The act is not impulsive, for you have thought about it well in advance. In Oregon, you discuss it with two physicians ahead of time; there is ample time to think about it and be evaluated for depression.

- **Lets you self-administer.** Unlike palliative sedation, Nembutal does not require that a physician or RN administer the medication. You, not the physician, are able to perform the final act that terminates your life. This gives you full control of the process until the very last moment of your life. And, you can always change your mind, up to the very last second.

- **Increases your chances of dying at home.** You can self-administer the Nembutal anywhere, including in your own home. In contrast, palliative sedation requires a morphine pump. Consequently, you must either be admitted to a hospice facility or make arrangements to have round-the-clock RN coverage at home (an out-of-pocket expense).

- **Reduces the grieving pains of your loved ones.** With Nembutal, death is quick and peaceful. There are no traumatic images of unbearable suffering etched in a survivor's memory. So, there is less grieving pain. In contrast, terminal sedation is a slow process. Typically, the survivors witness pain followed by a long comatose period of slow dying. During that period, the body deteriorates slowly from starvation, dehydration, or the advancing disease. The memories can be traumatic. Also, the survivors may witness some distressing scenes like the "death rattle." The dying person appears to be choking, but we are told there's no pain. Nevertheless, it's painful to watch. These final scenes can override a lifetime of good memories and have a huge impact on grieving. In my opinion, this dying slowly and in a coma process is not respectful, nor dignified. For the survivors, it appears cruel and inhumane; it can translate into a lot of grief.

- *Lets you choose the level of dignity you want.* With Nembutal you can decide how much of yourself you want left when you go. In contrast, terminal sedation will only be given if there is unbearable physical pain. The NHPCO guideline does not deal with the emotional and existential pain associated with dying. It doesn't address a dying person's need for dignity. Note: We each have our own definition of self-dignity. The dying person must be allowed to make that decision.

- *Lets you say goodbye.* With Nembutal the act is very specific and the intention is clear. You know when to say your goodbyes. In contrast, palliative sedation is cloaked in code. The dying part is not explicitly stated. The loved ones are often confused and then surprised by the finality of the act. Some request that the patient be revived from a coma to say their goodbyes.[28]

- *Provides a safer way to die.* Nembutal is immediate and peaceful. In contrast, palliative sedation involves a long process of decay, which can sometimes last several weeks or longer. Sometimes, the decay can be quite severe. For example, there could be uncontrolled bleeding from an eroding lesion. The hope is that the dying person is actually free of suffering during the process, as opposed to being simply unable to report it. There is no published evidence that sedation relieves pain and other symptoms, even if the dying person appears calm.[29] This situation may be similar to surgery, where patient awareness occurs between 2% and 3% of the time without the knowledge of the anesthesiologist. It's pretty scary stuff.

---

[28] Anemona Hartocollis, "Hard Choice for a Comfortable Death: Sedation," *New York Times*, December 28, 2009.

[29] Mellar P. Davis, "Does Palliative Sedation Always Relieve Symptoms?," *Journal of Palliative Medicine* (October, 2009).

From the above, you can see that the Nembutal approach has many advantages. In states where it is legalized, it has been added to the repertoire of palliative choices for the dying.

Nembutal and Palliative Care: The Synergy

You may remember that Dame Saunders, the founder of the modern hospice movement, was a firm opponent of euthanasia. She felt that hospice could do the job better; euthanasia was not needed. As I explained throughout this chapter, hospices are doing a marvelous job helping us through the dying process. However, their practice of palliative sedation does not offer the kindest of deaths. I made the case that, for some, the Nembutal provides an excellent alternative at the end. It makes palliative sedation almost seem barbaric.

To recap, palliative sedation, today, is a totally discretionary practice. The doctors decide if and when to give it. The patient does not choose the timing nor provide informed consent. Also, I'm not a big fan of the comatose, slow-death vigil that accompanies palliative sedation. It's painful to watch your loved one melt away before your eyes. You don't want to remember him or her as an unconscious, living cadaver. It violates the dying person's dignity—especially if a final directive expressed an unwillingness to be maintained in a vegetative state. For all these reasons, the Nembutal must be added to the hospice palliative care continuum of choices.

Luckily, things are changing. In 2007, the *American Academy of Hospice and Palliative Medicine (AAHPM),* the professional organization representing hospice doctors and nurses, softened its opposition to physician-assisted dying. Noting that its members were divided on the issue, the organization changed its stance from oppositional to neutral.[30]

The experience in Oregon continues to show that legalization of physician-assisted dying leads to improved palliative care. Oregon leads all other states in several important measures of the quality of

---

[30] Source: http://www.aahpm.org/positions/suicide.html.

palliative comfort care.[31] And Oregon doctors report that, since the passage of the *Death with Dignity Act*, several important steps have been taken to improve the quality of end-of-life care—including better use of pain medications, improved ability to recognize psychiatric disorders in the dying, and an increased number of patient referrals to hospice care.[32] Oregon leads the nation in terms of numbers of deaths occurring at home, the training of physicians in palliative care, and organized statewide use of POLST directives. Oregonians know that if they ever face a terminal illness, they will have control and choice over their manner of death. It appears that in states where the prohibition is lifted there is synergy between hospice and the Nembutal.

Modest Proposal for Palliative Sedation: Call 911

In the long run, the Nembutal may become a legal option everywhere. In the short run, we have palliative sedation for those who receive it. Is there a quick fix? Surprisingly, the answer is yes.

Here's my modest proposal for improving the practice of palliative sedation. I address it to the NHPCO and AAHPM:

Ladies and Gentlemen:

Thank you for all your work on behalf of the dying. Here's a modest proposal to improve your practice of palliative sedation. With these small changes, you can help millions die in less pain. My proposal is as follows:

- *Upon admission to a hospice program, patients will be provided with a bracelet identifying them as eligible for palliative sedation, should they request it. The hospice and patient must sign a legally binding agreement.*

---

[31] R. Steinbrook, "Physician-Assisted Suicide in Oregon: An Uncertain Future," *New England Journal of Medicine* (Vol. 346, 2002).

[32] Kathryn L. Tucker, "Choice at the End of Life: Lessons from Oregon," *American Constitution Society* (June, 2008).

- *A patient who feels hospice pain management is not alleviating excruciating pain has the right to dial 911 and report a terminal-pain emergency.*

- *The 911 emergency response teams will respond rapidly. Their normal goal is to have a paramedic on the scene within 6 to 10 minutes. If my proposal is implemented, the team will identify the call as a request from a terminal patient for unbearable pain relief. The responding paramedic can verify that the patient is indeed terminal from the bracelet and computerized data.*

- *The paramedic will then ask the patient if palliative sedation is wanted and explain the consequences. If the answer is yes, the paramedic will hook the patient to a morphine pump and other sedation drips. The ambulances will carry the pump as standard equipment along with a standing order from hospice doctors to use it on this class of patient. Currently, ambulances carry morphine but not the pump. All paramedics are already trained to provide IV support.*

- *The patient will not be moved to a hospital facility. The administration will be performed on-location (typically, the patient's home). The hospice team will be notified, but their permission is not required. They will attend to the patient as soon as possible.*

- *The total elapsed time between the patient's call to 911 and the morphine starting to take effect must be less than one hour.*

Our taxes have financed the EMS system, which is responsible for saving millions of lives. This modest proposal says we should use this proven and familiar service to relieve the suffering of the dying. Excruciating dying pain is a reason to dial 911. The hospice movement must take advantage of 911, not avoid it.

While I have your attention, I also propose that your palliative care specialists issue bracelets to terminally-ill patients when admitted to hospitals and ICUs. This will allow any patient suffering unbearable pain to request immediate sedation. Hopefully, your teams will be on location to ensure it all happens.

Respectfully,

Robert Orfali

I won't hold my breath waiting for something to happen.[33] The benefit of this proposal is that it rationalizes the terminal process within the current system. No new laws are required. Under my proposal, palliative sedation becomes an explicit right for the terminally ill; it's a contract. All hospices and ICUs must provide it on demand. Bringing 911 into the process guarantees response times of less than an hour.

In addition, the proposal standardizes the process. It's not ad hoc any longer. The patients and families will be involved. Everything becomes very explicit and transparent. This eliminates the vagaries of the current system. Instead of the act being performed at the discretion of doctors, it becomes a patient's right. As part of informed consent, the patient will be able to request it. Most importantly, the practice can be expanded to the ICU. Of course, there will still be a slow-death vigil. We must keep pushing for the Nembutal option.

Bottom Line

We have two health-care systems in America today: modern medicine and hospice. (Palliative care is mostly associated with hospice, but it also has pockets within the medical system.) In the age of slow dying and chronic illnesses, we need both systems. The ICU works well for us, most of the time. It does what it was designed to do, and it does it very well. There is no need to change something that works. We have a superb illness-fighting machine. Hospice is also a superb system; it provides outstanding end-of-life care for the dying (except for terminal sedation). So, we are lucky to have two systems that work, each one superb in the function it was designed to perform.

---

[33] Note: I will submit the proposal after this book is published, in order to provide the necessary background.

So what's the problem? The problem is that we live in a death-denying culture that makes it very hard to transition from one system to the next, when the right time arrives. We, and our doctors, have a very hard time accepting death. Consequently, most of us won't make the transition in time. We will end up dying in the ICU—a modern torture chamber for the dying. As Dr. George Lundberg, a former editor of the *Journal of the American Medical Association (JAMA)*, describes it: "A sophisticated hospital is the last place you want to be when terminally ill. Once you're in the hospital setting, you're trapped. The staff owns you, and they will do those terrible things they have been trained to do to prolong life, no matter how artificially or hopelessly."[34]

Note: *Moving to hospice sooner may even prolong our lives. In a recent study, the mean survival was 29 days longer for hospice patients than similar patients who did not choose hospice.*[35] *In another study, patients with terminal lung cancer who began receiving palliative care immediately upon diagnosis not only were happier, more mobile, and in less pain as the end neared, but they also lived nearly three months longer.*[36]

The ICU was never designed to help us die; it was designed to fight disease to the end. We want our illness-fighting machine to continue doing what it does best. Instead of changing the ICU, we must change our death-denying attitude. We need to better understand the end-of-life hospice option, so that we can die in peace. In other words, we must have these open *conversations* that help us make the transition to

---

[34] George D. Lundberg, *Severed Trust: Why American Medicine Hasn't Been Fixed* (Basic Books, 2000).

[35] S. Connor et al., "Comparing Hospice and Non-Hospice Patient Survival," *Journal of Pain Symptom Management* (Vol. 33, 2007).

[36] Jennifer S. Temel et al., "Early Palliative Care for Patients with Metastatic Non–Small-Cell Lung Cancer," *New England Journal of Medicine* (Vol. 363, 2010).

hospice care at the right time (i.e., before we end up in the ICU end-of-life torture chamber).

I used Jeri's end-of-life experience to demonstrate the nature of these conversations, which happen over a period of time. I showed that there are at least three conversations on death and dying that you must have. They're not easy. Where available, the palliative care people can help you understand your options. If you're lucky, you will make the transition to hospice and won't become another ICU death statistic.

Again, I used Jeri to explain what hospice is all about. It's a wonderful, caring system for the dying. It provides top-notch pain management, most of the time. We have the best dying specialists anywhere and they're trained to be compassionate and gentle. They really understand the needs of the dying. We're lucky to have hospice as an option.

I also used Jeri's example to demonstrate the weak link in hospice today: palliative sedation. It's a slow, and often messy, way to die. It can torture the dying and leave the survivors with painful memories, which will have a big impact on their grieving. Hospice must be a torture-free zone. So, I proposed a quick fix. If the hospice people insist on terminal sedation, then they must also provide a rapid response-time system to deal with the excruciating final pain. They must connect a morphine pump in less than an hour to a patient who requests it. Yes, dying pain is an emergency. I proposed that we be able to dial 911 from within the hospice system.

Good palliative care and the availability of the Nembutal are not mutually exclusive. I made the case that no dying patient should go without good palliative care; but, currently, good palliative care does not alleviate the suffering of all dying patients. In states where it is legal, the Nembutal provides another palliative care option—an alternate way to die. It allows us to combine the beautiful hospice end-of-life experience with a "gentle and easy death." I made the case that the Nembutal is far superior to the current terminal sedation approach, with its slow and often agonizing route to death.

Of course, we must each be allowed to decide what works best for us (i.e., how we want to die). The Nembutal is the drug of choice for those who do not want to be sedated into oblivion. For others, it serves as insurance; it's there, just in case they need it. Death remains the great "untamed." We need to keep *all* our palliative care options open. There is no right way to die. Every effort must be made to improve end-of-life palliative care. We must provide a continuum of palliative options to control pain and to prevent end-of-life suffering. To sum up, we have almost all the ingredients to make dying a gentle journey and death a dignified final exit. All we have to do now is legalize the missing ingredient, the Nembutal.

Chapter 4

Euthanasia: Modern Milestones

"In recent years the qualities that morally distinguished the living from the dying have been blurred. With our life prolonging techniques and medications, we have transformed death.... Logically and emotionally, we cannot intervene at one phase and then be inactive at another, more painful phase. We cannot modify nature and then plead that nature must be allowed to run its unhindered course.... Our best medical and religious traditions accept euthanasia when it assists the person who is imminently dying toward a less devastating and more peaceful demise."

—Kenneth L. Vaux, Professor of Ethics[1]

The topic of euthanasia has been on society's agenda since the dawn of civilization. In this chapter, I go over key milestones in the evolution of modern euthanasia. My focus is on democratic societies that place high value on the liberty and autonomy of citizens. What can be modern about euthanasia when we've been dying forever? The answer is that medical technology has radically transformed the way we die. Modern euthanasia grew in reaction to this new and quite often painful way of dying. It's our search for an "easy and gentle death" in the age of high-tech death and life support.

Large segments of society and the medical profession have now accepted that strict adherence to the preservation of life at all cost is

---

[1] Kenneth L. Vaux, "Debbie's Dying: Mercy Killing and the Good Death," *JAMA* (Vol. 259, 1988).

not always desirable: it submits us to the tyranny of modern medical technology. About 20 years ago, passive euthanasia ("letting die") became a morally acceptable medical practice. One decade later, slow euthanasia ("terminal sedation") became a morally acceptable palliative practice. In the last ten years, the fight has revolved around voluntary euthanasia ("physician-assisted dying"). It's all part of the same moral continuum. It's about the right of the individual to achieve a good death in the age of high-tech medical interventions that prolong life. It's been a long and hard-fought battle. The good news is that we have now achieved some control over the medical machine with advance directives, hospice care, and palliative sedation. Legalizing the Nembutal will complete the project.

In the U.S., it's a slow, uphill battle that is being fought state by state. In Europe, the battle is being fought one country at a time. This chapter traces the major U.S. and European milestones. It gives you a feel for what's been accomplished and where we stand today. Ultimately, this is about who has control over our death. It's the long battle for "our life, our death, our choice."

Major U.S. Milestones

In the U.S., the major driver for the *right to die* movement has always been the patient's rights in the age of high-tech dying. In 1970, Dr. Elizabeth Kübler-Ross published *On Death and Dying,* which made the subject of death less taboo in America; she made it possible to openly discuss the end-of-life in a death-denying culture. In the 1980s, women's struggle to control their bodies and reproductive rights was a major source of influence; it was a stepping stone to patient autonomy. In the 1990s, the AIDS epidemic brought death out of the closet in a big way. The heart-breaking pictures of young people dying from this horrible disease shocked the country. The visuals of extreme suffering demonstrated that our end-of-life support system was broken.

Here are the major U.S. milestones in the modern struggle over the "right to die":

- *In 1972,* the first *Patients' Bill of Rights* was published. It asserted that the patient has the right to refuse treatment. It also asserted the right to *informed consent*—doctors are now required to disclose the knowledge and facts that patients may need to determine what happens to their bodies. In the United States, patients now have the right to medical self-determination.

- *In 1976,* California became the first state to pass a *living will* law. In 1979, the state of Washington followed in California's footsteps. In response to public needs, state legislatures soon passed laws in support of living wills in virtually every state in the union. By 2007, 41% of Americans had completed advance directives.

- *In 1980,* the *Hemlock Society* was formed by Derek Humphry who helped Jean, his terminally-ill wife, die. He then wrote a book about it. By the mid-1990s, the society grew to 46,000 members. In 2005, Hemlock merged with Compassion in Dying to form Compassion & Choices.

- *In 1990,* in *Cruzan v. Missouri,* the U.S. Supreme Court decided for the patient's right to refuse artificial nutrition and hydration when there is "clear and convincing evidence of the refusal." The ruling affirmed the right of Americans to refuse unwanted medical treatment through the use of advance directives. It also affirmed their right to appoint *health-care proxies* to speak for them when they cannot.

- *In 1994,* Oregon voters passed the *Death with Dignity Act* by a vote of 51% to 49%. The Act was obstructed for the next three years by a failed lawsuit. In 1997, opponents tried to repeal the Act through another ballot initiative. Their efforts also failed; and, this time, the Oregon voters reaffirmed the initiative by a decisive 60% to 40% margin. The Dignity Act became fully effective in 1998. However, its opponents continued their efforts to thwart the initiative. They requested that the *Drug Enforcement Administration (DEA)* revoke the registration of physicians who prescribed the Nembutal. They argued that "assisting suicide is not a legitimate medicinal purpose."

In January 2006, the U.S. Supreme Court heard the landmark case *Gonzales v. Oregon.* In a 6-3 decision, the justices affirmed Oregon's Dignity Act and state rights by rejecting the back-door attack through the DEA. Oregon's Act has been implemented without interruption for the last 12 years.

- *In 1996,* the Ninth Circuit Court of Appeals (in *Glucksberg v. Washington*) and the Second Circuit Court of Appeals (in *Quill v. New York*) both ruled that the U.S. Constitution protects the choice of a competent, terminally-ill patient to choose aid in dying. The Ninth Court wrote: "We see no ethical or constitutionally cognizable difference between a doctor's pulling the plug on a respirator and his prescribing drugs which will permit a terminally ill patient to end his own life. In fact, some might argue that pulling the plug is a more culpable and aggressive act on the doctor's part. To us, what matters most is that the death of the patient is the intended result as surely in one case as in the other."[2] The Ninth Court trivialized both *double effect* and *letting die*; it dismissed both principles as "moral hypocrisy." The states of New York and Washington filed for review in the U.S. Supreme Court.

- *In 1998,* the U.S. Supreme Court heard both *Glucksberg* and *Quill.* The Court declined to find federal constitutional protection for aid in dying, leaving the possibility open that it will do so in the future, and referred the issue to the states. In that same ruling, the Court recognized a federal constitutional right for dying patients to receive as much pain medication as necessary to obtain relief, even if this advances time of death.[3] This means that there is a right to slow euthanasia by means of palliative sedation. It's justified by the principle of *double effect.*

---

[2] Kathleen Foley and Herbert Hendin, Editors, *The Case Against Assisted Suicide: For the Right to End-of-Life Care* (Johns Hopkins University Press, 2002).

[3] U.S. Supreme Court, *Washington v. Gluksberg* (1997).

- *From 1990 until September 1998*, Dr. Jack Kevorkian became a folk hero, for many in the U.S., by helping at least 93 patients die. Kevorkian was acquitted four times by sympathetic juries. He was helped by the relatives of his patients, who testified that they appreciated Kevorkian's help and compassion in ending their loved ones' suffering. All the patients appeared to be sound of mind; all were suffering. However, Kevorkian's critics claim that many of those patients had more than six months to live.

- *On November 22, 1998,* Dr. Kevorkian actively euthanized Thomas Youk who was suffering from advanced stages of ALS. He gave him a lethal injection and then sent the videotape to CBS's *60 Minutes.* Previously, all his patients had self-administered the lethal medicine. The airing of the video on CBS was seen as a direct challenge to the legal authorities. Kevorkian stood trial on charges of first degree murder. This time the jury could not ignore the law; Kevorkian was found guilty of second-degree murder. The judge sentenced him to a prison term of 10 to 25 years. She said: "No one, sir, is above the law. No one. You had the audacity to go on national television, show the world what you did, and dare the legal system stop you. Well, sir, consider yourself stopped." She maintained that the trial was not about the political or moral correctness of euthanasia; it was about lawlessness. Kevorkian was released on parole on June 1, 2007. (In 2010, HBO released the film *You Don't Know Jack,* in which Al Pacino plays Kevorkian.)

- *In 1999,* the U.S. House of Representatives passed the *Pain Relief Promotion Act (PRPA).* The bill's intention was to criminalize "aid in dying" and nullify the Oregon law. In 2000, Oregon Senator Ron Wyden threatened a filibuster to keep the PRPA from reaching the Senate floor.

- *In 2006,* the *American Medical Women's Association (AMWA)* came out in support of Aid in Dying.

- *In 2007,* the *American Academy of Hospice and Palliative Medicine (AAHPM),* the professional organization representing hospice doctors and nurses, softened its opposition to physician-assisted dying. Noting that its members were divided on the issue, the AAHPM shifted its stance from oppositional to neutral.[4]

- *In 2008,* the *American Medical Student Association (AMSA)* adopted a policy reiterating its 1997 endorsement and broadening its support of Aid in Dying.

- *In 2008,* the *American Public Health Association (APHA)* adopted a position supporting death with dignity for terminally-ill patients.

- *In 2008,* the *American College of Legal Medicine (ACLM)* adopted a position supporting death with dignity for terminally-ill patients.

- *On November 4, 2008,* state of Washington voters decisively approved *Initiative 1000,* modeled after Oregon's *Death with Dignity Act.* The vote was 58% to 42%. Washington became the second state to legalize aid in dying. In March 2009, the *Washington Death with Dignity Act* went into effect.

- *On December 31, 2009,* the Montana Supreme Court ruled in favor of the landmark case *Baxter v. Montana* affirming that it is not against public policy of the state of Montana for a physician to provide aid in dying to a mentally competent, terminally-ill individual. The Montana Supreme Court is the highest court available to decide on state issues. In April 2010, survey results showed that 63% of Montana voters supported their recent Supreme Court ruling. 70% of voters did not want the legislature to reverse the decision. In July 2010, a bill was drafted by the legislature in support of the Montana Supreme Court ruling. If it passes, Montana will have its *Death with Dignity Act.* As I go to press, the Montana Supreme Court ruling is being honored in the state.

Obviously, this is an ongoing struggle and there will be a lot more to come. Watch this space.

---

[4] Source: http://www.aahpm.org/positions/suicide.html.

Major European Milestones

The European movement was sparked by Dutch physicians out of a sense of compassion for their patients. As a society, the Dutch have a deep respect for the principle of self-determination. They are not afraid to legalize previously underground practices and bring them into the open. Instead of "don't ask, don't tell," the Dutch prefer to understand the issues and openly deal with them. They've become the social laboratory for post-modern Europe. Here are the modern European milestones:

- *On November 28, 2000,* the Dutch parliament's lower chamber passed the *Euthanasia Act.* The vote was 104 in favor, and 40 against. On April 10, 2001, the vote was ratified by the upper chamber of the parliament. This ended two decades of underground tolerance. During that experimental period, doctors were held guilty until proven innocent. In April 2002, after two decades of debate and research, the *Euthanasia Act* became law.

- *On May 28, 2002,* the Belgian parliament passed the *Law on Euthanasia,* which was largely similar to the Dutch law. On June 14, 2002, the parliament also passed the *Law on Palliative Care* which includes a "palliative filter procedure." It insures that when a patient requests euthanasia, all pertinent caregivers are informed. This includes physicians, nurses, and palliative-care experts. The team will review all the patient's options for palliative care.

- *On March 18, 2009,* Luxembourg became the third European country to legalize euthanasia. In December 2008, the Grand Duke of Luxembourg, a devout Catholic, announced that he would not be willing to affix his signature to the new law. To solve this problem, parliament simply enacted legislation removing the Grand Duke's veto power. In his new role, the Grand Duke can only announce parliament's decisions. According to the Luxembourg bill, the patient must make the request through a living will or advance directive. A doctor is required to consult with a colleague to ensure that the patient has a terminal illness and is in a "grave and incurable condition."

- *On Jan 27, 2010,* a *British Social Attitudes* survey indicated an 82% overall support for assisted dying for those who are suffering from an incurable disease. Survey results showed 92% support by the non-religious and 71% by the religious. Surveys have consistently shown that at least 80% of the U.K. population supports a change in the law on assisted dying. So, what is being done? The British *Dignity in Dying* organization has over 100,000 supporters; it advocates legislation modeled on Oregon's *Death with Dignity Act.*

- *In March 2010,* PBS's *Frontline* aired a documentary called *The Suicide Tourist.* It's the story of Professor Craig Ewert, an American ALS patient, who travelled to Switzerland to receive assistance in dying. The documentary was a surprise to most American viewers, who were not aware that assisted dying has been legal in Switzerland since 1941. Every year, there are about 400 cases of assisted dying in Switzerland; 132 of these involve patients from abroad, mainly Germany and England. Here's how it works. The request to die is made to a volunteer society such as *Exit* or *Dignitas.* A volunteer (often a clergyman, social worker, or nurse) goes over the requirements on the phone, asks for some supporting paperwork, and then directs the patient to a consulting doctor. Typically, the doctor meets with the patient and reviews the prognosis. If the patient meets the requirements, the doctor writes a prescription for 15 grams of Nembutal in powder form. The drug is not handed to the client. Instead, the prescription is picked up by the right-to-die organization. When the patient decides it's time to die, two volunteers will be present. They will hand to the patient the previously prescribed Nembutal and guide him or her through the dying process. The volunteers are skilled in providing a calm and re-assuring environment. Swiss law requires that no one is to profit from the act. Most "suicide tourists" receive the Nembutal in a pleasant Zurich clinic run by *Dignitas.* As we go to press, the Swiss parliament is considering a much tighter set of guidelines modeled after Oregon's *Death with Dignity Act.*

Most European countries support passive and slow euthanasia. The current debate centers on lifting the prohibition against assisted dying and voluntary active euthanasia. The Netherlands, Belgium, Switzerland and Luxembourg have already decided. Which country will be next? Public opinion polls show that there is strong support for physician-assisted dying and euthanasia in Denmark, France, Sweden, Great Britain, Spain, and Germany; Italy is divided.[5] On the other hand, doctors seem to have more reservations than the general public, particularly in Denmark, France, and Sweden. So, it's a toss-up.

I'll leave the final predictions to Professor John Griffith and his colleagues: "All in all, we are inclined to predict that legal change in the direction of widely held values will occur first in England, France, Denmark, and Sweden." My bet is that England will be next.

Canada and Australia: Dead Ends?

If England is next, then the chances are that Australia and Canada won't be far behind. After all, they do share "widely held values." Here's what's happening in Canada and Australia:

Canada

- *On September 30, 1993,* the Canadian Supreme Court denied dying ALS patient Sue Rodriguez the "right to die." The vote was 5 to 4 in the landmark case *Rodriguez vs. British Columbia.* At the time, 77% of Canadians supported the right-to-die. On February 12, 1994, Sue Rodriguez took her own life with the help of an anonymous physician.

- *In June 2007,* an *Ipsos* poll found that 76% of Canadians still support the right-to-die. It seems the public is very consistent in its support of assisted dying.

---

[5] John Griffith et al., *Euthanasia and Law in Europe* (Hart Publishing, 2008).

- **On May 13, 2009,** Bill C-384 was introduced, by MP Francine Lalonde, to legalize euthanasia and assisted suicide in Canada. On April 21, 2010, the bill was soundly defeated by the Canadian parliament. Unlike the Oregon Act, C-384 did not limit assisted suicide to the terminally ill. On September 7, 2010, the province of Quebec began public hearings on "assisted dying." Like most Canadians, the public in Quebec is strongly in favor of an Oregon-style bill. More importantly, organizations representing doctors in Quebec have been outspoken about making changes to laws governing euthanasia. It seems that Quebec may be heading for a public referendum.

Australia

- **In 1995,** Australia's Northern Territory became the first state in the world to approve assisted suicide. Using a computer program devised by Dr. Philip Nitschke, a total of three patients were able to self-administer the Nembutal and benefit from the law before it was challenged in court. The law was repealed on March 29, 1997, by a vote of 38 to 34. At the time, about 400 patients were on standby, waiting. Ironically, an opinion poll published during that same period showed that Australians' support for the right-to-die stood at 70%.[6]

- **In 2006,** the Australian parliament passed *The Suicide Related Materials Act*. It's a law without parallel: it restricts, controls, and censors end-of-life material. The law prohibits the use of a "carriage service" (phone, fax, e-mail, or the Internet) to discuss the practicalities of end-of-life issues.[7]

- **In 2009,** a survey by *Newspoll* of 1,201 Australian adult respondents showed that support for euthanasia was at an all-time high. The

---

[6] Sue Woodman, *Last Rights: The Struggle over the Right to Die* (Perseus Publishing, 1998).

[7] Philip Nitschke and Fiona Stewart, *The Peaceful Pill Handbook* (Exit International US, 2009).

results revealed that 85% of Australians support voluntary euthanasia; 10% are opposed; and 5% are unsure. The support was strong across the entire country. There was a 5% increase in support over a similar survey conducted in 2007.

To sum up, prohibitions do not work; they simply create opportunities for bootleggers. The polls consistently indicate that there is a problem with the end-of-life system in most modern societies, and the public knows it. The politicians act paternalistically, and think they know what's best for all of us. They believe that the polls must be wrong or that the public is not informed. They believe people will change their minds when they better understand the wonders of modern palliative care.

Obviously, the legislators did not do their homework, or perhaps they're simply trying to avoid this "hot button" issue. In any case, they appear not to understand the limits of palliative care, as explained in the previous chapter. Of course the public does. Why? Because death is universal; it happens in every family. Year after year, large majorities persistently tell us that they did not like what they saw with their own eyes. Thirty years of polling results show that, in the age of hospice, there's still work to be done. Eventually, legislators in democratic countries will get the message.

This ongoing struggle to control end-of-life suffering is part of the "Faustian bargain" we have made with modern medicine: "It lets us live longer but the price we pay is prolonged dying, often with increased suffering." I'll conclude with the following call-for-action from Dr. Tom Preston, professor of medicine:

"In the years ahead, medical technologists will find still more ways to extend our dying processes, meaning that end-of-life suffering may become an even greater problem. We need to act now to change how we are allowed die.... Our society must acknowledge its intervention in changing the forms of human life, and should allow a parallel human intervention to help humans die without unnecessary suffering. We need to legalize aid in dying as a humane response to life that has been extended medically beyond the bounds of nature." [8]

In the next chapter, I'll tell you how this challenge was met in both Oregon and the Netherlands.

---

[8] Tom Preston, *Patient-Directed Dying* (iUniverse Press, 2006).

Chapter 5

Euthanasia in the Real World

"At the heart of the controversy is a specific relationship, that between physician and patient. Patients are patients because they are in the care of physicians, and physicians are physicians because they care for patients. In an individualistic and mechanistic age, it may be difficult to acknowledge the power of the connection between them that is brought on by sickness. In that context, it was not rare in the past for physicians to assist in the death of patients who were overmastered by their suffering, and current surveys confirm the continuance of the practice. I know this from personal experience and a lifetime spent among doctors."

— Dr. Eric J. Cassell, M.D.[1]

Today, there are two distinct schools of euthanasia: American and European. The American school is primarily a patient's rights movement to control the end-of-life. In contrast, the European school is largely a physician-led movement. Oregon is the American prototype, while the Netherlands represents the European way. The Oregon lab has accumulated twelve years of real-world experience; the Netherlands lab has accumulated almost thirty. The Oregon experience was always above ground; it started after voters passed the *Death with Dignity Act*. In contrast, the Dutch experimented with their system for eighteen years before their parliament made it legal in 2001. Each

---

[1] Timothy Quill and Margaret Battin, Editors, *Physician-Assisted Dying: The Case for Palliative Care and Patient Choice* (Johns Hopkins University Press, 2004).

model is being cloned within its respective continent. In 2008, the state of Washington passed a measure that was modeled upon Oregon's *Death with Dignity Act*. In 2002, Belgium passed a law that was modeled after that of the Netherlands.

Oregon's law permits only the writing of a prescription for a lethal drug, but it does not permit active euthanasia. It requires that the patient be terminally ill, but makes no mention of suffering. In contrast, the Netherlands permits both voluntary active euthanasia and physician-assisted dying. Dutch law requires that the patient be facing intolerable suffering, but it does not state that the patient be terminally ill nor even that the suffering be physical.

Despite such differences, both models provide major advances in palliative care. They both allow the patient to initiate a final and explicit conversation about how he or she would like to die. This is the *missing conversation* I referred to in Chapter 3. It allows patients, doctors, palliative care specialists, and family members to conduct an open discussion about all the options that are available as death approaches. It's the fourth palliative conversation we must have.

Note: Why the fourth palliative conversation? It's a therapeutic narrative that attempts to restore some order and coherence in the face of the forthcoming onslaught that is death. It openly deals with questions that are seldom discussed in our death-denying culture. For the first time, it provides an official venue where a terminally-ill patient can ask questions such as: How much will I suffer? How will my pain be treated? How much of myself will I lose along the way? What help do I need? What help is available? How will I die? There are many more such questions. Of course, there are major differences in how the Europeans and Americans conduct this very important conversation.

The Oregon model is both practical and efficient. It was designed, from the top down, to work within an American context. Oregon does a great job preserving the autonomy of the individual while providing maximum safeguards that inform and protect the patient. Until the very last second, the individual retains maximum control over every aspect of the end-of-life decision. Besides prescribing the Nembutal, the physicians serve as guides and consultants. They inform the patient and provide options. They're neither being paternalistic nor in charge. It's a delicate balancing act; but, most importantly, it works.

This chapter focuses on the Oregon experience, which I advocate in this book. I will explain the palliative conversation and then analyze the results: how has the system performed over the last twelve years? I also briefly cover the Netherlands experience because there is so much we can learn from it. I go over recent data that conclusively proves there is no "slippery slope" in the Netherlands—a claim persistently made by anti-euthanasia advocates. I conclude with lessons learned and make recommendations on how to improve the Oregon model. Yes, I couldn't resist! As a system's analyst, I'm constantly looking for improvements.

How Do I Die? The Oregon Conversation

If you live in Oregon and are terminally ill, you'd be crazy not to ask for the Nembutal—even if you have no intention of using it. Why? First, it provides insurance, just in case. Second, and most importantly, it guarantees that you will get the best end-of-life care available in America today. Yes, you'll receive better care than even a U.S. senator. You'll be treated like a VIP, with all the protection that comes with it. Every aspect of your dying will be scrutinized. Your treatment will be first-class all the way: the system will roll out the red carpet for you.

For starters, at least two physicians will pour over your medical records and review your diagnosis and prognosis. They will inform you about all your remaining options. For each option, they will explain the outcomes, benefits, and risks. They will have a conversation with you about all your dying concerns—including pain management, coping with disability, loss of dignity, existential angst, home-care needs, terminal anxiety, dread of the future, what to expect, being a burden on others, concerns for your loved ones, and so on.

The physicians will involve others, if necessary. Typically, they will enlist the help of hospice doctors who, in turn, have access to a wide spectrum of palliative care resources—including spiritual counselors, home-care specialists, disability experts, social workers, community volunteers, and pain-management specialists. Psychologists or psychiatrists may be called upon to help you deal with your anxiety, existential pain, search for meaning, anticipatory grieving, fear of death, and depressed thoughts. With your permission, your family and loved ones will be drawn into the conversation.

The state will track your case. If everything goes well, your privacy will not be invaded. If anything goes wrong, many people will be on top of it. This includes state watchdogs, members of the press, and opponents of euthanasia. Distilled, this is the missing conversation every dying person must have. You'll understand your options and prepare yourself for your forthcoming death. You'll be able to enlist resources that can shepherd you through the dying process. If nothing works, you always have the Nembutal: it provides the ultimate peace of mind. Today, in the U.S., this conversation about dying is only available in the states of Oregon, Washington, and Montana—and only for people who request the Nembutal.

People who have this conversation early will have their wishes respected. They will also receive the best palliative care available, and they will be referred to hospice sooner. In contrast, and if at all, most patients are only referred to hospice when they are close to death. In part, this is because they never had that last conversation with their physicians. Over the years, the median length of stay in hospice was, sadly, only 17 to 19 days, with 33% enrolled for just eight days or less. The next three sections explain the mechanics of this conversation and the "safeguards" that it provides.

Oregon: A Finely-Tuned Balancing Act

Safeguards are a delicate balancing act. They must allow the patient to autonomously choose the way they want to die. The state must ensure that the choice is truly voluntary. The patient must be made aware of all the alternatives. Finally, there must be checks and balances on physicians to ensure the integrity of the medical profession. All this must be done with a minimum amount of bureaucracy, rules, and invasion of privacy. Consequently, we're dealing with a delicate balancing act that must protect:

- *The patient's autonomy and right to choose.* The decision must be made voluntarily and without coercion. The patient must be competent and fully informed of the alternatives. In other words, the final decision must be made by an informed patient. The medical team offers help that may or may not effect the decision. In all cases, the physicians must not act paternalistically. They must respect the patient's right to medical self-determination while providing top-notch comfort care to relieve the pain.

- *The integrity of the medical profession.* Doctors must provide the best medical advice and offer the best palliative care until the very end. The decision to prescribe the Nembutal must be peer-reviewed by doctors and audited by the state. It's not a curative action; it's all about the patient's choosing the right time to die. The doctors are there to help the patient think it through. The patient must never feel abandoned by the doctors.

- *The well-being of the vulnerable.* The Nembutal must not become an easy and low-cost solution for society to dispose of its vulnerable members. The safeguards must protect them from prejudice, societal indifference, and negative and inaccurate stereotypes. For example, "We won't do anything else for you because you're better off dead" is not acceptable. All the alternatives must be presented before the Nembutal is prescribed. Only the patients can decide when to go, and they can always change their minds. In the meantime, they must be given the best palliative care.

This may all sound pretty simple, but in this case the devil is in the details. Luckily, Oregon came up with a solution that is both elegant and simple. The next section goes over the mechanics.

Physician-Assisted Dying, Oregon Style

The Oregon *Death with Dignity Act* defines a set of procedures that any adult resident of the state of Oregon must follow to obtain the Nembutal. First, you must initiate the procedure by making an oral request to a physician, preferably someone who is treating you, and inform him or her that you want the Nembutal. The physician must determine that you are suffering from an incurable and irreversible illness that will, in the physician's judgment, result in death within six months; this diagnosis must be confirmed by a consulting physician. Your primary physician will inform you of your diagnosis and prognosis. Then, you must wait 15 days and repeat your request both verbally and in writing. The written request must be witnessed. The waiting period establishes that your request is persistent, genuine, and not impulsive.

Note: Who can witness? The written request must be witnessed by two people whom you know personally. These witnesses must be able to attest that your decision is an informed one. As an added precaution, at least one witness cannot be related to you by blood, marriage, adoption, or be entitled to any portion of your estate. No individual acting in a professional capacity as your health-care provider may serve as a witness.

The two physicians must establish that you are capable of making medical decisions. The prescribing physician must inform you of feasible alternatives, including comfort care, hospice care, and pain control. Your decision must be informed. If you appear to be clinically depressed or if you are suffering from a psychiatric disorder that impairs judgment, either physician may refer you to a psychiatrist for counseling. The prescribing physician must request that you notify your next of kin and family—it's a recommendation, not a requirement.

Before writing the prescription, the physician will inform you of the probable results of the medication. You will be told that it's important to have another person present when you take the medication. You will also be told that you can always change your mind until the very last second. Finally, you will receive instructions and ancillary medications to minimize your discomfort and achieve the desired outcome.

With your written consent, the physician will contact the pharmacist who will dispense the medication. Either you or your designated agent may pick up the medication. Both the physician and pharmacist must notify the state and fulfill the necessary paperwork. Note: No person—including the physician, pharmacist or health-care provider—opposed to assisted dying on moral grounds is required to participate.

The state must annually publish a statistical report of the information it has collected. Oregon's Act requires you be terminally ill, but makes no mention of pain or suffering. Also, the state stipulates that the termination of life under the Act "shall not, for any purpose, constitute suicide, assisted suicide, mercy killing or homicide under the law." In the eyes of the state, it's a natural death. Why? Because the person was already dying. The state views the Act as allowing the patient to choose one form of dying over another. It's "Death with Dignity" because those who choose it view it as a more humane, peaceful, and dignified way to die. On the death certificate, the cause of death is listed as the underlying disease. Consequently, it will not invalidate an annuity or life insurance policy.

Oregon's Death with Dignity: Mrs. Dunn's Death

Mrs. Dunn, a cancer patient, took advantage of Oregon's Act when she decided it was her time to go. Previously, she had discussed this option with her physicians, and she had fulfilled all the legal criteria to obtain the Nembutal. As required by the Act, she had enrolled in hospice and received excellent palliative care. She had the full support of her primary doctor. Here's how her daughter described her death:

"Her doctor stirred up the sleeping pills in the chocolate pudding. One thing I'll always be grateful for is, before he gave Mother the pudding, he said to her, 'Now I know we're all around your bed, and we've all come over here and made a special day to do this but, if there is any reason you don't want to do it, we'll just all go home, and that will be the end of it.' And Mother was adamant. She said, 'I want to do it.' ...Mother had to eat the pudding within five minutes. And I think she ate it in about a minute and a half. And within 15 minutes she was gone. My sisters and I were just all there for Mother. And very supportive of her. We all held her hand. I held her head up and stroked her neck for the whole time. And we all just really did pour love on Mother.... It was so painless; I mean, it was terribly traumatic and heartbreaking, but it was so easy for my mother."[2]

The lifting of the prohibition in Oregon made it possible for Mrs. Dunn to experience an "easy and gentle" death in the presence of her loved ones. The Oregon Act does not require that a physician be present. Any family member could have stirred the pudding. Mrs. Dunn self-administered the pudding as required by the law. The physician was there at Mrs. Dunn's invitation; it was a final act of bonding between doctor and patient.

Oregon: A System That Works

So how did Oregon's *Death with Dignity Act* perform in real life? I will answer this question by analyzing the yearly data reported by the state of Oregon from 1998 to 2009.[3] Where possible, I augment the data with the latest findings by medical and academic researchers. Unless I specifically mention a year, the numbers I present are 12-year aggregates. Here's a quick synopsis of how the Act performed:

• *It led to many conversations and a small number of deaths.* Only 460 patients died using the Act, accounting for 1 in 1000 deaths in Oregon. However, 1 in 50 dying Oregonians now talk to their

---

[2] Helene Starks et al., "Family Member Involvement in Hastened Death," *Death Studies* (Vol. 31, 2007).

[3] Oregon Department of Human Services, *Twelfth Annual Report on Oregon's Death with Dignity Act* (March, 2010).

physician about the possibility; and 1 in 6 talk to family members about it. Physicians only granted about 1 in 6 requests for aid in dying; only 1 in 10 requests resulted in hastened death.[4] This shows that legalization has resulted in a more open conversation about death. It also shows that many who request it use it as a form of insurance. Most importantly, opponents' dire predictions of a "death stampede" did not materialize. The safeguards worked.

- *All experienced a peaceful death.* The technology worked as advertised. The median time to unconsciousness was 5 minutes. The median time to death was 25 minutes; the longest time to death was 4.5 days. With one exception, no patient regained consciousness (see Note). 95.5% did not experience any complications; 4.5% experienced some regurgitation but their secretions were cleared by attending nurses or relatives. The prescribed lethal medication was either Nembutal (pentobarbital) or secobarbital. Over the last 12 years, both proved to be 99.9% effective and resulted in very peaceful deaths. There were no calls to 911 for complications.

Note: *In 2005, a patient regained consciousness 65 hours after ingesting the medication. He was subsequently treated in the emergency room where he recovered quickly; he declared the whole thing to be "a miracle." He died from the illness within two weeks. Oregon doctors later concluded that the patient woke up because he had taken a laxative to mask the bitter taste of the lethal drug; it prevented his body from absorbing the drug quickly enough.*

- *No physician interventions were required.* Contrary to opponents' predictions, no physician interventions were required; there was no need to perform active euthanasia. In 83% of cases, physicians or nurses were present when the medication was ingested; in 82% of cases, they were present at the time of death. They were there to provide moral support and a comforting presence.

---

[4] Timothy E. Quill, "Legal Regulation of Physician-Assisted Death—The Latest Report Cards," *New England Journal of Medicine* (Vol. 356, 2007).

- *Most informed their families about the decision*. Even though the Act does not mandate it, 93.5% informed their family of their decision; 4.7% chose not to inform their families; and 1.8% had no family to inform.

- *Most died at home.* 94.6% died at home; 4.1% died in long-term care facilities; and 1% died in hospitals.

- *Most were enrolled in hospice.* Over the last 12 years, 88.2% were enrolled in hospice. In 2009, 91.5% were enrolled in hospice. High hospice utilization also means that patients were being monitored by hospice doctors, nurses, and social workers. The hospice people detect and report issues such as poor mental health, potential family abuse, and depression. In a *2005 Congressional Testimony,* Ann Jackson, executive director of the *Oregon Hospice Association (OHA),* reported: "The Act has been responsibly implemented, with none of the predicted dire consequences. Hospice workers agree that the most important reason patients use a prescription is to control the circumstances of death. The least important reasons include depression, being a financial drain on others, and lack of social support."

- *Most had health insurance.* 98.7% were insured; 1.3% had no insurance. Only 2.6% were concerned about financial implications of their treatments; 36.6% expressed concern about being burdens on family, friends, and caregivers. According to hospice workers, "being a burden" was not the primary motivation for requesting the Nembutal. The state reports that the primary concerns were loss of autonomy (90.8%), not being able to engage in life's activities (87.3%), and loss of dignity (85.2%).

- *Most were highly educated.* 44.4% had a bachelor's degree or higher; 22.9% had some college; 25.5% were high school graduates; and 7.2% never completed high school.

- *Most died within the six-month window.* Over the last 12 years, the median time between the first request and death was 43 days.

- *It helped reduce anxiety of terminally-ill Oregonians.* According to family surveys, dying Oregonians are approximately 100 times more likely to consider assisted dying than to follow through with obtaining a lethal prescription. Knowing that they have that choice appears to relieve anxiety among the dying and their families. Many healthy Oregonians also find it psychologically reassuring to have that choice.

- *Racial and ethnic minorities were not placed at risk.* In the last 12 years, the people who used the Act were 97.6% White; 1.5% were of Asian descent; 0.4% were Hispanic, and 0.2% were African American. (Note: 2.65% of Oregonians are African American.)

- *Poor people were not placed at risk.* The data does not include direct measures of income, employment, or assets. However, the data shows that most had insurance and at least a high school education. Over 12 years, only 2.6% reported that financial implications of their treatment was a concern.

- *Uninsured people were not placed at risk.* Over 12 years, only 1.3% did not have medical insurance. In contrast, 17% of non-elderly adults in Oregon are uninsured.[5]

- *People with disabilities were not placed at risk.* Almost all dying people are to some extent physically disabled toward the end. The data from Oregon does not indicate whether a person had a disability before becoming terminally ill. However, over the last 12 years, no one received aid in dying for disability alone—they were all terminally ill. There is no evidence that physician-assisted dying poses a heightened risk to people with disabilities.

- *Elderly populations were not placed at risk.* 11% of patients who died from the Act were 85 or older; in comparison, 21% of all Oregon deaths are in this age category. 60% of the people who died using the Act were aged between 18 and 74.

---

[5] Source: Kaiser Family Foundation, *State Health Facts.*

- *The privacy of patients and doctors was respected.* The state was able to collect information while still respecting the privacy of the physician-patient relationship. It did not disclose any information that identified patients, physicians, pharmacists, witnesses, or other participants in activities covered by the *Death with Dignity Act*.

- *There was no rush of suicide tourists.* Everyone who died from the Act was an Oregon resident. There has not been a migration to Oregon for the purpose of using the Act.

- *It helped loved ones grieve better.* Studies of grief outcomes consistently show that survivors of those who used the Act had a shorter grieving period than survivors of those who did not die by lethal ingestion. For example, a major 2009 study reports: "The family members of those who died using the Act were more likely to believe their loved one's choices were honored and less likely to have regrets about how the loved one died. They felt more prepared and accepting of the death than comparison family members.... We found that 14 months after death that family of those who died using the Act had a low prevalence of depression and grief, and few negative perceptions about the death."[6] In addition, survivors are less likely to be afraid of their own deaths, probably because they witnessed a relatively peaceful and dignified death with aid in dying. Opponents of the Act have long made unsubstantiated claims that families would experience the complicated grief associated with suicide; this empirical study disproves those claims. The shortening of life at the end is not analogous to classical suicide.

- *It turned Oregon into a leader in palliative care.* Rather than undermining palliative care, the Act has improved end-of-life care for all the dying. Oregon leads the nation in terms of per capita opioid prescriptions, hospice referral rates, numbers of deaths occurring at home, the training of physicians in palliative care, and

---

[6] Ganzini et al., "Mental Health Outcomes of Family Members of Oregonians Who Request Physician Aid in Dying," *Journal of Pain and Symptom Management* (Vol. 38, 2009).

organized statewide use of POLST directives.[7] Oregon has hospices in all its counties both rural and urban. All state public hospitals provide palliative care.[8]

- **There was no documented evidence of abuse.** The Act requires the Oregon *Department of Human Services (DHS)* to monitor compliance with the law. The information compiled over the last 12 years shows that the procedures were followed. The law provides immunity to physicians only if they follow *all* the procedures. Also, the drugs used in Oregon are Schedule II narcotics that are closely monitored. When such a prescription is filled, it must be matched to the original report which indicates when the prescription was written. There are severe penalties for not reporting. It would be virtually impossible for a patient to *legally* obtain a life-ending medication without leaving behind a paper or electronic trail that could be followed.

- **Most were not depressed.** Over the last 12 years, only 8.4% of the patients who died from the Act were referred for psychiatric evaluation. The rest were found to be competent by two examining physicians. Approximately 20% of the yearly requests were made by depressed patients, but none were accepted. In 2009, the mental health of none of the patients who died from the Act was in question; consequently, 0% were referred to psychiatrists. Most people who are sent for psychiatric evaluation during the early part of the process end up not receiving a prescription. None of the patients who died from the Act had prior mental illness. Of course, it's possible that some patients became depressed after receiving the prescription; it's also possible that the two evaluating physicians may have missed signs of depression in a patient. However, there is no direct evidence that depressed patients are at higher risk for receiving assistance in

---

[7] Robert Steinbrook, "Physician-Assisted Death — From Oregon to Washington State," *New England Journal of Medicine* (Vol. 359, 2008).

[8] Goldsmith et al. "Variability in Access to Hospital Palliative Care in the United States," *Journal of Palliative Medicine* (Vol. 11, 2008).

dying. A large cross-sectional study found that all patients who received a prescription were mentally competent and able to give informed consent; they were significantly less anxious or depressed than those who did not receive a prescription.[9] The researchers also noted that non-psychiatric MDs have sufficient competence to make this type of diagnosis.

Note: In the U.S., general practitioners treat the vast majority of depressed patients and prescribe 90% of psychotropic drugs. The psychiatrists deal with more complicated mental illnesses such as schizophrenia and acute bipolar disorders.

- *It improved the integrity of the medical profession.* It's almost impossible to obtain hard data on the practice of clandestine euthanasia. However, it's safe to say that the Oregon Act reduces the need for underground euthanasia. The Act regulates the practice of euthanasia and makes it less ad hoc and dangerous. The patient is better protected. Most importantly, the Act facilitates the end-of-life discussion. At the end of their lives, the patients do not feel abandoned by their physicians. Many Oregon physicians now report that the process has increased their confidence and assertiveness in discussing these difficult issues. As noted earlier, the Act certainly improved the practice of palliative medicine in Oregon.

In summary, the Oregon laboratory has performed superbly during the last 12 years. The data proves that physician-assisted dying can be made to work in the United States. As you read in the last chapter, the evidence convinced four of the top medical professional and health organizations in the U.S. to adopt policies in support of aid in dying.[10] They include the *AMWA,* the *AMSA,* the *AHPA,* and the *ACLM.* Their

---

[9] Ganzini et al., "Prevalence of Depression and Anxiety in Patients Requesting Physicians' Aid in Dying," *British Medical Journal* (Vol. 337, 2008).

[10] Kathryn Tucker, "At the Very End of Life: The Emergence of Policy Supporting Aid in Dying Among Mainstream Medical and Health Policy Associations," *Harvard Health Policy Review* (Vol. 10, 2009).

endorsements were made after careful review of the Oregon data and arguments presented by groups that opposed the Act.

In 2008, the voters in the state of Washington carefully scrutinized the Oregon record. After a heated campaign, the voters decided to adopt the Washington *Death with Dignity Act* by the significant margin of 58% to 42%. It was a resounding vote of confidence for Oregon's performance by their neighbor state.

Washington's Learning Curve

In February 2010, the state of Washington released its first annual report. Because the law took effect on March 2009, the report covers only the last nine months of that year. During that period, 36 patients died after ingesting the medication. Their profiles were very similar to those in Oregon. However, two small errors were incurred as part of the learning curve. The state reported that two patients woke up shortly after taking the medication, but they died a little while later. No one called 911, but what happened?

According to Dr. Thomas Preston, the first patient threw up part of the medication because he drank six cans of Pepsi, his favorite drink, in the hour before taking the drug. The patient woke up and fell back asleep several times before finally dying 28 hours later—the longest time to death reported among the 36 Washingtonians. Most patients lapsed into unconsciousness within 10 minutes and died within 90 minutes.

The second patient swallowed the drug too slowly because she kept stopping to say goodbye to the people around her. She fell asleep after drinking less than half the full cocktail, then awakened before dying a short time later. The lethal drug used in assisted dying in Washington was, in most cases, secobarbital mixed with a sweet-tasting liquid or custard.[11]

---

[11] Harris Meyer, "First Year Complications with Assisted-Suicide," *Crosscut*, March 23, 2010.

Dr. Preston explained that the problem in these two cases was that the patients refused to have a physician or trained volunteer present to ensure that proper procedures were followed. In Oregon, trained volunteers are present in 95% of deaths.

Note: "Compassion & Choices" counsels patients not to eat for four to five hours beforehand; to take an anti-nausea tablet an hour ahead of time; to refrain from ingesting laxatives or acidic beverages such as orange juice; to drink water or soda only at room temperature; and to say their goodbyes before drinking the lethal cocktail all at once.

Netherlands: The Doctor-Patient Relationship

First and foremost, euthanasia in the Netherlands is based on the very deep and personal bonds that exist between the Dutch people and their family physicians, or *huisarts*. In 2005, 87% of all euthanasia deaths were handled by these huisarts; the patients died at home. Euthanasia is only performed in hospitals or hospices when the huisarts cannot control the patient's pain at home.

The literal translation of the word "huisarts" is physicians of the house, which is exactly what they are. They live in the neighborhood. Typically, they have office visits in the mornings and then spend their afternoons making house calls or visiting patients in nursing homes. They wear street clothes and often ride their bicycles.

Over the years, the huisarts get to know their patients and their families intimately. Even though they have access to the best technology, the huisarts favor a more holistic and talk-centered approach to medicine. They understand their patients' domestic circumstances, job stresses, child-rearing issues, and any family support or pressure that may be relevant in a request for euthanasia. Their goal is to treat the "whole patient."

Dr. Frances Norwood is an American medical anthropologist who spent two years in the Amsterdam area observing the communication between the huisarts and their patients, including the very intimate "euthanasia talks." You can read more about that incredibly compassionate practice in her book *The Maintenance of Life*.[12]

The second thing you must know about the Dutch system is that it provides full-coverage health care for everyone. In the Netherlands, insurance includes full hospital coverage, home care, hospice care, nursing home care, physical therapists, nutritionists, and other providers. Everyone has a huisart. The Dutch have full access to palliative care in homes, hospices, or institutional settings. The entire Dutch population is 100% insured to cover the cost of long-term illness. In the Netherlands, requests for euthanasia are almost never motivated by financial pressures or medical costs.

Netherlands: "Euthanasia Talk"

In the Netherlands, a patient's request for euthanasia starts as a conversation with the family huisart. The Dutch call it "euthanasia talk" and consider it to be a palliative function. The conversation serves as a venue for openly discussing death, the meaning of life, and the needs of the dying.

Typically, the huisart uses the conversation to respond to the needs and fears of the patient. Following that, the huisart organizes the social and palliative resources that the patient will need for end-of-life care. Eventually, the living room is transformed into a hospital room. The conversation continues: it now evolves into an ongoing discourse on dying. It brings together patient, family, nurses, and doctors. Together, they examine all the options and go over the palliative choices.

The huisarts devote a lot of time to these conversations. They make house calls at night, during weekends, and at other times. They take life and death very seriously. At the end, the conversation rarely culminates in a euthanasia death. In 2005, fewer than 1 in 10 who initiated requests died as a result of euthanasia or assisted suicide.

---

[12] Frances Norwood, *The Maintenance of Life* (Carolina Academic Press, 2009).

In some cases, the palliative treatment fails and the conversation then moves to the next step. The patient must *concretely* request euthanasia in a written declaration. Dutch law requires that: 1) the patient make a voluntary, informed, and well-considered request; 2) the patient must be facing unbearable and hopeless suffering, either currently or in the immediate future, with no outlook for improvement; 3) the physician must agree with the patient that no reasonable alternative treatment is available (the patient has the right to refuse treatment); 4) the physician must consult with an independent physician not involved in the case; and 5) the action must be performed with due care and reported to the authorities.

Netherlands: Death by Euthanasia

Typically, when these concrete requests are made, the huisart conducts lengthy meetings with the patient and each family member, and reviews all the options. There is no waiting period, but time must be allocated to reach a consensus. As one huisart put it, "I need the time, not only to make sure the patient is consistent, but also to prepare myself and the patient's family."[13] Because of the very personal relationship with their huisarts, patients also recognize that the physician may need time before the decision is really shared. One patient said of his physician, "I need to give him time to learn to accept that he will help me end my life."

Eventually, a consensus is reached. The patients can then set a date. Of course, they can change their minds as many times as they wish. The second doctor must come to see the patient, talk about it all, and, in the process, perform a very thorough palliative evaluation; it's all part of the conversation.

On the technical side, the patient must decide whether to have a drink or a needle. Typically, the whole family gathers around when the death takes place. The huisart is like any other family member; it's all very

---

[13] Timothy Quill and Margaret Battin, Editors, *Physician-Assisted Dying: The Case for Palliative Care and Patient Choice* (Johns Hopkins University Press, 2004).

intimate. Later, the huisart helps each of the family members cope with individual grief. Remember, the huisart is the personal physician for the entire family. The conversation itself is a form of anticipatory grief therapy for both patient and family.

Once the patient makes a decision and feels in control, he or she can then focus on the goodbyes. This prepares the family for the upcoming death and allows them to obtain closure. Solid empirical data shows that these bereaved families suffer significantly less traumatic grief than their counterparts who lost a loved one through "natural death."[14]

In 2005, only 1 in 3 who made concrete requests died from euthanasia or assisted suicide. That year approximately 1.7% of all Dutch deaths were from voluntary active euthanasia and 0.1% by physician-assisted dying. In the Dutch physician-patient context, it seems that active euthanasia makes more sense. It's the huisart's final act of compassion for the patient; it's the culmination of a long relationship based on trust and a shared humanity. In the U.S., the act is a patient's declaration of autonomy. Consequently, the patient performs the act.

Netherlands: Top-Notch Palliative Care

In the past, the Netherlands was often criticized for its presumed lack of palliative care—mainly because there were few hospices. Of course, home care has always been a big part of the Dutch health-care system; palliative care takes place in people's homes. In any case, the Dutch accepted some of the criticism and have worked on improving their system. The first hospice facility was set up in 1988. By 2006, there were about 200 facilities for terminal palliative care. Some of these institutions are hospices, some are "almost-home houses," and the rest are wards in nursing homes and hospitals. In most palliative care institutions euthanasia is an option.

The majority of palliative care, however, is provided by the country's 8,000 huisarts with help from hospital-based palliative care

---

[14] N. Swarte et al., "Effects of Euthanasia on Bereaved Family and Friends: A Cross-Sectional Study," *British Medical Journal* (Vol. 327, 2003).

professionals. The huisarts treat their dying patients at home or in institutions such as nursing homes. Increasingly, the Dutch choose to die at home. In 2005, the huisarts were the attending doctors at 44% of all deaths and at 87% of all euthanasia deaths; specialists attended 33% of all deaths and 9% of all euthanasia deaths. The rest died under the supervision of nursing-home doctors. In recent years, the huisarts were given more advanced palliative-care training, especially in pain management. With the help of huisarts, about 65% of cancer patients in the Netherlands now die at home.

Over the years, the Dutch developed a network of huisarts and other physicians who are trained in both palliative care and all aspects of euthanasia. The network, known as *Support Consultation Euthanasia Netherlands (SCEN),* serves as a center of competence for all things related to the practice of euthanasia in the Netherlands. In 2006, there were 532 SCEN-trained doctors. They served as the independent consulting physicians in 90% of euthanasia cases.

On the average, SCEN doctors spend about four hours reviewing each request for euthanasia. In 75% of all cases, the SCEN doctor agreed that all the requirements had been met. Note: The SCEN network, not the huisart, picks the consulting physician; the consultation is truly independent.

When you put it all together, "The quality and availability of palliative care in the Netherlands is currently considered, relative to other countries, very advanced."[15]

So, why is euthanasia still practiced? The answer: Almost two-thirds of Dutch physicians do not agree with the suggestion that adequate treatment of pain and terminal care could make euthanasia redundant.[16] They believe that, even with the best palliative care, there is still a need for euthanasia.

---

[15] John Griffith et al., *Euthanasia and Law in Europe* (Hart Publishing, 2008).

[16] Jean-Jacques Georges et al., "Physicians' Opinions on Palliative Care and Euthanasia in The Netherlands," *Journal of Palliative Medicine* (Vol. 9, 2006).

Netherlands: No More Secrets

The Dutch did not go into euthanasia lightly. They debated and researched every aspect of it. As a result, they collected more empirical data on how people die than any other society on earth. Over the last 20 years, they conducted four major studies of life-shortening medical practices. Each study includes extensive data on the practices of termination of life support, palliative sedation, voluntary active euthanasia, physician-assisted death, and the termination of life without request. This last category is not murder. It's a standard medical practice in all societies. Typically, it's "don't ask, don't tell" stuff. The Dutch were the first to openly discuss this medical practice. And until 2002, euthanasia was illegal in the Netherlands. Yet, the Dutch collected all the data they could on euthanasia and published it. They revealed underground medical practices. Everything was published, measured, and accounted for. The Dutch made their doctors tell the world everything; and the skeletons came out of the closet—all of them.

Think about it. How much do we know about clandestine euthanasia in the United States today? How much do we know about mercy killings that take place in our hospitals and nursing homes? How much do we know about how palliative sedation is actually practiced? Except for the Netherlands, this type of hard data cannot be found anywhere today.

The four Dutch studies were conducted in 1989/1990, 1995, 2001, and 2005/2006. The first two studies generated an explosion of headlines, articles, books, and commentary. They fueled an incredible amount of debate. There was praise and there were attacks. Interestingly, not much was written about the last two studies. I will be focusing on their data in the next sections.

Back to the first two studies. As you would expect, they generated a feeding frenzy among anti-euthanasia groups, who were mostly non-Dutch. The Dutch were busy analyzing their data and writing reports, but not in English. In contrast, their opponents were busy writing accusations in English, but they did not read Dutch. The opponents accused the Dutch of being in denial. They claimed the data was evidence that there was a slippery slope in the Netherlands and that the Dutch proved to be "remarkably fast skiers." The Dutch doctors were accused of having gone wild. The integrity of the medical profession had rapidly degenerated: safeguards were not working, doctors were not reporting euthanasia, palliative care was not practiced, and doctors had turned into killers. They killed babies, the disabled, the comatose, and the demented. No one was safe in the Netherlands; euthanasia was out of control. As you will soon read, these claims are pure fantasy.

To get a reasoned and non-inflammatory version of the criticism generated by the Dutch studies of 1990 and 1995, read Dr. Herbert Hendin's book *Seduced by Death*.[17] He and others were rebutted by Professor John Griffiths and colleagues from the Netherlands. In their very detailed book, *Euthanasia and Law in the Netherlands,* they translated much of the internal Dutch discussion into English for the first time.[18]

Netherlands: Is Euthanasia Slippery?

In 1997, U.S. Supreme Court Judge David Souter observed that there was a "substantial dispute" about what the Dutch experience shows. This is what he wrote in *Washington v Glucksberg*: "The day may come when we can say with some assurance which side is right, but for now there is the substantiality of the factual disagreement..."[19] He then used the disagreement to reject the claim for a constitutional right to physician-assisted dying in the United States.

Fast-forward to the year 2010. Euthanasia is now a legal and accepted practice in the Netherlands and we have a lot more data about how it is

---

[17] Herbert Hendin, *Seduced By Death: Doctors, Patients, and the Dutch Cure* (Norton, 1997).

[18] John Griffiths et al., *Euthanasia and Law in the Netherlands* (Amsterdam University Press, 1998).

[19] U.S. Supreme Court, *Washington v. Gluksberg* (1997).

performed. The day has come "when we can say with some assurance which side is right." I will present the new data and then let you decide if the Netherlands is on a slippery slope.

My source for the data is the Dutch national study conducted in 2005/2006.[20] I will tell you how the results compare with the previous three national studies. In addition, I was fortunate to be able to draw information from Professor Griffiths's timely new book, *Euthanasia and Law in Europe*.[21] Again, he provides valuable information that was previously only available in Dutch. Here are the numbers:

- *Voluntary active euthanasia:* In 2005, 1.7% of all deaths in the Netherlands were the result of euthanasia, as compared with 2.6% in 2001, 2.4% in 1995, and 1.7% in 1990. The numbers for euthanasia seemed to have peaked in 2001 and are now going down.

- *Physician-assisted death:* In 2005, 0.1% of all deaths were from physician-assisted dying as compared with 0.2% in 2001, 0.2% in 1995, and 0.2% in 1990. The numbers are going down.

- *Reporting rates from physicians:* In 2005, 80.2% of euthanasia and assisted dying cases were reported by physicians. The number is up from 18% in 1990 when both practices were illegal. This is a dramatic improvement. In comparison, the reporting rate is zero in countries where euthanasia is not legal.

- *Palliative consultation:* In 2005/2006, 90% of second consultations were conducted by SCEN-trained palliative care specialists. No comparable numbers are available for previous years. No slippery slope to report here. Note: The SCEN consultation allows palliative care specialists to provide *before death* verification. It's a major step forward.

---

[20] Agnes van der Heide et al, "End-of-Life Practices in the Netherlands Under the Euthanasia Act," *New England Journal of Medicine* (Vol. 356, 2007).

[21] John Griffith et al., *Euthanasia and Law in Europe* (Hart Publishing, 2008).

The data is all good. It's case closed for voluntary active euthanasia and assisted dying in the Netherlands. There are no slippery slopes to report.

Netherlands: Is Involuntary Euthanasia Slippery?

What about claims that Dutch doctors are practicing involuntary euthanasia? Remember, critics accused them of killing babies, the demented, the comatose, and the disabled. Here's the data:

- *Ending of life without explicit request by the patient:* In 2005, 0.4% of all deaths in the Netherlands were in that category, as compared with 0.7% in 2001, 0.7% in 1995, and 0.8% in 1990. These deaths, too, are on the decline. Usually, doctors perform these deaths to relieve the unbearable suffering of patients who are imminently dying. Typically, they administer morphine. In 2001, there were no cases in which the procedure was performed on a competent patient There is no equivalent data for 2005.

Doctors everywhere perform these types of mercy interventions on patients who are not competent. Typically, they do it with the approval of the patients' families or colleagues. Most of these cases are handled discretely and do not receive wide attention. The Dutch, on the other hand, are meticulously documenting the practice and informing us that it is being done. A Dutch Government report explains:

> "These were patients who were terminally ill and who were suffering very badly but who were no longer able to express their wishes. Either the doctor and the patient had discussed the matter at an earlier stage, or the patient had previously expressed a wish that his or her life be terminated in such a situation."

In other words, the dying patients had lost their ability to communicate but had previously stated that if such a situation were ever to occur, they wanted their life to be terminated. The Dutch rates in this category are in the middle range of other European countries that don't practice euthanasia. For example, comparable numbers are 0.67% for Denmark, 0.33% for the U.K., and 0.23% for Sweden. Furthermore,

116

the Dutch have documented every case. Their reports show that doctors have either obtained prior permission from the patient and relatives, or they have consulted with other doctors.

We may not like the practice of involuntary euthanasia, but there is no slippery slope. If there is a suspicion of abuse, the police will be called to investigate. Note: I don't have comparable numbers for the U.S., but it's being done here, too.

Netherlands: Is Palliative Sedation Slippery?

Are we finished? Can we declare that there are no slippery slopes in the Netherlands? Not yet. There is one statistic that's on the rise: palliative sedation. I'll present two sets of numbers that demonstrate this trend. The first is for all instances of "double effect." The second is for instances of "double effect" that include deep continuous sedation with the probable withholding of hydration and nutrition. Here are the numbers:

- *Pain relief with life shortening effect:* In 2005, 25% of all deaths in the Netherlands were from pain control and sedation, with possible hastening of death, as compared with 21% in 2001, 19% in 1995, and 19% in 1990. This is a significant increase.

- *Continuous deep palliative sedation:* In 2005, 7.1% of all deaths in the Netherlands were from deep palliative sedation, with possible hastening of death, as compared with 5.6% in 2001. This, too, is a significant increase.

The numbers indicate that the practice of palliative sedation accounts for one in every four deaths in the Netherlands. (Note: the 7.1% number for continuous deep sedation is a subset of the 25%.) In this respect, the situation is not different from other advanced countries where palliative sedation is medically and morally accepted based on the principle of "double effect."

Personally, I find these numbers troubling. As you know, I'm not a big fan of palliative sedation, especially in places where the Nembutal is a legal alternative. Why? Because palliative sedation may serve as a shortcut for doctors. It may provide a way to perform euthanasia without dealing with safeguards, second consultations, and reporting forms. It gives the doctors a lot more power and puts them back in control. The decision to end life is not made by the patient; it happens as part of the palliative treatment which is under the control of doctors.

It takes an informed patient to ask for euthanasia. Ethics require that the patient must autonomously request it; doctors must not be the first to suggest it. At the end of their lives, many patients are too weak and exhausted to request euthanasia. In contrast, it takes a lot less effort for a doctor to perform terminal sedation. There's no fuss, no paperwork, no safeguards, and no SCEN reports to be filed. The patients are put out of their misery and their deaths are reported as natural. End of story.

Of course, this is not the type of slippery slope the opponents of euthanasia had in mind. On the contrary, many will applaud the move and call it a good palliative practice. Like their counterparts in other countries, Dutch doctors are starting to get the hang of the wonders of "double effect."

Who loses? The patients, of course. Unlike euthanasia, terminal sedation is not something a patient can explicitly request. Only physicians can initiate it. As noted earlier, the practice suffers from a disturbing lack of consistency. It's pure luck of the draw; the decision rests firmly in the hands of the attending physician. The patient does not get to choose when or how to die. There is no "euthanasia talk" and the final conversation does not take place. For many, terminal sedation will happen by default. The few patients who understand the ins and outs of terminal sedation may explicitly request euthanasia to avoid being sedated into oblivion. (In Chapter 3, I covered in detail the pros and cons of palliative sedation versus the Nembutal.)

In my opinion, the rising trend of terminal sedation in a country that supports euthanasia and physician-assisted dying is not a step in the right direction. However, no one else seems to be complaining.

Consequently, the rise of palliative sedation is not viewed as a slippery slope.

Netherlands: Slippery Slope for the Vulnerable?

Can we now report back to Justice Souter that there were no slippery slopes in the Netherlands? We're getting there. However, there's one more question to be answered: What was the impact on vulnerable groups during these years? Luckily, there is a very detailed study that answers this question.[22] The authors of the study examined the evidence from 1998 to 2006 in both Oregon and the Netherlands and this is what they found:

> "Rates of assisted dying in Oregon and in the Netherlands showed no evidence of heightened risk for the elderly, women, the uninsured, people with low educational status, the poor, the physically disabled, the chronically ill, minors, people with psychiatric illnesses including depression, or racial and ethnic minorities, compared with background populations.... While extra-legal cases were not the focus of this study, none have been uncovered in Oregon; among extra-legal cases in the Netherlands, there was no evidence of higher rates in vulnerable groups."

It's all good. Now, we can tell Justice David Souter with much assurance: "There were no slippery slopes in the Netherlands. The euthanasia side was right. It is unfortunate that you did not have access to this hindsight knowledge in 1997, when you issued your Supreme Court ruling. It would have saved us many battles at the state level. Also there would have been a lot less suffering among the dying."

Netherlands' Lesson: "Let the Doctors Do It"

In 2005, 43% of the Dutch died with assistance from their doctors. Here's how the numbers break down: 25% died from slow euthanasia

---

[22] Margaret Battin et al., "Legal Physician-Assisted Dying in Oregon and the Netherlands: Evidence Concerning the Impact on Patients in Vulnerable Groups," *Journal of Medical Ethics* (Vol. 33, 2007).

(by terminal sedation and the "double effect"); 16% died from passive euthanasia (by withdrawing or withholding life support); 1.7% died from voluntary active euthanasia (by lethal injection); 0.4% died from involuntary euthanasia (by morphine overdose); and 0.1% died from physician-assisted dying (by self-administering the Nembutal).[23]

What do these numbers tell us? They seem to indicate that 42.5% of the dying population prefer to have their physicians directly assist in their death (i.e., pull the plug or insert the needle). In the case of active euthanasia, the patient tells the doctor when to do it. However, only 0.1% prefer to perform the act themselves. Perhaps it's the nature of human beings. We will not take our own lives. We would much prefer that our physicians do it for us.

What are the implications for Oregon, where active euthanasia is not an option? In the Netherlands, when given a choice, 1.7% chose active euthanasia; 0.1% chose to self-administer. In Oregon, where there is no such choice, the Nembutal is only used by the 0.1% who are willing to self-administer instead of spending the rest of their lives drugged into oblivion. You will notice that the 0.1% number is consistent in both countries. This begs the question: Could a large number of dying patients be suffering in Oregon because they are afraid or unwilling to self-administer?

As I wrote in Chapter 2, the Nembutal provides an answer for strong-willed, empowered patients who are willing to self-administer. I'm totally in favor of self-administration; it would have worked fine for Jeri. The Oregon numbers demonstrate that the Nembutal works as advertised, and there is no need for a physician's assistance. But what happens to patients who want their doctors to perform the act on their behalf? They're out of luck. In the U.S., the right-to-die activists believe that we must do it ourselves. Those of us who can't will have to depend on a physician to do it for us by administering a morphine pump instead of a needle. When the time comes, we must hope that

---

[23] Note: These percentages take into account all deaths in the Netherlands including accidents.

our doctors will put us out of our misery by sedating us into oblivion. The doctors, not the patients, make that choice.

Note: Why isn't active euthanasia also on U.S. ballots? There is really no moral difference between a physician handing a consenting patient a bottle of Nembutal versus pouring the liquid down the patient's throat. However, there are practical differences. Self-administration maximizes the patient's autonomy; it insures that the act is truly voluntary. It also separates the doctors from the physical act of administering the Nembutal, and so they prefer it. On the other hand, should patients require it, there is no good ethical reason not to legalize the active euthanasia approach. Of course, the safeguards will have to be tighter than they are in Oregon. For example, the law could require that a second independent doctor be present during the act. It's all doable. At the end, we must do whatever is best for the dying patients. The numbers from the Netherlands demonstrate that we must further research this question: What do U.S. patients truly need? Maybe the research will conclude that Americans are not like the Dutch; we may prefer to do it ourselves. In any case, let's find out. The voters will pass whatever law is best for the dying patients, but we must first tell the voters what the patients want.

The Bottom Line: Oregon It Is

The Dutch model works as advertised and there are no slippery slopes to report. However, I still prefer the Oregon model. Why? Because self-administration provides maximum insurance that the final decision belongs to the individual. The *Death with Dignity Act* provides insurance for everyone, greatly improves end-of-life palliative care, and allows the dying to openly discuss their forthcoming death. Only a tiny percentage end up using the option. Consequently, the Nembutal provides insurance for all, while being used by the few. It's the best of all worlds. Of course, there's always room for improvement. Here's my list of fixes for Oregon, and it's very short:

- ***The second consultant must be drawn from an expert pool.*** Over time, Oregonians will develop the type of expertise that is embodied in the Dutch SCEN. When that happens, the second consultation must be provided by physicians trained in both palliative care and euthanasia.

- ***Collect information on the previously disabled.*** The state must include information on the previously disabled in its yearly reports. Currently, this information is obtained by interviewing the physicians and families of patients who use the Act. Both sides of the debate would like the state to collect this information as part of its yearly statistics.[24] (Note: Most of the dying are disabled at the end but were not *previously disabled.*)

- ***Publicize the benefit of the final conversation.*** Ideally, the conversation must start at least six months before death when patients still have stamina and when their minds are still clear (i.e., before opiates fog the brain). After the Nembutal is procured, the patient can decide when (or if ever) to take it. In Oregon, the request for the Nembutal is not made soon enough. The median duration between the first request and death is only 43 days. Many of the requesters die before obtaining the Nembutal. It's last minute stuff. Hospices face the same problem. Typically, patients will delay for as long as possible any discussion of death. In the end, that delay does not work in their favor. They may end up missing out on the benefits of both hospice and the Nembutal. It would be nice if someone would produce a documentary explaining the palliative benefits of this final conversation—hint, hint. Somehow, this information must be made widely available. (Late News: In 2011, HBO released the documentary *How to Die in Oregon* by filmmaker Peter Richardson. It provides an intimate portrait of what it means to die in dignity.)

- ***Shorten the duration between requests to one week.*** Two weeks is much too long. People must have the conversation while they're still

---

[24] Gloria L. Krahn, "Reflections on the debate on disability and aid in dying," *Disability and Health Journal* (Vol. 3, 2010).

coherent and lucid. At the end, dying people are too exhausted to have any type of conversation. It's best to conduct the conversation early. Every day counts when you're close to dying. Shaving a week helps the process.

This concludes a long chapter on how euthanasia performs in the real world. The data from both Oregon and the Netherlands prove that safeguards work. It's all in favor of the proponents of euthanasia. There were no slippery slopes. The next two chapters deal with the remaining concerns. Yes, the opponents still have a long list of issues that need to be addressed.

Chapter 6

The Great Debate

"Why would you deny this to me when I want it so much and it is the only way that I can see to relieve my suffering?"

— Sue Rodriguez, Dying ALS patient

In 1994, Sue Rodriguez, a 44-year old mother suffering from ALS, asked this heart-breaking question during a face-to-face televised debate with anti-euthanasia campaigner Margaret Somerville. Previously, a specialist had described Sue's situation as a "living hell." The ALS was killing her. Sue went public and expressed a wish to have a physician end her life. She was desperate to find a doctor to help her die before muscle wastage would choke her to death. Her request made it all the way to the Canadian Supreme Court which narrowly rejected it, in a 5-4 landmark decision, even though 77% of Canadians supported her right to die. Sue ended up taking her own life with the help of a sympathetic physician. The televised debate took place one week before her death.[1]

What I find fascinating is Margaret Somerville's response during the debate. She just said no. She completely disregarded a competent dying patient's explicitly stated preferences and goals; she discounted Sue's best interests as stated by Sue herself. Margaret later wrote that she denied Sue the right because she believed that legalizing euthanasia would do great harm to society and to our respect for

---

[1] Raphael Cohen-Almagor, *The Right to Die with Dignity: An Argument in Ethics, Medicine, and Law* (Rutgers University Press, 2001).

human life. It would change one of the most fundamental norms on which society is based: we must not kill one another.[2] Margaret placed hypothetical societal concerns above Sue's immediate cry for mercy. Sue was tormented in her last days because of some ideological speculation about how society would change.

Sue Rodriguez died on February 12, 1994. Fast-forward to the year 2010. Physician-assisted dying has been legal in Oregon for the last 12 years. We can now safely say that there were no slippery slopes in Oregon. Civilization did not collapse. Physicians did not turn into killers. The disabled were not euthanized. Grandmas did not commit suicide en masse to avoid being burdens on their families. Vulnerable groups were not abused. The pharmacies did not shut down in protest. The integrity and ethics of the medical profession did not go down the tube. And hospice palliative care advances were not abandoned in favor of the Nembutal.

There was no Armageddon in Oregon. Human life is still being preserved. From a media perspective, the whole thing turned out to be a non-event. A big yawn! The Nembutal simply became a legalized transaction between dying patients, like Sue, and their physicians. The state reported the statistics and ensured the safeguards. It was a very civilized process. So, after years of wild speculation about the corrosive dangers of euthanasia, we were finally able to examine the empirical facts in the previous chapter. As you read, the fears did not materialize. This is the reality.

Why am I writing this chapter and the one that follows? Because, when assisted dying appears on a state ballot, you'll hear the same old stories repeated. The opponents won't give up. Some don't care about reality or the facts. They live in a parallel reality that has its own rules. I'll try to present their viewpoints as clearly as possible, and then rebut them. If Oregon's experience has already convinced you, then you may want to skip over these two chapters. But, be forewarned: you're going

---

[2] Margaret A. Somerville, "Death Talk in Canada: The Rodriguez Case," *McGill Law Journal* (Vol. 39, 1994).

to hear about every one of these concerns in TV ads, on radio talk shows, and in newspaper columns. So you may want to read this material anyway to prepare yourself for the onslaught.

Who Is Against Physician-Assisted Dying?

The anti-euthanasia arguments fall into three broad categories: 1) the sanctity of life must be preserved, 2) the slippery slopes must be prevented, and 3) the medical system can alleviate end-of-life pain. In Chapter 3, I thoroughly covered the gaping holes in the medical and palliative care systems. I explained in great detail why they do not have all the answers for alleviating end-of-life suffering. This leaves us with only two issues to cover: sanctity of life and the slippery slopes. *Warning*: These two issues will take us on many tangents. So I'll need two chapters to cover them all. Just hang in there.

The opposition to euthanasia is spearheaded by some very strange bedfellows. The Catholic church has always been opposed, based on religious morality, even though they run hospices. The pro-life groups entered the fray in a big way after the Terri Schiavo case. Their extreme wing's agenda is to turn back the clock on many of the advances in palliative care. The AMA hierarchy has always been opposed to physician-assisted dying, but it is countered by other large medical professional groups like the *American Medical Women's Association (AMWA)*. Then there are disabled rights groups, such as *Not Dead Yet*, who fear they may become the unwilling targets of a slippery slope. In fact, they were not too fond of Dr. Kevorkian, whom they helped put in jail. Finally, there are some people on the left who are worried about the rationing of medical resources. Their fear is that euthanasia may be used to cut down on medical costs for the poor, the disabled, and other vulnerable groups.

The Law: Murder vs. Suicide

We will start this discussion by looking at the big picture, namely, society's stake. As you know from Chapter 2, our criminal law makes no distinction between mercy killing and murder. Shortening life by a few days, even for people who are terminally ill, is murder. In the eyes of the law, the relief of unbearable pain is no justification for murder.

Voluntary euthanasia, Oregon style, provides an easy answer to this legal dilemma. Technically, it's an act of suicide, not murder. In this case, the dying patient voluntarily expresses the wish to die and the physician assists by prescribing the Nembutal. The physician is now an accomplice in the suicide. The idea is to make this assistance legal in the eyes of the law.

Until recently, suicide itself was a crime under *common law*. The act was perceived as a direct challenge to the sovereign's power over life. A person's life belonged to the monarch or God; it could not be taken away by suicide. In fact, there were some severe penalties against the crime. The crown would confiscate the possessions of the person who committed suicide and the church would mutilate the body by driving a stake through it. During the first part of the 19th century, these sanctions were still on the books.[3] Today, suicide is not a crime throughout the U.S. as long as the person doing it is competent. However, survivors of suicide attempts who are deemed irrational may end up in a psychiatric ward. Government has an interest in the prevention of suicides; it provides hotlines and counseling services.

Why is assisted suicide a crime when suicide itself is not? The law's answer is that it deters abuse. In the case of Nembutal, abuse is almost impossible because the act consists of two separate actions. The physician writes the prescription and, later, the person takes her or his own life. There is no assistance or coercion during the actual suicide. Society is being asked to legalize the prescribing part of the act as long as the appropriate safeguards are followed by the physician. If the public wills it, the legal problem can easily be solved. Eventually, it comes down to a vote that legalizes or decriminalizes the prescription with appropriate safeguards. In the United States, Oregon provides a legal precedent that is easy to clone.

---

[3] Shai Lavi, *The Modern Art of Dying: A History of Euthanasia in the United States* (Princeton University Press, 2008).

Is It Ordinary Suicide?

From a mental health perspective, there is a stark difference between suicide associated with clinical depression and the choice of a terminally-ill patient to self-administer the Nembutal to bring about a peaceful death. The *American Psychological Association* now clearly recognizes the difference.[4] In fact, psychiatrists now speak of *rational suicide*—an idea that has roots in antiquity. In Chapter 1, I briefly mentioned that euthanasia was widely practiced in ancient Greece and Rome. The early Christian church was ambivalent about the practice. It became a church taboo with the writings of St. Augustine. In *City of God,* he argued that man is created in God's image and thus has no right to end his own life, no matter the motivation. A rejection of life is a rejection of God. In the year 578 AD, the church forbade all forms of suicide making it an offense against God, which resulted in damnation.[5]

In the United States, the idea of rational suicide for the dying took hold in the 1980s and early '90s when the AIDS epidemic was devastating the gay community. In those pre-viral medicine days, suicide was seen, by many, as the only escape from the horrible suffering. It also allowed the dying to maintain their dignity—they were not victims of the disease. Isolated from mainstream society, the gay community created its own rules and rituals for death and dying. Suicide at the end of life became a public act. Typically, it was preceded by a living wake attended by loved ones and family. They talked story, recalled the good times, and said their goodbyes.

The lesson that psychiatrists learned from that painful period is that suicide for the dying can be a rational act. The young people with AIDS were not suicidal in the clinical sense. They did not want to die. It was the disease that was killing them. They chose the timing of their

---

[4] Kathryn L. Tucker, "Choice at the End of Life: Lessons from Oregon," *American Constitution Society* (June, 2008).

[5] Georges Minois, *History of Suicide: Voluntary Death In Western Culture* (Johns Hopkins University Press, 1999).

death to escape from the ravages of the disease. According to Supreme Court Justice John Paul Stevens: "Terminally ill individuals are faced not with the choice of whether to live, only of how to die."[6] For the terminally ill, the decision to take their lives is akin to declining life-sustaining measures, which is based on judgment and reason. Consequently, they are hastening their death during a period when death is imminent. Their act is not analogous to what is commonly termed "suicide" which is an act of self-destruction typically based on clinical depression. The state of Oregon does not count physician-assisted dying as suicide. In Oregon's view, the patient's death is caused by the underlying disease. The official report of death reflects that view, which is also shared by major professional medical associations.

Sanctity of Life: Everyone's First Choice

Like "pro-life," the slogan "sanctity of life" is information-free. Most of the terminally ill are pro-life and believe in its sanctity. Those who don't would have committed suicide a long time before their end-of-life. So let's agree that people on both sides of this debate believe in the sanctity of life. Near the end, most people may value their life even more and want to have as much of it as possible. For some, however, there may come a time when the disease has progressed to a point where life is not worth living. The death alternative is better than continuing to live. In their calculus, the nothingness of death beats the end-of-life suffering.

In Jeri's case, she wanted to live as long as possible. She believed life was precious and she fought hard to preserve it. However, a time came when she hit a cross-over point "when her life was more bad than good." So based on her quality-of-life values, she made a decision that she "had stayed too long." Sue Rodriguez went through her own quality-of-life calculus and reached that same conclusion. Each person must make his or her own cost-benefit calculus; it usually factors in

---

[6] Amicus brief of AUTONOMY. Filed in *Gonzales v. Oregon* (2005).

things like dignity, suffering, and meaning of life. If you believe in an afterlife, then you must also factor that into the equation. For example, if you think your next destination is Hell, then you're better off alive for a while longer—unless you believe Hell is better than your current situation. The calculus is purely subjective. There are no absolute measures; it's totally up to the individual. It's your life and therefore your decision. For most people, the calculus works out in favor of life.

The alternative is to let the government or the medical profession decide on a set of quality-of-life criteria that works for all people. Worse yet, we could require them to be the arbiters of what works best for each competent individual. Thank you, no! It's best to let competent individuals make the decisions that affect them directly, as long as they're not hurting others.

Note: Disabled groups, like Not Dead Yet, remind us that life can still be precious even when the body starts to break down. A dying patient can find pleasures in things never appreciated before. People are resilient and they learn to cope with their new situation. I fully agree with them and so did Jeri. However, a time may come when life is all suffering. Who determines this state? Answer: the persons who are experiencing the suffering. It's their suffering and no one else's. The people at Not Dead Yet are not experts in dying. Like their name implies, they're "not dead yet." And judging from their blogs and participation in anti-euthanasia protests, they still have much life left in them. This discussion is about dying people not the disabled. The dying must be allowed to make their own quality-of-life decisions; it's their calculus. Even the disabled will die some day; it may be in their interest not to oppose the rights of the dying.

To sum up, there are circumstances when autonomous human beings could decide to give up on the most precious thing they own—their lives. They may do this to put an end to their suffering. Some may even view life as being too precious to allow the disease to slowly obliterate it. They do not want to be kept alive at all costs—intubated or permanently sedated. That would negate the meaning of their lives; it would degrade their view of what was intrinsically precious about life itself. So the sanctity of one's life is an individual decision. Each person brings their own sense of meaning to it. We each have our own calculus.

Sanctity of Life: The Societal Exceptions

What about society at large? Society has an interest in the preservation of life, but it can be outweighed by other considerations. For most societies, the sanctity of life is not an absolute. Every society makes exceptions. For example, most societies say it's okay to execute criminals, kill in self-defense, and kill your enemies during war. Typically, they justify these acts in the name of "defending life itself." Of course, many wars, especially the ones fought in the name of religion, have nothing to with the defense of life. Yet they are sanctioned. In the name of mercy, we are asking society to make one more exception. Legalize the Nembutal for the dying. Is it too much to ask?

Sanctity of Life: Whose Life Is It?

We've been assuming here that our life is ours to take. What if our life wasn't ours? No, I'm *not* kidding! There were long periods in history when human life was not the property of the individual. It belonged to someone else: a monarch, a slave owner, or God. Today, in the United States, you are the master of your life; it's all yours if you're a competent individual. However, there are some religious groups who do not see it this way. In their interpretation of the Bible, our life belongs to God. But, isn't life still ours because it's God's gift to us along with free will? According to the interpretation of these religious groups, the gift is more like a loan. We are the *trustees* of this gift which we must protect at all cost. We can't dispose of it at will. There is no free will when it comes to human life—it is sacred and holy. The sanctity of life is absolute. Life itself is intrinsically valuable. This sanctity, obviously, does not apply to religious wars.

Sanctity of Life: The Pro-Life Vitalists

People with this extreme religious view are called *pro-life vitalists*. In the past, their energy was focused on the anti-abortion campaign. The Terri Schiavo case gave them a new cause to add to their repertoire. Unlike the Catholic church which is involved in hospice, this group also seems to challenge the whole idea of palliative care. They do not view end-of-life suffering as a terrible thing that needs to be ameliorated. These people number in the millions and they're not wackos. It took me a while to discover that they're perfectly rational. Their parallel world view is totally consistent. It's just another way to look at things. It's a different paradigm.

Here's a sketch of what the end-of-life looks like from this alternative paradigm. The entry-point in this paradigm is that life is sacred because it belongs to God. Consequently, the sanctity of life dictates that the most aggressive treatment must be used to prolong life. The dying must fight the disease to the very end. They must defend life with one heroic treatment after another. They must have faith in last minute miracles as hope stimulates action and prevents helplessness: death follows when hope is gone. So the dying must think positively to the end, constantly praying, and looking for cures. Intubation and life support must always be accepted and must never be discontinued. In this paradigm, end-of-life counseling is to be rejected: life is absolute and there's nothing to discuss. Some pro-life activists have labeled the end-of-life discussion a "death panel."

What about extreme suffering? In this paradigm there is dignity in suffering; it provides an opportunity to find meaning and be brave. Suffering provides redemption. The experience of suffering discloses essential truths that cannot be discovered, nor known, in any other way. What are these truths? I really don't know. Maybe it's that "humans are fundamentally weak creatures."

In some ways, I admire the consistency of this outlook. It all hangs together. The views that I present in this book, however, are diametric opposites. Based on the right to autonomy, I believe that these people have the right to do whatever they please with their lives, as long as they don't hurt others. Of course, I believe that they're on the wrong path and many will end up dying in excruciating pain in an ICU. I don't wish to see them die in pain, but it's their choice to make. The million dollar question is: Why can't they grant us the right to choose our own death? In other words, why are they fighting our right to choose? Why do they feel they must impose their will on autonomous individuals who do not share their paradigm?

Sanctity of Life: Pro-Life vs. Palliative Care

In his new book *No Good Deed*, Dr. Lewis Cohen, a palliative care specialist, examines the danger that the pro-life vitalist paradigm poses to his field. He paints a scary picture. Here's what he has to say about the pro-life coalition that emerged after Terri Schiavo's death:

> "I was unaware of the power of this other side and ignorant of the negative reactions that palliative medicine elicited from some segments of the general public.... Activists in this coalition claim that organized medicine has become seduced by death, and some of them—but certainly not all—are steadfastly opposed to every medical decision that accelerates dying, including the withdrawal of or withholding of medical technologies, vigorous use of narcotics, and so forth. For many of the religiously motivated members of the coalition—and they constitute the majority—the term *pro-life* has now been expanded beyond abortion to encompass the terminus of life and all practices that foreshorten human existence.... A backlash is occurring against palliative medicine shattering the illusion that there is a societal consensus on end-of-life care."

Ouch! It looks like a "take no prisoners" fight is brewing. Of course, the coalition will have its crosshairs set on any initiative that supports assisted dying. In the meantime, they've been busy in 23 states introducing 51 separate legislative measures to change or nullify the use of advance directives. And, it doesn't stop there. Hospices may well be their next target. During Terri's ordeal, hundreds of pro-life protestors descended on Hospice House Woodside, a winner of the prestigious Circle of Life award, shouting "murderers" and holding signs denouncing "Hospice Auschwitz." [7]

In this alternative paradigm, the withdrawal of life support is the same as murder. The paradigm deals in moral absolutes. There's no room for justifications like "allowing to die." There's no wiggle room for doctrines like the "double effect." Sanctity of life is an absolute; it is a mortal sin to assume control over the manner of one's death. Physicians must not "play God" by shortening life. Instead, they must prolong life by any means because it belongs to God. Euthanasia, in all its forms, is never an option and must always be fought—it's a crime against the sanctity of life. The paradigm is consistent, from top to bottom.

Sanctity of Life: The Clash of Paradigms

This new pro-life paradigm can do some serious damage; it can have a horrific impact on how we die. Consider this: Two million Americans die each year from the withholding, withdrawal, or limitation of treatment.[8] The pro-life paradigm attacks the very foundations of our palliative care system. If it gains traction, untold millions will suffer. We will die in high-tech dungeons, stripped of any protections.

What is to be done? It's time for the *American Medical Association (AMA)* to join our world. Yes, there is a slippery slope. It goes like this: First, they came for the Nembutal; then, they went after the termination of life support; next, they came for the palliative sedation; finally, they went after the hospices and morphine. The pro-life vitalists will brand all palliative medicine as euthanasia—slow, passive, active, or whatever branding they pick.

We're dealing with a populist movement. The debate will be televised. It certainly won't take place in obscure ethics journals or the *JAMA*.

---

[7] Lewis Cohen, *No Good Deed: A Story of Medicine, Murder Accusations, and the Debate over How We Die* (Harper, 2010).

[8] Source: *No Good Deed*.

The populists will make their case on cable channels, using sound bites. It will take less than ten seconds for pro-life pundits to demolish the sophistries of "double effect" and "letting die." It will all be euthanasia to them, which is why I tried to reclaim the word "euthanasia" in this book, even though I am advocating physician-assisted dying, Oregon style. I wanted to address their anti-euthanasia concerns—slow, passive, or assisted.

On cable TV, there is no demarcation line that separates the Nembutal from the removal of a dialysis machine or a feeding tube. The pro-life commentators know that Terri's disease did not kill her—she died because the feeding tubes were removed. To these commentators, it's all euthanasia and therefore murder. Remember, this is the same movement that enacted *Terri's Bill* in one day. Yes, it took them less than one day to line up the U.S. Senate, the U.S. House of Representatives, and the vacationing U.S. President to pass the bill. So where does this leave us? We'd better get our act together. We must let the public know that this is a battle between two very different end-of-life approaches:

- *The first paradigm is the "gentle and easy palliative death."* The dying make full use of the best palliative techniques, including hospice. Through advance directives, they can hasten their death if they choose to do so. This puts the dying somewhat in control over the high-tech medical machine. The addition of the Nembutal to the repertoire optimizes this option. It provides another level of insurance; it allows the dying to maintain some dignity and control.

- *The second paradigm is "life at all cost."* The dying must continue the fight to the very end. Death is surrender. Existence is an end in itself, and any attempt to shorten life is murder. This paradigm allows the medical machine to remain unchecked and perform its grind till the very end. The dying find their dignity in suffering. Apparently, dignity is in the act of staying alive as long as possible.

The choices could not be clearer. The public has a huge stake in this debate, and the outcome will greatly affect how we will die. You may ask: "What's the problem? The individual can choose to die either way." Yes, as long as the adherents of the second paradigm do not destroy the palliative care system on which the first paradigm is based.

In some ways, the proponents of the second paradigm are introducing a medieval view of death in the age of high-tech, slow dying. Their paradigm is more suited for a time when death was more immediate. End-of-life has evolved, but their paradigm has not. Even worse, they make use of the high-tech medical machine to prolong life at any cost. In their defense, I can say that the second paradigm is not morally ambiguous: it is clear and consistent. Its entry point is religious faith. There is no need for double talk. The proponents of this paradigm can speak from the heart. Their moral clarity may sway voters who are not well versed in the subtleties of the "double effect."

Proponents of the first paradigm must deal with the moral ambiguity issue. We must come out of the closet and level with the voters. We must clearly tell them what is needed to improve palliative care and to reduce end-of-life suffering; we must legalize whatever is required. We must explain the prevailing practice of euthanasia in unambiguous terms—no "double effects." If compassion for the dying requires it, the public will understand. There is no need for double talk. When informed, the public will choose the path of least suffering. The polls indicate that a majority already supports euthanasia in its passive, slow, voluntary, active, and physician-assisted versions. Involuntary euthanasia is the red line we must never cross. The Nembutal explicitly addresses the issue of assisted death; it brings it out of the closet. A vote for the Nembutal is also a vote in support of palliative medicine.

Eventually, I think physician-assisted dying may become an acceptable option for the Catholic church, the AMA, and Not Dead Yet. On the other hand, I have a strong feeling that the pro-life movement will never accept any of it. We are willing to coexist with their paradigm. Unfortunately, they will not reciprocate. As pro-life California Assemblyman Anthony Adams put it: "You better darn well believe I want to impose my morality on these people."[9] The pro-lifers are determined to control the way we die. They want us all to die their way—the hard way.

Sanctity of Life: Which Way, Catholic Church?

When it comes to palliative care, the Catholic church is a house divided. Its hospitals and hospices provide top-notch palliative care. Catholic ethicists have traditionally supported the withdrawal of medical treatment and life support at the end of life. Most Catholic hospices provide palliative sedation and support the withdrawal of hydration. On the other hand, the more conservative Catholic theologians are squarely in the pro-life vitalist camp. For example, the Vatican's Cardinal Martino called Terri Schiavo's death, "A victory for the culture of death over life." He added, "This is a grave step toward the legal approval of euthanasia in the U.S."

In 2004, Pope John Paul II surprised the medical world with his strong statement that health care providers must provide artificial food and hydration to patients in a persistent vegetative state or coma. His successor Pope Benedict XVI is also a theological conservative. Under his leadership, the church hierarchy is now leaning towards the pro-life vitalist camp. On November 17, 2009, the *U.S. Conference of Catholic Bishops (USCCB)* issued a revised version of its *Directive #58*. It now says that there is an "obligation" to provide feeding tubes to patients to stay alive. Anyone requiring a feeding tube must have one surgically implanted, and it must be kept "indefinitely." According to the directive:

> "This obligation extends to patients in chronic and presumably irreversible conditions (e.g., the 'persistent vegetative state') who can reasonably be expected to live indefinitely if given such care."[10]

---

[9] http://www.religioustolerance.org/euthca5.htm.

[10] U.S. Conference of Catholic Bishops, *Ethical and Religious Directives for Catholic Health Care Services, Fifth Edition*, November 17, 2009.

I pity the Catholic hospitals, hospices, and nursing homes who are required to enforce this directive. Every year, about one in six Americans receive their health care in Catholic institutions. In some states, they provide over 30% of the available health care; so it may be hard for patients to switch. About 300,000 Americans receive feeding tubes each year. I find it hard to believe that these Catholic institutions will not honor their patients' advance directives.

However, here's what Father Thomas G. Weinandy, executive director for the Secretariat of Doctrine at the USCCB, had to say about compliance:

> "If a patient or person comes to a Catholic hospital and has an advance directive [stating] that if they are diagnosed with being in a permanent vegetative state, that even if they could live indefinitely with nutrition and hydration that they would want the nutrition and hydration to cease, then that advance directive could not be honored in a Catholic hospital because that would be seen as participating in passive euthanasia.... I would like to think that for the government to require Catholic hospitals to abide by these patient advance directives would be against the First Amendment freedom to practice one's religion without being intimidated or coerced into doing something that is opposed to one's religion."[11]

This is not good for patients' rights. In addition, the Catholic church has always been strongly opposed to euthanasia. The church fought the Oregon bill all the way to the U.S. Supreme Court. Their rationale: "As Catholics we oppose euthanasia or assisted suicide because we believe that human life is a gift from God, that we are the stewards— not owners—of that life, that we are made in God's image."[12] Their constituents, however, are divided on the issue. For example, in a 2006

---

[11] Charles Stanley, "Do No Harm: Catholic Clergy, Hospitals Torn Over New Church Directives," *The SundayPaper,* December 20, 2009.

[12] Source: California Alliance Against Assisted Suicide (CAAS).

poll, 64% of Roman Catholics were in favor of California's *AB 651* initiative, which was modeled on Oregon's *Death with Dignity Act*.[13]

Over the years, the Catholic church was able to adapt to the requirements of modern medical technology and meet the practical needs of its congregations. It is conceivable that a future pope may have a different position on removing feeding tubes (i.e., passive euthanasia). An enlightened, future pope may even support physician-assisted dying if it becomes a legal and accepted palliative practice. Of course, he will never call it euthanasia. And, he will justify the practice by using the principle of "double effect."

Sanctity of Life: Doctors Must Not Kill

Doctors are deeply involved in life or death decisions every single day. As you read in Chapter 3, modern medicine has the capacity to artificially prolong life, even if it results in unlivable conditions. Under such conditions, medicine, not fate, controls the timing of death. Doctors are shortening life or hastening death every day when they stop dialysis, remove a ventilator, or discontinue an antibiotic drip in a person with pneumonia. Many of these actions invite death within hours or days. So we can agree that doctors are already in the business of shortening life.

When physicians do not have a cure for a dying patient, they are not obligated to treat the disease. Their role becomes palliative. They must then try to relieve the excruciating suffering. Very frequently, they hasten death by removing life support. The Nembutal is simply a more humane option for hastening death, especially when the final act is performed by the patient. It becomes the final act in palliative care.

For most physicians, the Nembutal is not in conflict with existing practices. Physicians manage the timing of death every day. By prescribing the Nembutal, the physician is helping terminally-ill patients manage the timing of their own death. The patients self-

---

[13] Mervin Field and Mark DiCamillo, "The Field Poll: Continued Support for Doctor-Assisted Suicide," (March, 2006).

administer the Nembutal when the time is right. In states where the Nembutal approach is legal, there is no conflict with existing medical practice.

Physicians do not see themselves as murderers when they shorten life. Absolutely none of these healers see themselves as "executioners" and neither does society. These decisions are all part of the modern practice of palliative medicine. In medicine, killing implies the termination of a healthy life. In the case of physician-assisted dying, the life is already being terminated by the disease—it's on life support. The decision is about who pulls the plug and when. When a patient is dying, the guiding ethical principle for physicians must not be the preservation of life at all costs. Instead, their guiding ethic must be to alleviate the suffering and help the patient die in comfort.

Modern medicine is responsible for prolonging life. Now, we're asking the physicians not to abandon the patient at the end. The hot potato has landed squarely in their lap. They must not abandon their patients in pain or leave them to the whims of technology.

Physicians have the ability and, hence, the responsibility to resolve the problem of end-of-life suffering. We're holding them responsible for solving the problem their technology may have caused. Dealing with pain and suffering is part of their mission. It's their responsibility to treat the dying. We're asking them to prescribe the medicine that will hasten death for terminally ill patients who request it. Of course, this can only happen if the practice is legal.

I'll have more to say about the role of physicians in the slippery slope arguments. For now, let's agree that the Nembutal at the end does not violate palliative medical practices.

From a moral perspective, prescribing the Nembutal is not different from pulling the life support plug, performing palliative sedation, respecting DNR instructions, or withholding life-saving treatment. In many ways, it is even better because the death-causing act is the patient's, not the physician's. Consequently, abuse is less likely to occur.

Slippery Slopes: FUD vs. Real Issues

Sanctity of life was the opening salvo in this debate. Hopefully, we can agree that human beings are masters of their lives. As they approach death, some rational people, who normally would want to preserve life, may reach the conclusion that their own life is not a virtue that must be preserved at all costs. Death with dignity does not imply an inherent desire to die. It simply means that, for some, a protracted terminal illness can mean a fate "worse than death."

Can we close this debate now? Not yet! Sue Rodriguez's opponents have more arrows in their quiver. Over the years, they've concocted a variety of scenarios that depict how helping the likes of Sue will have dire implications. If we violate the taboo, there is hell to pay. They've imagined a series of plagues that will hit us—all terrible.

It's always a good idea to exercise caution when dealing with death. We must do due diligence and investigate all claims to see if there is any truth to them. There are people out there who thoughtfully disagree with euthanasia, and I will try to thoughtfully address their concerns. Then there are those who indulge in wild speculation. Their goal is to create *FUD*—an acronym for *Fear, Uncertainty, and Doubt*. The FUD must be debunked.

Who Is the FUD Targeting?

The FUD targets the vulnerable and those who mistrust the system—the elderly, the disabled, the poor, and members of minority groups. The message to these people is simple: If doctors are allowed to kill, they will come for you next. A vote for the Nembutal is the beginning of the end—a decline down a slippery slope that we are unable to stop until it reaches the dreaded bottom. Typically, the dreaded bottom is the involuntary killing of the most vulnerable in society—the disabled, elderly, or poor.

Some opponents of euthanasia go so far as to claim that the dreaded bottom is Nazi-like genocide. A vote for the Nembutal will lead to "a far more morally abhorrent practice."

The FUD comes from a variety of sources. There are those who believe that the taboo is part of a bigger scheme of things and that we "shouldn't be messing with the way things are." Their belief in the taboo is so unshakable that they will allow the likes of Sue Rodriguez to be tortured to death. In their bigger scheme of things, patients must not attempt to control death. A tortuous death is the price we pay for being human beings. In a strange way, they believe we should be humane to pets precisely because they're non-human.

The FUD is also generated by some on the left who believe that giving the Nembutal to Sue will expose a class of people who are vulnerable. They fear that if the Nembutal becomes available, the vulnerable will take it to escape from their predicament. Or, society may encourage the vulnerable to take their lives by handing them the Nembutal. In a more extreme scenario, our resource-strapped society may encourage doctors to prescribe the Nembutal to the vulnerable as a cost-cutting measure. Consequently, it's best to protect the vulnerable from ourselves by maintaining the status quo; the Nembutal must not be legalized. The likes of Sue will be left to suffer to protect the vulnerable.

The Reformers: "First, Fix the System"

The opposition also includes reformers who believe that the current system is broken and must be fixed. Until then, the Nembutal must not be made available to Sue. It's a hostage situation. Sue cannot have the Nembutal as long as the health care system is broken. She must wait until an "ideal" standard of palliative care takes shape. She must wait until the disabled receive proper home care. She must wait until doctors learn how to manage terminal pain. She must wait until poverty is eradicated. She must wait until affordable insurance becomes universally available. She must wait until there is no more discrimination based on age, sex, disability, or race. Unfortunately, people like Sue Rodriguez cannot wait. They have no more than six months to live. So, they must suffer. They won't be allowed to take the easy way out. The reformers are holding them hostage until the system is fixed, which may be never.

The opposition also includes some palliative care specialists. Why? Because their system still has a long way to go, and they need to buy time to make it work. In the meantime, they're afraid that physician-assisted dying may gain traction and become the health consumer's preferred option. There are also medical ethicists who hope to gain respectability by attacking euthanasia, even though it's part of the standard medical practice. Of course, they don't call it euthanasia.

Bottom Line

This chapter covered the issues that lie at the heart of the debate over assisted dying: the deep moral concerns based on the sanctity of life. In some ways, the "slippery slope" arguments are just secular smoke screens for the moral arguments. Only the vitalists openly base their attacks against euthanasia on religion-based, moral arguments. For them, the issue is "good versus evil." I respect their moral clarity. However, the problem is that they are trying to impose their morality on everyone else. They want us all to die their way—the painful way.

In this chapter, I argued that vitalists do not have a monopoly over sanctity of life: both sides of this debate believe life is precious. In the words of professor Ronald Dworkin: "In both cases, the crucial question is not whether to respect sanctity of life, but which decision best respects it." On one side, people may refuse to be kept alive in a state of permanent sedation, intubated, and tended as vegetables. In their view, this condition degrades what has been "intrinsically valuable in their living." Others disagree; they believe that mere biological life is so inherently precious that nothing can justify deliberately ending it. This disagreement is among people who believe that human life is sacred but disagree about how to die in light of that conviction. In the words of Dworkin: [14]

---

[14] Ronald Dworkin, "Life Is Sacred. That's the Easy Part," *New York Times Magazine*, May 16, 1993.

"The disagreement is an essentially religious or spiritual one and a decent government, committed to personal integrity and freedom, has no business imposing a decision. Dictating how people should see the meaning of their own lives and deaths is a crippling, humiliating form of tyranny.... If we realize that we are arguing not about whether abortion and euthanasia are murder but about how best to honor a humane ideal we all share, then we can cure the bitterness in our national soul. Freedom of choice can be accepted by all sides with no sense of moral compromise, just as religious groups and sects can accept, with no sense of compromise, freedom for other versions of spiritual truth, even those they think gravely mistaken."

Religious groups are represented on all sides of the assisted-dying debate. The original ballot initiative to legalize assisted dying in Washington State was conceived in a Seattle church basement by Reverend Ralph Mero who also formed the prominent right-to-die group *Compassion in Dying*.[15] The organization played a major role in passing the Oregon *Death with Dignity Act*. During the Oregon debates, the religious community was pretty much divided.

Public policy debates are usually not argued in religious terms. Religious arguments alone are not enough to win majorities. The separation of church and state requires that religious arguments remain private: they have no place in the public realm. In debates of this type, the public is more swayed by secular arguments. Consequently, most anti-euthanasia groups base their attacks on secular slippery slopes.

Note: Even the Catholic church de-emphasized religious arguments in its long battle against the Oregon Dignity Act. Instead, it fought the Act on the basis that it provided inadequate safeguards. Towards the end of the campaign, the church put doctors instead of priests into the pulpits.

---

[15] Robert P. Jones, *Liberalism's Troubled Search for Equality* (University of Notre Dame Press, 2007).

From the anti-euthanasia camp, you'll be hearing very little about God's wrath. Instead, the opponents will claim that they are protecting the public from the hypothetical dangers (slippery slopes) that will be unleashed when people like Sue are prescribed the Nembutal. Of course, the slippery slopes tend to generate much FUD, which in turn helps maintain the status quo (the prohibition). In the next chapter, I will attempt to address every one of these slippery-slope arguments and present counterpoints.

Chapter 7

Point and Counterpoint

"Do those of us with deep moral reservations about the morality of physician-assisted suicide have any business using the coercive power of government to try to prevent those who disagree with us from doing what they believe is right?... When all things are considered, the arguments in favor of continued prohibition of physician-assisted suicide are not particularly compelling. This is not to suggest that those of us with deep reservations about physician-assisted suicide should swallow our scruples and spearhead legalization campaigns. But it does suggest that we should not stand in the way of thoughtful individuals who favor legalization."

—*Daniel E. Lee, Professor of Ethics*[1]

In the previous chapter, I introduced the concept of slippery slopes and the uncertainty they create. The debate over assisted dying is being fought on those slippery slopes. They provide the necessary sound bites that help generate FUD (an acronym for *Fear, Uncertainty, and Doubt*). The FUD is meant to frighten people; it works against the legalization of assisted dying. The slippery slopes are mostly based on speculation and imaginary threats, which makes them particularly hard to refute. At the end of the day, it's all about finding some contrived reason for denying the Nembutal to the likes of Sue Rodriguez.

Here's how it works. The opponents of assisted dying dream up some alleged societal concern, and then connect imaginary dots that begin

---

[1] Daniel E. Lee, *Navigating Right and Wrong: Ethical Decision Making in a Pluralistic Age* (Rowman and Littlefield Publishers, 2003).

with the legalization of the Nembutal. They imagine steep descents down slippery slopes that result in horrific outcomes. Once they establish the possibility of a negative consequence, the burden of proof (or disproof) falls upon the shoulders of the people who want to legalize the Nembutal. Mostly, it's FUD, but the whole idea is to stop us in our tracks: the Nembutal must not be legalized.

The FUD, when combined with wild speculation, creates problems for me: How to prove a negative? How to prove that various doomsday scenarios will not come to pass? How to prove that Hitler's ghost won't reappear? How to disprove apocalyptic predictions? It seems to me that the burden of proof must be on the parties who are making the claims. They must quantify the risk. Of course, they don't. Even worse, they seem to ignore the empirical data. Regardless, I'll do my best to address every one of these claims by analyzing both the risks and the logic. I ask for your patience.

This chapter deals with some very convoluted slippery slopes and other concerns. I'll present points and counterpoints. The points are my best rendition of what the other side is saying; when possible, I directly quote their words. Remember, each one of these points makes a claim for denying the Nembutal to patients like Sue Rodriguez. My counterpoint rebuts the claim. As always, my prime concern is for the terminally ill. I support their autonomy. I also believe that the medical system must present valid alternatives and then let the patient decide. It's all about "our life, our death, and our choice." You may want to take a deep breath and enjoy the show.

Note: I could have easily closed the remaining debate by making two points. First, none of the anticipated slippery slopes have occurred in either Oregon or the Netherlands. Second, the same slippery slope arguments could be made, and have frequently been made, against the termination of life support ("allowing to die"). In the U.S., people have been allowed to die since the "Nancy Cruzan" Supreme Court decision in 1990. In the last 20 years, millions have died through the termination of life support; there were no slippery slopes. However, I

*did write this chapter to flesh out the issues and then let you decide if
there are valid concerns.*

Slippery Slope to Nazi Eugenics?

Point:

John S. Keown, professor of ethics at Cambridge University, argues
that a slide to involuntary active euthanasia is inevitable because
safeguards to prevent it cannot be made effective.[2] Others have argued
that we will then not be able to draw the line between "acceptable and
unacceptable killings" and thus we will slide toward the bottom of a
slippery slope, killing any group that is deemed "unfit" for continued
existence. The notorious death camps of Nazi Germany are frequently
offered as evidence of humans not being able to avoid the slide down
the slippery slope.[3]

Counterpoint:

The evidence from both Oregon and the Netherlands clearly
demonstrates that there is no such slide. The data shows that there
were no slippery slopes. If slippage from voluntary euthanasia to
involuntary euthanasia is possible, then slippage is also possible from
the withdrawal of life support. With 20 years of palliative care behind
us, we would have been way down that slope to the extermination
camps. Look around you. We are not. Clearly, this argument is meant
to generate FUD. As Professor Jocelyn Downie points out, there are
significant differences between the Nazi experience and the
contemporary assisted-dying movement. She writes:

> "First, the Nazi program did not slide from voluntary to
> involuntary. It was, from the beginning, involuntary. Second, the

---

[2] John. S. Keown, *Euthanasia, Ethics, and Public Policy: An Argument
Against Legalisation* (Cambridge University Press, 2002).

[3] Michael Manning, *Euthanasia and Physician-Assisted Suicide* (Paulist
Press, 1998).

Nazi program was motivated by jingoism, racism, and a fascist political ideology. By contrast, the movement to decriminalize assisted suicide and voluntary euthanasia is motivated by a desire to alleviate suffering and respect for individual autonomy. Third, pre-Nazi Germany did not have as a part of its collective consciousness an awareness of the horrors of the Holocaust. The example of Nazi Germany could actually deter the very slippage it is taken to indicate is possible." [4]

The opponents of assisted dying will have to do better than invoking the Nazis. The weakness in their argument was recognized by Professor Daniel Callahan, a well-known critic of euthanasia.[5] He points out:

"Those of us who use such arguments against euthanasia should realize that, for all their intuitive plausibility, they rest upon a calculus of probabilities that has little grounding in history or experience. The often-invoked Nazi analogy has little value in our situation. The Nazis did not start with voluntary euthanasia and move on to involuntary euthanasia; they started with the latter, and their rationale for involuntary euthanasia had nothing to do with either self-determination or the avoidance of medical over treatment. These slippery slope arguments are, then, not fully adequate."

Slippery Slope for Minorities and the Poor?

Point:

For minorities and the poor the problem has never been medical "over treatment." Instead, the problem they face is medical "under treatment." Typically, they can't afford to pay for supplemental insurances that cover end-of-life services. They must choose between

---

[4] Jocelyn Downie, *Dying Justice: A Case for Decriminalizing Euthanasia in Canada* (University of Toronto Press, 2004).

[5] Jonathan D. Moreno, Editor, *Arguing Euthanasia* (Simon and Schuster, 1995).

bankrupting their families or going without the much-needed health care. Many end up very sick, with no money, lingering in pain, and soiling themselves in state-run hospitals or nursing homes. Many states are in deep financial crisis and are cutting down on services. Medicaid, on which the poor rely, is under the gun. The "have nots" and the "have not enoughs" are primary candidates for triage. End-of-life suffering with lack of access to palliative care makes them very vulnerable. The Nembutal may be their only way out and society may push them in that direction. So the Nembutal becomes a "final solution" for minorities and the poor. In the words of Joanne Lynn and Felicia Cohn:

> "The availability of physician-assisted suicide may itself become coercive in a society where health care services are not a right but a privilege that is circumscribed by individual finances..."[6]

In its 2007 campaign against Assembly Bill 374, the anti-euthanasia group *Californians Against Assisted Suicide* was even more explicit in its claim:

> "It is remarkable that the legislature is considering assisted suicide at a time when millions of low-income Californians and their families still have no access to health care. Is the legislature saying to low-income people, 'we won't provide health care, but we will make it easier for you to commit suicide when you're at your most vulnerable and uninsured'?"[7]

Counterpoint:

Empirical data from Oregon and the Netherlands shows that the poor and minorities are not currently at risk. Of course, this may change if society decides to deeply ration health-care resources. Ironically, if

---

[6] Kathleen Foley and Herbert Hendin, Editors, *The Case Against Assisted Suicide: For the Right to End-of-Life Care* (Johns Hopkins University Press, 2002).

[7] Californians Against Assisted Suicide, *Points to Remember: Opposition to Bill AB 374* (2007).

things get worse, the Nembutal offers the best protection for minorities and the poor. Why? As soon as they ask for the Nembutal, they become protected VIPs. Doctors, palliative care specialists, and social workers will bend over backward to find available resources and provide end-of-life care. The Oregon safeguards are designed to protect the vulnerable. Instead of languishing in decrepit state-run nursing homes and hospitals, the poor and minorities may find themselves in the hospice system. This would give them access to the best palliative care available.

Of course, the Nembutal is purely voluntary; there is never an obligation to take it. However, if all else fails, the Nembutal will provide a peaceful death, which is a lot more humane than the alternative. It's win-win for the poor and minorities. The egalitarian philosopher Ronald Dworkin writes: [8]

"Our current two-tier system discriminates against the poor by putting physician-assisted suicide exclusively in the hands of the elite, who have connections to a doctor who *will know what to do*."

Legalizing the Nembutal makes a highly-coveted universal good available to poor people. In states that maintain the prohibition, Nembutal is an underground luxury good not available to the poor or middle class. The rich, on the other hand, have the right connections. They can illegally obtain the Nembutal from friendly veterinarians. They can also procure it on the black market where it sells at exorbitant prices. For example, a 100 ml bottle that contains 6 grams of Nembutal would retail to a vet for less than $50. On the black market, that same bottle could fetch over $5000.[9] Two bottles may be required for a total cost of $10,000. The rich can also afford to travel

---

[8] Robert P. Jones, *Liberalism's Troubled Search for Equality: Religion and Cultural Bias in the Oregon Physician-Assisted Suicide Debates* (University of Notre Dame Press, 2007).

[9] Philip Nitschke and Fiona Stewart, *The Peaceful Pill Handbook* (Exit International US, 2009).

to Switzerland where they can consume their Nembutal in spa-like conditions.

There is no reason for the poor not to have the Nembutal choice, too. Just because they're poor does not mean that they must die in pain. We must work on eradicating poverty, but in the meantime the Nembutal must also be made an option to the terminally-ill poor. To withhold the Nembutal from them, if they choose it, is callous. The anti-poverty activists can make their case without requiring the dying poor to endure extreme suffering in their last days. They must not hold them hostage until the system is fixed. It's hard enough to be poor and dying without also being bullied and tortured.

Note to opponents: *In the name of mercy, please take your fight elsewhere. The Nembutal does not stand in the way of social justice.*

Slippery Slope for the Elderly?

Point:

Our aging population is consuming a disproportionate share of our dwindling health-care resources. Medicare is in a financial bind with over a quarter of its budget spent on those who are within a year of dying. Nursing homes for the elderly cannot get enough staffing or funding. The elderly must compete against other portions of the population for health-care services.[10] The situation will only get worse as large numbers of baby boomers begin entering the end-of-life queue and start vying for these medical resources. With Medicare on the verge of bankruptcy, some form of triage can be expected. A future rationing of health-care resources would not favor the elderly. The Nembutal provides an inexpensive way out. It's a form of triage that puts the elderly on a slippery slope. The Nembutal must not be legalized.

---

[10] D. Callahan, "Controlling the Costs of Health Care for the Elderly: Fair Means Foul," *New England Journal of Medicine* (Vol. 333, 1996).

Counterpoint:

Empirical data from both Oregon and the Netherlands shows that the elderly are not at risk. They are not on a slippery slope. The above scenario is totally hypothetical. However, it does not hurt to refute it.

Unlike minorities and the poor, the elderly as a group have a tremendous amount of political clout. Many held important positions in the system during their younger years. In their later years, they are members of powerful lobbying groups like the AARP. They form a huge voting block and they do cast their votes. They are joined by the baby boomers, who perceive that they are next in the end-of-life queue. The elderly are also protected by their children, as well as social networks to which they belong.

The Nembutal cannot be forced on the elderly against their will. The safeguards provide maximum protection against any form of coercion. The request for a prescription is scrutinized by doctors, hospices, families, psychologists, pharmacists, and the state. The Nembutal does not endanger the elderly as a group.

Slippery Slope for the Disabled?

Point:

Unfortunately, all are not equal when access to health care is the issue. This is especially true of the disabled who depend on the medical system and caregivers to keep them alive every day. Both Medicare and private insurance provide insufficient home-health and personal-assistance services. Many disabled are trapped in nursing homes in abysmal conditions. As Wesley Smith writes:[11]

"The disabled are among the most discriminated-against people in our society. Many disabled are poor and must rely on Medicaid, resulting in their often experiencing profound difficulties gaining

---

[11] Wesley J. Smith, "A Doctor Death Runs for President," *National Review Online*, September 4, 2003.

access to quality medical care. Frequent studies have shown that lack of health care can lead to suicidal ideation."

In their brief to the U.S. Supreme Court, *Not Dead Yet (NDY)* argued:

"As long as society, including the medical profession, demonstrates ignorance and prejudice regarding the lives of people with disabilities, no safeguards can be trusted to contain the torrent of discrimination that will be unleashed by lifting the ban on assisted suicide."[12]

NDY argues that disabled people will be coerced into physician-assisted death by caregivers, doctors, and insurance companies. Why? Because NDY believes that our society is "repulsed by disability and fears it." It claims that doctors and other health care professionals cannot be trusted. Like the rest of society, they are biased against people with disabilities and may, therefore, feel that the disabled are better off dead. So, they will just prescribe the Nembutal. Members of NDY report having been "repeatedly requested and pressured to sign *Do Not Resuscitate (DNR)* requests." In the case of insurance companies, the prejudice has more to do with cost cutting. Furthermore, the disabled themselves may end up internalizing the societal prejudices and regard themselves as burdens. Consequently, NDY considers that, in today's society, the Nembutal is not a truly free choice for the disabled. In the words of the NDY brief to the Supreme Court:

"Cloaked in the false rhetoric of personal *autonomy*, physician-assisted suicide threatens the retaining rights of a profoundly oppressed and marginalized people."

In other words, people with disabilities are so oppressed by the lack of options offered by society that any decision to end their lives could only have been coerced. In the words of Paul Longmore: "It is one

---

[12] Amicus brief of Not Dead Yet et al. Filed in *Washington v. Glucksberg* (1996).

thing to make fundamental choices; it's another to have the society that's oppressing us set up mechanisms to facilitate our suicides."[13] The solution according to NDY's President Diane Coleman:

"We have no idea what it would be like to live in a society that welcomed and accommodated each individual, regardless of his or hers abilities and disabilities. We should try that first—respecting and valuing everyone by according them real dignity and human rights. People will feel much better if they do not have to fear being devalued and disrespected, or abandoned by families, friends, and health care resources, with nowhere to turn to for support. We can do better than that. In the meantime, the right to a natural death is sufficient. The right to be killed...is premature at best."[14]

Counterpoint:

Empirical data from both Oregon and the Netherlands shows that the disabled are not at risk. The safeguards worked. However, I'm really moved by the concerns expressed by NDY and would like to deal with them. First, I agree that the disabled need better access to home care and health resources. Second, I agree that society must change its attitude towards the disabled. The *Americans with Disabilities Act (ADA)* is a first step in that direction. As a society, we need to better understand the deep social and physical needs of the disabled and provide the necessary help—dumping them into nursing homes is not the answer. The disabled are us. Most of us will be disabled as we age and start to die.

Having said this, I find that NDY's argument fails to make a case against legalized assisted dying. The Nembutal cannot be held

---

[13] B. Corbet, "Assisted Suicide: Death Do Us Part," *New Mobility* (Vol.8, 1997).

[14] Kathleen Foley and Herbert Hendin, Editors, *The Case Against Assisted Suicide: For the Right to End-of-Life Care* (Johns Hopkins University Press, 2002).

responsible for society's failure to provide adequately for people with disabilities. On the contrary, asking for the Nembutal puts terminally-ill people with a disability on the VIP track for palliative care and counseling. Because of NDY's briefs, the disabled are now getting a ton of extra attention. In Oregon, doctors, hospices, and social workers go out of their way to find life-asserting solutions to disabled clients' problems. Asking for the Nembutal is actually the start of a suicide-prevention process on steroids. When it comes to the terminally-ill disabled, the danger is that Oregon doctors may "err on the side of life," which can also be a problem.

What do the disabled rank and file want? In a 2001 nation-wide Harris Poll, 68% of people with disabilities were in favor of physician-assisted dying.[15] In 2005, the U.S. Supreme Court heard the following brief from AUTONOMY, a disability-rights organization opposed to NDY's prohibition on choice: [16]

"The danger posed by coercion and societal indifference is that the patient will be pressured to choose a path that he or she otherwise would not choose. Opponents to assisted dying seek to do just that by substituting their own moral, philosophical, or religious view for that of all patients through the elimination of choice."

The Supreme Court voted in favor of the Oregon experiment. Shortly before he died in 2003, AUTONOMY's cofounder Andrew Batavia wrote the following:

"I have fought hard to live my life as I choose to live it, to make my own life decision choices. I will not give up this autonomy of life decisions on my deathbed.... The contention that all people with disabilities are so oppressed, simply by virtue of their

---

[15] Carrie L. Snyder, Editor, *Euthanasia: Opposing Viewpoints* (Thomson Gale Press, 2006).

[16] Amicus brief of AUTONOMY, Inc., et al. Filed in *Gonzales v. Oregon* (2005).

disability status, as to be presumed incapable of making end-of-life decisions reflects the same paternalism that the independent living movement was established to abolish. The right to assisted suicide is based on respect for the autonomy of terminally ill individuals during their final days. Moreover, it does not deprive people with disabilities of anything, and therefore does not violate the ADA or the Equal Protection Clause of the Constitution. It does not deny people with disabilities suicide prevention services, protection against murder, or other abuses.... Those who oppose a right to assisted suicide predict that a substantial number of people with disabilities would be killed if assisted suicide were legalized. However, there is no evidence that this has happened."[17]

On January 6, 2003, Andrew Batavia died at the age of 45. His powerful words still live. Andrew had been disabled since age 16; he helped write the landmark ADA act. He was also a strong advocate of assisted dying. The latest data from Oregon and the Netherlands demonstrate that he was on the right side of the debate. Had he lived, Andrew Batavia would have felt vindicated by the 2005 U.S. Supreme Court ruling in *Gonzales v. Oregon*. The AUTONOMY brief was based on his arguments.

On the other side, you heard from NDY an equally powerful voice for the rights of the disabled. I believe that the latest evidence on assisted dying does not support NDY's case. The Oregon safeguards really work. In addition, hospice workers understand the needs of the disabled and provide added safeguards. There are no slippery slopes for the disabled in either Oregon or the Netherlands.

Given the empirical evidence, NDY is not doing the disabled a favor by continuing its attacks against the right-to-die movement. There is no good reason for the disabled to die in pain. At this point, NDY can only justify its continuing attacks by resorting to pro-life vitalist

---

[17] Timothy Quill and Margaret Battin, Editors, *Physician-Assisted Dying: The Case for Palliative Care and Patient Choice* (Johns Hopkins University Press, 2004).

arguments.[18] However, the vitalist position is completely at odds with the principles of self-determination and informed consent. Autonomy and self-determination are at the heart of the struggle of people who are living with disabilities. The movement used the principle of self-determination in support of the right to independent living and personal assistance services; the ADA is based on the principle of autonomy. NDY must decide which side it is on: autonomy or vitalism.

Does It Discriminate Against the Disabled?

Point:

On this issue, criticism can be heard from both sides of the disabled community. Barry Corbet, a pro-NDY disabled advocate, asks:[19]

"Why offer physician-assisted dying to people who are physically capable of taking their own lethal dose, and deny it to those who are not? Whose asses and assets are we covering?"

Andrew Batavia, the pro-euthanasia founder of AUTONOMY, agrees with Corbet. He wrote:[20]

"The distinction between self-administration and administration by others is a difference without real meaning. We believe that assistance should be permitted in the manner in which the individual needs it and that people who are not capable of self-administration should not be deprived of any right simply by virtue of their disabilities or arbitrary distinctions."

---

[18] David J. Mayo and Martin Gunderson, "Vitalism Revitalized: Vulnerable Populations, Prejudice, and Physician-Assisted Death," *Hastings Center Report* (2002).

[19] Barry Corbet, "Physician-Assisted Death: Are We Asking the Right Questions?," *New Mobility* (May, 2003).

[20] Timothy Quill and Margaret Battin, Editors, *Physician-Assisted Dying: The Case for Palliative Care and Patient Choice* (Johns Hopkins University Press, 2004).

Counterpoint:

As I explained in Chapter 2, liquid Nembutal allows even ALS patients to self-administer. The Oregon data shows that the Nembutal is very effective; there is no need for a physician to complete the act. Consequently, it's best to insist on self-administration. It ensures that the act is truly voluntary. From a moral perspective, I agree that the distinction has no meaning. In the Netherlands, doctors are allowed to administer. However, I still prefer self-administration. Ultimately, we must do whatever works best for the dying while providing the necessary safeguards.

Does It Discriminate Against the Non-Terminal?

Point:

The terminally ill are not the only ones who suffer. Non-terminal patients also suffer and may have a lot longer to suffer. For example, there are those who are in the early stages of chronic, incurable disease; and there are those who have emotional pain or deep depression but no physical disease. What happens to autonomy, compassion, and right-to-choose in those cases? In the words of Supreme Court Justice Anton Scalia: "Why does the voice just arise when death is imminent?"[21] Professor John S. Keown adds, "For if voluntary euthanasia is justified by respect for patient self-determination, how can it be right to deny it to any patient who autonomously asks for it." More broadly stated, the question is: Why not extend the right of assisted suicide to everyone?

Counterpoint:

In the Netherlands, the right to euthanasia is extended to all patients who "suffer unbearably." In Oregon, however, the right is only asked for the terminally ill. Why? I'll let Katherine Tucker answer the question. This is what she told the U.S. Supreme Court in *Washington v. Glucksberg*:

---

[21] U.S. Supreme Court, *Washington v. Gluksberg* (1997).

"We do draw the lines at a patient who is confronting death because unlike other individuals who wish to die by suicide, one on the threshold of death *no longer* has a choice between living and dying but only the choice of *how* to die."

Is it discrimination? No, it is not. Death does not discriminate; eventually, we all die. The Nembutal is an equal-opportunity benefit for people who are nearing the end of life. It's similar to hospice care where the benefit is only available to those with no more than six months to live. The state of Oregon also has two practical reasons for insisting on the "six months before death" requirement: 1) it ensures that hospice care, with its added safeguards, can be made available to those requesting the Nembutal; and 2) it allows the state to attribute the cause of death to the underlying disease, instead of suicide. This makes it possible for survivors to claim insurance and annuities that may be denied when suicide is the cause of death. It also does not interfere with the last rites of certain religions.

Finally, does legalizing the right for the terminally ill create a legal precedent for the general right to assisted suicide? The Oregon law has been in effect for 12 years; I am not aware of any lawsuits that have claimed it as a legal precedent. If challenged, the state could easily defend its firewall around the terminally ill. Personally, I support the Oregon law "as is." It serves its function while providing maximum safeguards. However, if it's the right thing to do, there is no moral justification for society not to extend the right to competent patients with unbearable suffering. The Netherlands demonstrates that extending the right can safely be accomplished with no resulting slippery slopes.

Does It Discriminate Against Alzheimer Patients?

Point:

Dr. John Keown, professor of ethics at Cambridge University, makes the following argument:

"If voluntary euthanasia were to be made available to competent people who requested it, it would soon be argued that it should be extended to the incompetent, either on the ground that it would be discriminatory to deny them this benefit because of their incompetence or because this is what they would have wanted had they been competent to ask for it."[22]

Keown makes that argument to demonstrate that slippery slopes are inevitable. The incompetent will end up being euthanized. Consequently, the Nembutal must not be legalized.

Counterpoint:

The Oregon safeguards are absolute and have held for the last 12 years: the patient who is making the request must be competent. In some cases, this may result in denying the request of a previously competent patient. For example, Oregon does not have a solution for terminal patients with Alzheimer's who may have previously requested (by way of an advance directive) that they should be given the Nembutal when they become fully demented. This decision was made when the patient was still competent. However, as the disease progresses another question arises: Is it still the same person? The Oregon Act avoids the issue by simply denying the request to incompetent patients. Although this can seem heartless, the alternative is to breach the safeguards by letting the health-care proxy decide. The state of Oregon rejects this alternative in favor of the safeguards. I agree.

Will It Be Used to Ration Health Care?

Point:

The government is deeply in debt. The states are in fiscal crisis. There is no way to finance entitlements like Medicare and Medicaid. When these programs were first conceived the average lifespan was lower

---

[22] John. S. Keown, *Euthanasia, Ethics, and Public Policy: An Argument Against Legalisation* (Cambridge University Press, 2002).

than 70 years. The aging baby boomers will bring the end-of-life medical system to its knees. There is no way to pay for their health-care costs in the age of slow dying and chronic disease. If the Nembutal is legalized, it will be used to ration health care. The government will use the Nembutal to solve its Medicare and Medicaid crises. Of course, the vulnerable will be the most at risk. The Nembutal must not be legalized.

Counterpoint:

The Nembutal is purely voluntary. The government can't shove it down peoples' throats. The legalization of the Nembutal is accompanied by safeguards that proved to be very effective in Oregon. The rationing argument in connection with the Nembutal is completely hypothetical; it's used to generate FUD. Regardless, I'll take a stab at it by looking at the numbers.

The Nembutal cannot be used to solve the government's fiscal crisis. Why? Let's do some quick math. Over 90% of those who take the Nembutal are also enrolled in hospice; most use the Nembutal to curtail their lives by a few days. Think of the Nembutal as a substitute for terminal sedation. Let's assume it takes, on the average, 10 days to die from palliative sedation. In contrast, death from the Nembutal is almost instantaneous. Consequently, the Nembutal saves 10 hospice days. How much is this saving?

In 2009, Medicare's reimbursement rate to hospice providers was about $100 per day. That's a total savings of about $1000 per patient. Now, let's assume that 1% of the dying population in the U.S. takes the Nembutal route. That's about 25,000 patients per year. Medicare would then save about $25 million per year—a drop in the bucket. In 2009, Medicare spent $420 billion.[23] Medicaid spent about $270 billion. That's a grand total of almost $700 billion. Even if 10% (a total of 250,000 patients) choose the Nembutal every year, the savings would only amount $0.25 billion—also, a drop in the bucket. (Note:

---

[23] Kaiser Family Foundation (see http://facts.kff.org).

The true cost of hospice is a lot more than $100 per day; the government is getting a deal.)

When you add it all up, the Nembutal is really part of the hospice course of treatment. It may save 10 days of hospice stay, which isn't much money. On the other hand, there are savings to be made by cutting down on futile end-of-life ICU treatments and moving patients to hospice sooner. How big are the savings? I don't know. But here's a back of the envelope calculation to give you a feel for the numbers involved. In 2002, the average cost per day in the ICU was about $3500 without a ventilator and $5000 with a ventilator.[24] Let's say it's about $4000 on the average. A 10-day stay in the ICU costs $40,000 per patient. About a million Americans die in hospitals or the ICU each year. If they were *all* moved to hospice, the savings could amount to $39 billion. It's a nice chunk of change but not enough to solve the health-care financial crisis, as you will read next.

Rationing: The Elephant in the Room

Point:

We can't afford the current level of health care. Rationing will become mandatory. In 2009, Peter Singer, professor of bioethics at Princeton University, made the following case in the *New York Times*: [25]

> The case for explicit health care rationing in the United States starts with the difficulty of thinking of any other way in which we can continue to provide adequate health care to people on Medicaid and Medicare, let alone extend coverage to those who do not now have it. Health-insurance premiums have more than doubled in a decade, rising four times faster than wages. In May, Medicare's trustees warned that the program's biggest fund is

---

[24] J. Dasta et al., "Daily Cost of an Intensive Care Unit Day: The Contribution of Mechanical Ventilation," *Critical Care Medicine* (Vol. 33, 2005).

[25] Peter Singer, "Why We Must Ration Health Care," *New York Times*, July 15, 2009.

heading for insolvency in just eight years. Health care now absorbs about one dollar in every six the nation spends, a figure that far exceeds the share spent by any other nation. According to the Congressional Budget Office, it is on track to double by 2035.... Rationing health care means getting value for the billions we are spending by setting limits on which treatments should be paid for from the public purse. The debate over health care reform in the United States should start from the premise that some form of health care rationing is both inescapable and desirable."

Professor Singer explains in his article that there are ways to set a ceiling on how much we should spend to save a human life. He writes that the *quality-adjusted life-year*, or *QALY*, could be used to decide which medical treatments will be paid for with public money.

The opponents can then argue that people who have reached their spending limits will be allowed to die. The Nembutal provides an easy way out for financially-strapped people who have exceeded their maximum health-care benefit. Consequently, the Nembutal must not be legalized.

Counterpoint:

This scenario has nothing to do with assisted dying. Nevertheless, I will respond. In my view, medical rationing is a form of *involuntary* euthanasia. We must all stand firmly against it. If Medicaid and Medicare were to resort to it, large populations would be "allowed to die" based on their inability to pay for high-tech interventions. Only the wealthy and the healthy would be immune. Medical rationing is a potential death sentence for any poor or middle-class person afflicted with disability or chronic disease.

Yes, it could be argued that, if these people were to commit suicide, it would be more dignified for them to use the Nembutal instead of a gun. In this horrific scenario, the Nembutal only provides a more humane way to die. The system has already handed down a death sentence to these patients by denying them medical treatment.

Back to reality. Both Republicans and Democrats are firmly opposed to health-care rationing. In fact, the health-care reform act of 2010 has removed all life-time ceilings on insurance payments. The new act specifies that people cannot be denied health coverage because of previous medical conditions, disability, or chronic disease. Insurance pools will make health care available to the uninsurable. With the passage of the health-care act, the outlook for Medicare has improved substantially despite lower near-term revenues resulting from the economic recession. In 2010, the Medicare trustees reported:

> "The system is now expected to remain solvent until 2029, 12 years longer than was projected last year, and the 75-year financial shortfall has been reduced to 0.66% of taxable payroll from 3.88% in last year's report.... The projected program costs as a share of GDP over the next 75 years are down 23% relative to the costs projected in the 2009 report."[26]

This is all good news. Of course, there are many skeptics who do not trust these rosy numbers. They may still believe that we're headed for financial armageddon. Let's hope they're wrong. However, even if we are headed that way, we must never consider health-care rationing. Yes, the end-of-life system needs to be fixed, but rationing must never be the answer. It's a genocidal act; it must be resisted. It's also important not to compete for medical resources by saying: "Don't touch my Medicare. Go after their Medicaid." There are much smarter ways to improve the productivity of our health-care system and make it more cost-efficient. In the current system, costs seem unrelated to the quality of care delivered. For example, a 2003 *New England Journal of Medicine* study found that administrative costs make up a full 31% of health-care spending in the United States (it translates to $1,059 per capita). Note: In the U.S., we have 1,300 different insurance companies that all have different forms to be filled out and different methods for judging claims. Any cost-cutting can start here.

---

[26] Social Security and Medicare Board of Trustees, *Status of the Social Security and Medicare Programs* (2010).

To sum up, it should be clear by now that assisted dying, Oregon style, is totally orthogonal to this discussion; it has nothing to do with health-care rationing. Imposing a prohibition on the Nembutal would be a bit like saying: "The morphine in palliative sedation could be used to kill people if health care were rationed. So, we must prohibit the use of morphine and palliative sedation." The whole thing is ridiculous. However, it does generate a copious amount of FUD.

Does It Put Medicine on a Slippery Slope?

Point:

Doctors heal: they do not kill. By lifting the taboo against killing, we are endangering ourselves. We're making it easier for our doctors to kill, instead of doing the difficult work involved in curing. Doctors could be tempted to take the easy way out. Instead of doing the hard work involved in pain control, they might be tempted to just hand out the Nembutal. Doctors would stop doing their utmost to save lives. We're giving them too much power. We're allowing them to play God with our lives. Legalizing the Nembutal will destroy the integrity of the medical profession. Here's what Dr. Leon Kass, professor of medical bioethics, has to say:

> "To provide real safeguards against killing the unwilling or the only half-heartedly willing, and to provide time for a change of mind, they must be intrusive, cumbersome, and costly.... Should doctors cave in, should doctors become technical dispensers of death, they will not only be abandoning their posts, their patients, and their duty to care; they will set the worst sort of example for the community at large—teaching technicism and so-called humaneness where encouragement and humanity are both required and sorely lacking.... It is a bad idea whose time must not come— not now, not ever."[27]

---

[27] Leon Kass, "Neither for Love nor Money: Why Doctors Must Not Kill," *National Affairs* (No. 94, 1989).

Counterpoint:

The safeguards have worked in Oregon. The choice of the Nembutal is ours to make, not the doctor's. It's purely voluntary. When we ask for it, we're already in the process of dying; there is no cure available. We're just controlling the timing of our death. The doctors will continue the palliative-care treatment as long as we request it. In Oregon, over 90% of those who took the Nembutal were also enrolled in the hospice system. Once a patient is in hospice care, pain management continues until the patient decides it's no longer working. The doctors perform the "hard work involved in pain control."

Does legalizing the Nembutal allow doctors to play God with our lives? If you think about it, they are already doing that by elongating life, terminating life support, and performing terminal sedation. As a medical school joke puts it, "God is the one with the white coat." The taboo was lifted a long time ago. From a medical ethics perspective, the Nembutal does not add anything new. It only gives patients more control over their death, which may help alleviate their suffering. In this case, the patients are playing God, not their doctors.

Is the Nembutal destroying the integrity of the medical profession? No. There was no slippery slope for doctors in Oregon. The state is now at the forefront of palliative care in the United States. The Nembutal also improves the integrity of medicine by eliminating the need for clandestine euthanasia. In the United States, outside of Oregon, 18-24% of primary care physicians and 46-57% of oncologists report having been asked for their assistance in a patient's hastened death; about one-quarter of them complied.[28] Oregon-like safeguards are not available in states where euthanasia is clandestine.

Professor Kass issued his dire warnings in 1989. He was proved to be wrong by real-world experience in both Oregon and the Netherlands. The integrity of medicine is intact in both places. Doctors did not "cave in and abandon their posts." On the contrary, they are acting

---

[28] Helene Starks et al., "Family Member Involvement in Hastened Death," *Death Studies* (Vol. 31, 2007).

"humanely" and doing what's best for their patients; doctors won't abandon them near death and won't let them suffer. Incidentally, I do not subscribe to Kass's idea that because we are "human," we must be allowed to suffer at the end. In that same article, he wrote:

> "It is precisely because animals are not human that we must treat them (merely) humanely. We put dumb animals to sleep because they do not know that they are dying, because they can make nothing of their misery or mortality, and, therefore, because they cannot live deliberately—i.e., humanly—in the face of their own suffering or dying."

This is pure vitalism! Suffering is good for humans: "we can make something out of our misery." No, thank you. I'd rather have our doctors treat us "humanely" should we request it. Some of us may choose to be relieved of "our misery."

Of course, vitalists can choose to go their way. It's their moral choice to make. In this case, Kass is imposing a vitalist moral position on the entire medical profession; it affects us all. A vitalist physician can choose not to perform assisted dying. On the other hand, the entire profession cannot choose to be "cruel and inhumane" to humans.

Does It Cause Doctors to Undervalue Life?

Point:

The psychology of doctors will begin to subtly change as they grow more accustomed to the idea that they were given the license to kill. It may cause them to cheapen the value of their patients' lives. Instead of performing the hard work of healing, they may be more tempted to kill patients whose life they do not value. According to Professor Leon Kass:

> "Doctors need protection against themselves.... The taboo against physician-assisted death is crucial not only as a protection against physicians' weaknesses but even more, perhaps, against their arrogance—their willingness to judge on the basis of their own

169

private prejudices and attitudes, whether this or that life is unworthy of continued existence."[29]

Counterpoint:

The experience in both Oregon and the Netherlands shows that this is not the case. The checks and balances protect both the patients and their doctors. The safeguards work. In Oregon, doctors are bending over backward to redirect those who request the Nembutal to hospice and palliative care. As noted, in Chapter 5, prescribing the Nembutal is part of a larger palliative conversation about dying.

In the United States, doctors have already been given license to terminate life. The taboo was removed in 1990 by the U.S. Supreme Court in its *Cruzan* ruling. Over the last 20 years, millions have died by palliative sedation or through the removal of life support. Neither practice has turned doctors into killers nor made them more willing to kill. Legalized Nembutal provides more safeguards than either of these two practices. And, unlike these two practices, the patients self-administer the medication. Consequently, it's the patients, not the doctors, who are performing the final act.

Does It Undermine the Doctor-Patient Trust?

Point:

Providing the license to kill undermines the trust between physicians and their patients. It creates suspicions among patients that their doctors may be trying to kill them. According to Professor Leon Kass:[30]

"The patient's trust in the doctor's wholehearted devotion to the patient's best interests will be hard to sustain once doctors are

---

[29] Kathleen Foley and Herbert Hendin, Editors, *The Case Against Assisted Suicide: For the Right to End-of-Life Care* (Johns Hopkins University Press, 2002).

[30] Leon Kass, "Neither for Love nor Money: Why Doctors Must Not Kill," *National Affairs* (No. 94, 1989).

licensed to kill.... Fears of deadly abuse of the new license will attach even to the most honorable physicians."

In 1988, the *JAMA* published *It's Over Debbie*—an intern's personal story of how he had performed euthanasia on a young patient with advanced ovarian cancer by giving her an extra shot of morphine. The story caused a huge debate among doctors who came out on both sides of the euthanasia issue. Professor Kass was one of four prominent bioethicists who condemned the intern in the strongest terms.[31] Here's what he and his colleagues had to say:

"The very soul of medicine is on trial.... This issue touches medicine at its moral center; if this moral center collapses, if physicians become killers or are even licensed to kill, the profession—and, therewith, each physician—will never again be worthy of trust and respect as healer and comforter and protector of life in all its frailty."

Counterpoint:

Fast-forward 22 years. The year is 2010 and assisted dying has been legal in Oregon for 12 years. We can safely report that the "moral center of medicine" has not collapsed. Oregon simply added an extra palliative consultation at the end of life. This conversation takes place at the patient's request; it's totally voluntary. In Oregon, thousands of dying patients benefited—most of them did not take the Nembutal. If anything, the consultation added a new level of trust between patients and physicians: patients perceive that their physicians will not abandon them at the end. Consequently, they are more open to discussing their true fears and needs with their doctors. The result is better palliative care for most. The same can be said about the Dutch experience with their huisarts ("family doctors"). In both Oregon and the Netherlands, physician-assisted dying strengthens the doctor-patient relationship. The patients know that their physicians care enough about them to help them die with dignity.

---

[31] Willard Gaylin et al., "Doctors Must Not Kill," *JAMA* (Vol. 259, 1998).

Here's how Professor Dan Brock responded to the moral claims made by Kass and colleagues:

> "Might the authors, nevertheless, be correct that if physicians should become killers, the moral center of medicine would collapse? This question raises what, at the deepest level, should be the guiding aim of medicine. I believe that the two values of respecting patients' self-determination and promoting their well-being should guide physicians' actions as healers, comforters, and protectors of their patients' lives and should be at the 'moral center' of medicine. These two values support physicians' performance of euthanasia when their patients make competent requests for it."[32]

Finally, let me reiterate that, in 1990, the U.S. Supreme Court granted physicians license to terminate life and withhold medical treatment. None of these practices has destroyed the "moral center of medicine." Instead, they reinforced patients' rights to medical self-determination and informed consent. Likewise, legalization of the Nembutal bolsters the "moral center of medicine" by strengthening the doctor-patient relationship at the end of life. In Oregon, patients can now trust that their doctors will not abandon them at the end.

Does It Violate the Hippocratic Oath?

Point:

The Hippocratic Oath is etched in the minds of our society as the cornerstone for the profession of medicine. The Oath says: "I will neither give a deadly drug to anybody if asked for it, nor will I make a suggestion to this effect."[33] The Nembutal is in clear violation of this ancient tradition. According to Professor Leon Kass:

---

[32] Dan. W. Brock, "Euthanasia," *The Yale Journal of Biology and Medicine* (Vol. 65, 1992).

[33] Ludwig Edelstein, *Ancient Medicine* (Johns Hopkins University Press, 1987).

"In forswearing the giving of poison, the physician recognizes and restrains the godlike power he wields over patients, mindful that his drugs can both cure and kill. But in forswearing the giving of poison when asked for it, the Hippocratic physician rejects the view that the patient's choice for death can make killing him right. For the physician, at least, human life in living bodies commands respect and reverence—by its very nature.... The deepest ethical principle restraining the physician's power is not the autonomy or freedom of the patient; neither is it his own compassion or good intention. Rather, it is the dignity and mysterious power of human life itself, and, therefore, also what the Oath calls the purity and holiness of the life and art to which he has sworn devotion."[34]

Counterpoint:

Does the Nembutal really violate the Hippocratic Oath? It depends on your interpretation. The Oath does say, "I will give no deadly drug." In my interpretation, the intent was similar to "gun control" today. The physicians of Ancient Greece were in possession of lethal weaponry— in this case, deadly poisons that could kill without leaving a trace. When the Oath first appeared, the Athenian economy was collapsing and physicians were not being hired. There was great fear of "physician-poisoners" who might be tempted to use their skills for financial gain. Plato went so far as to label them "skilled and secret assassins."[35] The Oath prohibits physicians from using the poisons to either directly commit a murder or to be involved in a murder plot as the suppliers of effective poisons. The physicians were the guardians of the poison; it could only be used for medicinal purposes.

Medical historian Paul Carrick supports this wider interpretation of the Oath. He writes:

---

[34] Leon Kass, "Neither for Love nor Money: Why Doctors Must Not Kill," *National Affairs* (No. 94, 1989).

[35] Steven H. Miles, *The Hippocratic Oath and the Ethics of Medicine* (Oxford University Press, 2004).

"I hold that the author of this proviso may have intended at least a tacit reminder to the physician that under no circumstances does his profession morally permit him to be an accomplice to murder.... It is a documented fact that in the Greco-Roman era it was popularly believed that the physician who is skillful at curing was, in virtue of this knowledge, also peculiarly well suited to know how to kill.... Anyone could practice medicine, and many who did were quacks and charlatans. Money and greed were powerful motives for complicity in murder. Ancient physicians dispensed pharmaceuticals and so were in a position to sell the necessary poisons in order to enrich themselves." [36]

In Ancient Greece and Rome, prescribing the Hemlock for euthanasia ("the good death") was part of the normal medical practice. It was both morally and medically accepted by the society which gave the world the Hippocratic Oath. It was a compassionate use of the technology. The practice was totally legal during the Greco-Roman era.

In fact, most Greco-Roman physicians were not aware of the existence of the Oath, and it had no effect on their practice. They routinely performed euthanasia. The few ancient physicians who practiced the Oath belonged to a small sect of *Hippocratic healers*. Here again, these healers had the discretionary power to perform both abortion and euthanasia; they did not interpret the Oath as a prohibition. According to Professor Carrick: [37]

"The Hippocratic healer of the fifth and fourth centuries BC was never morally bound by positive duties to assist in abortion or voluntary euthanasia on request. He could, of course, assist in these practices without much risk of moral disapproval from either inside or outside the ranks of his craft, if he so chose.

---

[36] Paul Carrick, *Medical Ethics in The Ancient World* (Georgetown University Press, 2001).

[37] Paul Carrick, *Medical Ethics in Antiquity: Philosophical Perspectives on Abortion and Euthanasia* (Reidel Press, 1985).

Therefore, he possessed what may be described as a discretionary professional right to assist in abortion or voluntary euthanasia.... It was entirely up to his judgment and moral sense of things."

Now, fast-forward a millennium and a half, or so. By the twelfth century AD, the Oath was reinterpreted by Catholic theologians in more absolute terms—no more Hemlock. The practice was banned. Physicians were not allowed to play God. A natural and painful death was necessary for the redemption of the soul. The suffering was not to be alleviated. The Hemlock was interfering with God's intention.

Fast-forward to the present. ICUs and palliative interventions are redefining death. There's nothing natural about dying; it's high-tech interventions, all the way to the end.

To be relevant in today's high-tech world, the Oath must be re-conceived to deal with intubation, palliative sedation, and all sorts of life-termination issues. In a modern ICU, the Hemlock would be very low-tech in comparison with our other end-of-life interventions.

But isn't the Oath an absolute? No, it is not. For example, the Oath forbids surgery ("I will not use the knife") and abortion ("I will not give to a woman an abortive remedy"); and yet many modern medical practices do just that. Of course, these modern practices are in clear violation of the Oath.

Today, most medical schools have abandoned the fundamentalist interpretation of the Hippocratic Oath.[38] Cynics say it's probably because the Oath swears to take no fee for teaching students medicine. The medical school commencement recitations of the Oath are usually sanitized versions that omit references to sensitive topics such as abortion, surgery, euthanasia or free medical tuition.

Besides healing, the practice of medicine is based on two equally important principles: 1) doctors must alleviate suffering, and 2) doctors must never abandon their patients. Prescribing the Nembutal to

---

[38] Jonathan D. Moreno, Editor, *Arguing Euthanasia* (Simon and Schuster, 1995).

dying patients is in line with these principles. The final palliative consultation in both Oregon and the Netherlands is medicine at its best. When doctors cannot cure, they must alleviate the suffering of their patients. And, they must never abandon them.

Notice that Professor Kass uses the vitalist interpretation of the Oath in his critique. His moral vitalism transcends both compassion for the patients and respect for their autonomy. In the age of high-tech dying, his vitalist interpretation of the Oath is a pure recipe for suffering.

Does It Undermine Palliative Care?

Point:

If the Nembutal is made available, research in pain-control technology will suffer; palliative care will be neglected. Physicians will take the easy way out and prescribe the Nembutal instead of mastering the discipline of palliative care. Hospices will suffer. In 2002, Dr. Kathleen Foley wrote: "We believe there is convincing evidence that legalization of assisted suicide and euthanasia undermines the care provided to patients at the end of life." She then made the plea that palliative care must be made available for all citizens before physician-assisted suicide or euthanasia are legalized.[39]

Counterpoint:

The year is 2010. Palliative care and hospice are now widely available in the United States. Oregon and the Netherlands are both leaders in palliative care. Over 90% of the patients in Oregon who chose the Nembutal were enrolled in hospice. Patients in both Oregon and the Netherlands receive excellent end-of-life care. The availability of the Nembutal option has improved the palliative practice in both places. Hospice and the Nembutal have proved to be very complementary.

Placing the Nembutal option on the ballot seems to be the fastest way to improve palliative care in states where it is substandard. This is

---

[39] Kathleen Foley and Herbert Hendin, Editors, *The Case Against Assisted Suicide: For the Right to End-of-Life Care* (Johns Hopkins University Press, 2002).

exactly what happened in the state of Maine, in the year 2000, when voters put a *Death with Dignity* initiative on the ballot. At that time, the state ranked last in the U.S. for hospice use. It was also one of six states with no Medicaid hospice benefit for the poor. During the campaign, the *Maine Medical Association* pledged to change the situation. The initiative was narrowly defeated—the vote was 51% to 49%. In 2001, however, the Maine legislation passed a law to expand hospice coverage and to improve end-of-life care.

Note: During the campaign, the opponents resorted to FUD and even outright lies to distort the Oregon record, then in its infancy. Ten years later, the facts proved the opponents wrong.

Good palliative care and the availability of the Nembutal are not mutually exclusive. The Nembutal is simply another palliative care option. Mostly, it competes with palliative sedation. The Nembutal is the drug of choice for those who do not want to be sedated into oblivion. For others, it serves as insurance; it's there, just in case they need it. Death remains the great "untamed." We need to keep *all* our palliative care options open. There is no right way to die. Every effort must be made to improve end-of-life palliative care. We must provide a continuum of palliative options to control pain and to prevent end-of-life suffering.

Oregon demonstrates that the Nembutal approach works best when it is complemented by hospice care. Knowing the Nembutal is available as a last-resort option, the patients can choose to receive pain management in a hospice setting for as long as possible. The Nembutal gives them peace of mind and the courage to go on living a while longer. Here's how Barbara Coombs Lee, CEO of *Compassion & Choices,* explains the palliative benefit that the Nembutal provides in these situations:

"We would have been happy, if after the first year, there had been no persons using the Oregon *Death with Dignity Act*, as long as the option is there. We get calls all the time from families asking us

177

what happened to their mother, brother, or sister after they have received their lethal prescription. They have reengaged the world, started eating again. They have an insurance policy that they will be able to end their lives in the manner that they choose."[40]

To sum up, the Oregon experience proved Dr. Kathleen Foley's fears to be unfounded. There is no slippery slope to report here. In Oregon, the Nembutal and hospice have been shown to be highly synergistic. The final conversation is a major advance in palliative care. The Nembutal has set a new bar for pain management: no suffering will be tolerated at the end. In addition, the call to legalize assisted dying has served as a catalyst for the improvement of palliative care in states where it is substandard.

Is Taking Control of Your Death Narcissistic?

Point:

To want to control one's death is narcissistic and arrogant. Professor John Mitchell writes:

"Needing to control all things makes us incomplete, separated from the rich experiences that come when we do not control. The idea of a 'right' to control the time and manner of our death is a strange one, as if we could control death. Death defines us we do not define death." [41]

Counterpoint:

Mitchell is wrong, this time! Think about it. We define our own narrative—our life story. We define ourselves through our actions. Our death is part of the narrative. Controlling our death is a way to avoid an end that violates the character and integrity of our life story. Our survivors will remember us the way we want to be remembered. It's a

---

[40] Robert P. Jones, *Liberalism's Troubled Search for Equality* (University of Notre Dame Press, 2007).

[41] John B. Mitchell, *Understanding Assisted Suicide: Nine Issues to Consider* (University of Michigan Press, 2007).

form of dignity. In addition, controlling the final narrative can be very therapeutic. It helps the patient feel somehow in control of death at a time when there is very little control over anything else. For some, the Nembutal provides a dignified final exit; it maintains the coherence of their life stories. Finally, people try to control the narrative of their death through advance directives; it's an accepted practice. Autonomy takes the form of the inherent right to define ourselves through our own choices. It's "our life, our death, and our choice." We each make our own choices. Professor Mitchell can choose not to have any control over his death; it's his choice to make.

Can Right to Die Turn Into Duty to Die?

Point:

That a duty to die exists when a seriously ill patient faces the likelihood of financial hardship is an argument that is gaining traction. It's now part of bioethics and policy debates. In 1997, the *Hastings Center Report* featured a cover article by John Hardwig entitled "Is There a Duty to Die?" He writes: [42]

> "Modern medicine and an individualistic culture have seduced many to feel that they have a right to healthcare and a right to live, despite the burdens and costs to our families and society. But in fact, there are circumstances when we have a duty to die. As modern medicine continues to save more of us from acute illnesses, it also delivers more of us to chronic illnesses, allowing us to survive far longer than we can take care of ourselves."

The right to die creates another source of pressure for vulnerable people to end their lives. Even if the dying person does not want to die, he or she may now feel a duty to die so as not to be a burden on others. Hence, physician-assisted dying introduces a new source of pressure for the dying. They must now convince themselves that it's okay to

---

[42] John Hardwig, "Is There a Duty to Die?," *Hastings Center Report* (Spring, 1997).

live even while being a burden on others.[43] The Nembutal creates a slippery slope for those who may feel they have a "duty to die."[44] Consequently, it must not be legalized.

Counterpoint:

The safeguards in both Oregon and the Netherlands are designed to detect such coercive scenarios and prevent them from happening. In Oregon, those who request the Nembutal are made to feel that there is absolutely no obligation to die. The act must be truly voluntary. More options are made available to those who need them. According to the Oregon data, neither financial hardship nor perceived obligation to die appeared to be issues for those who requested the Nembutal.

In any case, I could make a parallel argument that the option of refusing life-prolonging treatment places similar burdens on the vulnerable. Unlike assisted dying, there are no safeguards in those situations.

Is There a Patriotic Duty to Die?

Point:

Here's a scary scenario. America faces a deep fiscal crisis. The country is on the verge of bankruptcy. Deep budget cuts are required including a triage in health-care spending. The Nembutal is an available option. Appeals are made to the elderly, the sick, and the disabled to die for their country: "Please take the Nembutal to allow the rest of us to live." The patriotic act enters into the calculus of dying.

Counterpoint:

This hypothetical scenario has absolutely nothing to do with physician-assisted dying. If that call is ever made, the patriots can use

---

[43] Yale Kamisar, "Some Non-Religious Views Against Proposed Mercy Killing Legislation," *Minnesota Law Review* (Vol. 42, 1958).

[44] Kathleen Foley and Herbert Hendin, Editors, *The Case Against Assisted Suicide: For the Right to End-of-Life Care* (Johns Hopkins University Press, 2002).

their guns to take their lives. If it has to be medically performed, there is always terminal sedation. The Nembutal does not add anything new.

I'm not a political expert, but I'm positive that our country will never make such a call. That's not who we are. In America, on matters of life and death, the right is pro-life, the center is for self-determination, and the left is compassionate. As long as we remain a democracy, this call will not be made. After all, the elderly, the disabled, and the ill are either us, or they're our flesh and blood.

Will Grandma Feel She Has a Duty to Die?

Point:

The right to die could be interpreted by a vulnerable patient as the "duty to die." For example, Grandma may feel considerable guilt for being a burden on her family. The legalizing of assisted dying will add yet another pressure on her to "bow out" quietly and graciously.

In 1992, syndicated columnist Nat Hentoff claimed that the legalization of the Nembutal would create "a stunningly steep slope."[45] In this scenario, grandmas would line up for the Nembutal out of a sense of duty to their families. They would seek assistance in dying to prevent imposing further burdens on their loved ones. The Nembutal puts dying grandmas at risk; it must not be legalized.

Counterpoint:

This scenario did not materialize in Oregon. Grandmas did not stampede en masse to obtain the Nembutal. According to hospice workers, some patients did feel they were a burden on their caregivers, but it was not their primary reason for requesting the Nembutal. In addition, family members of those who took the Nembutal were not particularly burdened by the caregiving. According to Professor Linda Ganzini:

---

[45] Nat Hentoff, "The Slippery Slope of Euthanasia," *Washington Post*, October 3, 1992.

"Hospice nurses reported that only 11% of family members of patients who received lethal prescriptions were more burdened by caring for their ill relative than other families of hospice patients; 31% were less burdened. My assessments of patients who have requested assisted suicide support this finding: their concerns about being a burden to their families appear to reflect patients' own perceptions of the dying process as being without value rather than attitudes communicated to them by others."[46]

The Oregon safeguards were designed to inform patients about all the caregiving options available to them, including hospice. This means that hospice social workers and volunteers can help reduce caregiver stress by working with the families. In both Oregon and the Netherlands, the conversation on dying always tries to include the families and caregivers. The dying are assured that they're still members of the human community.

The hospice setting encourages the family to reassure Grandma that "we love you and want to keep you around as long as possible." The final decision is Grandma's to make. This open conversation about death may factor into her calculus the knowledge that the family wants her to live for as long as possible. If Grandma decides to take the Nembutal, it won't be because she feels she has a duty to die.

Will Grandma Be Killed for the Inheritance?

Point:

Greedy relatives may want Grandma to "hurry up and die" so that their inheritance is not diminished by further health-care costs. Some may want Grandma dead because she's a financial drain on the family. In either case, the family could end up encouraging Grandma to take the Nembutal route. A newsletter from *Californians Against Assisted Suicide* makes the following point:

---

[46] Timothy Quill and Margaret Battin, Editors, *Physician-Assisted Dying: The Case for Palliative Care and Patient Choice* (Johns Hopkins University Press, 2004).

"Research has documented widespread elder abuse in this country. The perpetrators are often family members (two-thirds, according to the California Attorney General's Office). Such abuse could easily lead to pressures on elders to 'choose' assisted suicide. Despite extensive efforts by California's legislature and law enforcement to deter elder abuse, assisted suicide could facilitate the ultimate abuse."[47]

Counterpoint:

In this case, asking for the Nembutal provides Grandma with maximum protection from family abuse. The Oregon safeguards were designed to protect her and ensure that her request is an autonomous act. You may remember that at least one of the witnesses to Grandma's request cannot be related to her by blood, marriage or adoption, nor be entitled to any portion of her estate. In addition, the doctors and hospice workers will look for signs of family coercion.

In Oregon, volunteers and medical people are usually present when the Nembutal is self-administered. This makes it even more difficult for abuse by the family to take place. If you think about it, there is much more risk of family abuse when a health-care proxy requests that life support be terminated on an unconscious patient.

What if the relatives decide to murder Grandma by forcing the Nembutal down her throat? Anything is possible. However, it's not that easy: careful preparation is required. It would be much easier to put a plastic bag over Grandma's head. In our society, people who want to commit murder have no need for the Nembutal. They have plenty of other options.

Does the request for the Nembutal provide an alibi? Does it create a setting for the perfect crime? Margaret Dore, an elder-law specialist, argues: "By signing the form, the client is taking an official position

---

[47] Californians Against Assisted Suicide, *E-Newsletter*, February 26, 2007.

that if he or she dies suddenly, no questions should be asked."[48] True, but the same could be said for hospice. Autopsies are rarely performed on patients who die while under hospice care. In both situations, murders may go undetected. Regardless, the scenario is quite convoluted. It requires that Grandma be terminally ill with fewer than six months to live. Why not wait it out?

In any case, the Nembutal adds safeguards that could be an impediment for the killers. It would be easier for them to have Grandma admitted into home hospice care and then use some other means to kill her. Also, our society has severe punishments to deter people from committing murder. Maybe it would be best for the greedy relatives to let Grandma die in her own time.

Don't Worry, We've Got You Covered

Point:

We've got you covered. There are remedies for everything. Pain can be controlled most of the time with good palliative care. Depression can be cured by taking anti-depressants. Disability is something you learn to live with. Dying is a natural process that must be allowed to take its course. There is no need for the Nembutal.

Counterpoint:

The opponents like to focus on a single issue—such as pain, depression, or disability—and then claim to have solutions. Unfortunately, it's not that simple. Dying is much more complex; it is a multi-dimensional experience. Many things are happening at the same time, and the whole is much more than the sum of the parts. In addition to physical pain, there is other suffering; it involves the whole person, not just the body. In addition to depression, there is deep sadness, hopelessness, loneliness, existential angst, fear of the future, and anticipatory grief. In addition to disability, there is loss of control, loss of self, and the feeling of being under assault.

---

[48] Margaret Dore, "Death with Dignity: What do we Advise our Clients? *King County Bar Bulletin*, May 9, 2009.

All these things are interactive. For example, loss of function may aggravate fear which may then increase the pain and make it difficult to control. It's a negative feedback loop. As Dr. Eric Cassell explains:

"Only the patients know how awful their own suffering is.... While bodies may exhibit pain, only persons have meaning and ideas of the future.... Symptoms are not simply brute facts of nature; they are actively influenced by the person in whom they occur because they are affected by that person's meaning."[49]

In other words, dying is very personal, multi-dimensional, and non-deterministic; it defies reductionism and simplistic explanations. Consequently, only the dying patients can decide when enough is enough. If they make that choice, their cry for help must be met.

Hospice Is All You Need

Point:

In 2001, Dame Cicely Saunders wrote: "Those of us who think that euthanasia is wrong have the right to say so, but also the responsibility to help to bring this relief of suffering about."[50] Dame Saunders met the challenge by founding the modern hospice and palliative care movement. She changed the paradigm for the treatment of the terminally ill from "cure at all cost" to comfort care and pain control for the dying. Hospice is the solution. There is no need for the Nembutal.

Counterpoint:

I disagree. My counterpoint is Chapter 3. There, I explained why we need both hospice and the Nembutal. In addition, the practice of palliative sedation needs to be fixed. I proposed my 911 solution. The

---

[49] Timothy Quill and Margaret Battin, Editors, *Physician-Assisted Dying: The Case for Palliative Care and Patient Choice* (Johns Hopkins University Press, 2004).

[50] Kathleen Foley and Herbert Hendin, Editors, *The Case Against Assisted Suicide: For the Right to End-of-Life Care* (Johns Hopkins University Press, 2002).

Oregon experience proves that hospice and the Nembutal are synergistic; they provide complementary approaches to palliative care.

I will use this counterpoint to put a human face on the shortcomings of hospice and palliative care. I will present a story which graphically demonstrates why the Nembutal must be made an option. Shortly before her 31st birthday, Melbourne writer Angelique Flowers was diagnosed with Stage 4 colon cancer which had spread to her liver and ovaries. Angelique was admitted to Australia's foremost palliative care unit at Monash Medical Center, in Melbourne. The doctors had warned her that death would be painful.

A few weeks before she died, Angelique posted an incredibly articulate and moving video on YouTube.[51] In her video, she talks about her dire condition and makes a plea for the Nembutal. She explains that she fears a slow, painful death from a total bowel obstruction. She would like her life to end peacefully and on her own terms. She also makes the case for the legalization of voluntary euthanasia, which she knows will not happen in her lifetime. Here's a short excerpt of Angelique's direct plea to Australian Prime Minister Kevin Rudd:

"The law wouldn't let a dog suffer the agony I'm going through before an inevitable death. It would be put down. Yet under the law, my life is worth less than a dog's.... At a time when I want to spend what good days and precious moments I have left having meaningful time with the people I love, I've had to cut myself off, writing questions and notes, making inquiries, doing research. If euthanasia was legal, I could have ended my days as I chose, finding peace before leaving this world, not panic and more pain."

Angelique died on August 19, 2008, at age 31. Unfortunately, she suffered from the bowel obstruction she had feared. Her older brother Damian was with her at the time of her death. He believed Angelique was still in pain despite massive doses of morphine and other

---

painkillers. In her last hour, he held a bowl under his sister's chin as she vomited fecal matter. Here is what Damian told *The Age*:

"The peaceful ending wasn't there. From the death she could have had, taking the Nembutal, saying her goodbyes to friends and family, having everyone there for her and being where she wanted to be, compared to what she did actually go through, it just doesn't bear imagining.... How can that be right? How can society believe terminal patients should be put through awful agonizing deaths? Angelique wasn't afraid of dying; it was more the way she was going to die that she feared."[52]

I'm sorry, Angelique, that you had to go through such an agonizing death. You were a brave, beautiful, and articulate woman. Thank you for the YouTube video; I hope the entire world sees it. It helped me better understand why I had to write this book. Sadly, this all took place in Australia's foremost hospice and palliative care unit. It appears that Dame Saunders' movement does not have the means to completely "tame" death. In the case of Angelique Flowers, the morphine was not enough to keep the pain under control or prevent her from vomiting fecal matter. She wanted a "good death," which the hospice was not able to provide. The Nembutal must be added to the hospice palliative-care repertoire. Luckily, things are changing. As noted earlier, the *American Academy of Hospice and Palliative Medicine (AAHPM)* softened its opposition to physician-assisted dying and, in 2007, it declared a neutral position.[53]

Does It Devalue Human Life?

Point:

Physician-assisted dying devalues human life. The vulnerable will feel that their life is not worth living. A person with disability summarized

---

[52] Sherrill Nixon, "This Is Angelique: She Wanted to Die with Dignity," *The Age*, September 13, 2008.

[53] Source: http://www.aahpm.org/positions/suicide.html.

this aptly: "I'd like to have the option of physician-assisted dying for myself. But because that position risks devaluing the life that people like me have, I have to oppose it."[54]

Counterpoint:

There are two points that need to be addressed here. First, the devaluation of life; and, second, the perception that it may be used to devalue the life of people with disabilities. I'll let Dr. Marcia Angell, the former editor-in-chief of the *New England Journal of Medicine*, address the first point:

> "It is not a choice between life and death. It is a choice between a slow, agonizing death and a quick, merciful one. The Oregon *Death with Dignity Act* makes that choice much easier for patients and their families. But it does not preclude people from making a different choice. People who prefer a longer life to an easier death are not prevented from choosing that. It seems that Oregon has chosen a path that gives dying patients the opportunity to exercise the greatest possible self-determination with the full support of their families and communities. I cannot imagine why anyone would want to prevent that."[55]

Nicely said. Let me add that the removal of life support does not devalue life and neither does assisted dying. The latter is just one more palliative option that we have at the very end. It's mostly insurance, in case the other choices fail.

The second point was partially addressed by disability activist Andrew Batavia earlier in this chapter. Here, let me add that Oregon's Act does not devalue the life of people with disabilities. In fact, it goes out of its way to address their concerns. Nevertheless, I believe that some

---

[54] Gloria L. Krahn, "Reflections on the debate on disability and aid in dying," *Disability and Health Journal* (Vol. 3, 2010).

[55] Timothy Quill and Margaret Battin, Editors, *Physician-Assisted Dying: The Case for Palliative Care and Patient Choice* (Johns Hopkins University Press, 2004).

activists mistakenly believe that assisted dying is, at heart, a disability issue. Therein lies the problem. In the words of disability activist Suzanne McDermott:

> "Almost all people at the end of life can be included in the definition of 'disability.' Thus, the practice of assisted suicide results in death for people with disabilities. People with disabilities have been recognized as a health disparity group; they experience substantial discrimination in society, and yet they can live extremely high-quality lives." [56]

I agree that people with disability can live extremely high-quality lives. However, I totally disagree with the assertion that dying is a disability issue. It's not. I do not want to insult the disabled community, but disability is a very small part of the dying process. The dying are in a league of their own. In the case of the terminally ill, the real issue is the ravaging disease. The suffering is both emotional and physical.

As I explained in an earlier counterpoint, dying is a multi-dimensional experience. The breakdown is catastrophic—everything appears to be falling apart. Providing the dying with wheelchairs and walkers is always welcome, but it's a drop in the bucket. Towards the end, the dying *cannot* live "extremely high-quality lives." Death is brutal and messy; it's the nature of the beast. This whole debate has nothing to do with disability. It's about letting us choose how we want to die.

Does It Benefit Only the Few?

Point:

At the end of the day, very few patients end up taking the Nembutal. As Marilyn Golden points out: [57]

---

[56] Suzanne McDermott, "Assisted suicide: Why this is an important issue," *Disability and Health Journal* (Vol. 3, 2010).

[57] Marilyn Golden and Tyler Zoanni, "Killing us softly: the dangers of legalizing assisted suicide," *Disability and Health Journal* (Vol. 3, 2010).

"Moreover, anyone with a chronic but nonterminal illness is not eligible for assisted suicide in either Oregon or Washington State. Anyone with depression that affects his or her judgment is also ineligible. Thus, the number of people whose situations would actually be eligible for assisted suicide is extremely low, yet its harmful consequences would be significant."

It is not appropriate to make sweeping and potentially dangerous public policy changes to benefit a small class of individuals however compelling their stories might be. The Nembutal must not be legalized.

Counterpoint:

I'll let Professor Margaret Battin and Dr. Timothy Quill provide the main counterpoint. Here's how they rebut the claim:

"There are three things wrong with this claim: the assumption that if only a small proportion of dying people actually use it, the availability of physician-assisted dying isn't important to others who are facing death; the assumption that physician-assisted dying is dangerous; and the quite callous view that dismisses the rights and interests of those who would use it. The comfort provided by the possibility of an earlier, easier death, even if one never uses it, can be enormous. For those who do use it, the prospect of dying in a way of their own choosing rather than being gradually obliterated by disease can be of central importance in the meaning of their soon-to-be-completed lives."[58]

I couldn't agree more. Yes, there's a huge benefit multiplier. Oregon's experience demonstrates that for every person who took the Nembutal one hundred had considered it. Having that choice helps the people in Oregon feel less anxious about death. Throughout this book, I've made the case that the palliative benefits of the Nembutal are immense. Even opponents will agree that the debate has greatly improved end-of-life

---

[58] Timothy Quill and Margaret Battin, Editors, *Physician-Assisted Dying: The Case for Palliative Care and Patient Choice* (Johns Hopkins University Press, 2004).

care in America. When the Nembutal is an option, it raises the bar for pain management: patients will tolerate zero suffering at the end of life. This sets a new standard of quality for palliative care.

Could There Be a Cure on the Horizon?

Point:

Terminally-ill patients who contemplate taking the Nembutal have probably heard this familiar refrain: "You can't take your life prematurely. You might miss out on a cure. Who knows? Maybe they'll discover something on the day after you terminate your life."

Counterpoint:

In Oregon, the patient who makes the request must be terminally ill and have no more than six months to live. Two physicians must review the case to ensure that there are no cures on the horizon. How do they know? Cures just don't happen out of the clear blue sky. It takes years for a cure to obtain *Food and Drug Administration (FDA)* approval. Typically, there are three phases of clinical trials before the FDA approves a cure and allows it to be used by the general public. Interim results from these trials are presented at specialists' conventions.

Most patients are aware of every trial that affects them. For example, I tracked every ovarian cancer clinical trial on behalf of Jeri. I knew about every treatment that was in the pipeline. For each possible cure, I tracked the FDA approval cycle like a hawk. Support groups publish newsletters and websites with the latest information on new treatments. The *National Institutes of Health (NIH)* maintains a registry of federally and privately supported clinical trials conducted in the United States and around the world; its website lets you find all trials for a particular illness or medical condition.[59]

This is the age of the Internet. The information on possible cures is widely available to both patients and doctors. If a cure appears to be on

---

[59] See: http://www.clinicaltrials.gov.

the horizon, the doctors will most likely not prescribe the Nembutal. Instead, they may try to enlist the patient in a clinical trial. Of course, the patient has the right to refuse treatment. There is almost zero probability that the FDA will approve a cure, out of nowhere, on the *day after* a patient takes the Nembutal.

Could There Be a Last-Minute Miracle?

Point:

Some diseases may miraculously heal by themselves. Patients have been known to recover on their own, thus fooling modern medicine. For example, some cancer patients experience *spontaneous remissions*. The cancer either unexpectedly improves or totally disappears on its own. Last minute miracles are always possible. Consequently, assisted dying must not be legalized.

Counterpoint:

Everyone has heard of people who were expected to die of cancer in several months or a few years but who defied the medical prognosis and underwent spontaneous remissions. Unfortunately, these types of remissions are extremely infrequent—especially in late cancers. The probability is about 1 in 100,000 for advanced cancers. A recent study in the *British Journal of Cancer* estimates that "only about 1–10 spontaneous remissions per 1 million cancer cases can be assumed."[60] Patients considering the Nembutal must factor these odds into their calculus. However, the numbers appear to be too infinitesimal to sway the decision.

What about biblical miracles? For example, God may decide to cure someone at the last minute. Yes, anything is possible. On the other hand, God can also raise the dead. So, it doesn't matter to God if the patient takes the Nembutal first. God can take care of you, dead or alive. What if God can only resurrect a body that is intact? I don't see

---

[60] U. Hobohm, "Fever Therapy Revisited," *British Journal of Cancer* (Vol. 92, 2005).

why God should be so limited. However, let's go along with this assumption and explore the ramifications. According to Professor John Mitchell, it would imply "that we should never bury or cremate anyone."[61] It would imply that everyone should be "cryogenically frozen prior to death" to await future cures or miracles. This gives us a lot to speculate about. However, none of these arguments succeeds in making a case against the Nembutal.

Could There Be a Misdiagnosis?

Point:

Everyone's heard of people who were misdiagnosed and end up living long and healthy lives. Legalizing the Nembutal creates a risk. The misdiagnosed could take their lives prematurely.[62] Consequently, the Nembutal must not be legalized.

Counterpoint:

In Oregon, two doctors must go over the diagnosis and prognosis. In most cases, a hospice doctor is also involved. Could three doctors get it wrong? Maybe. However, the probability is infinitesimal. Why? Because we are not dealing with an initial diagnosis. We're talking about people with late-stage terminal disease—those who have less than six months to live. In its late stages, a disease has many pathological manifestations that can be seen on CAT scans, MRIs, and other such technologies. It's hard to see how three doctors, with all the high-tech imaging equipment, can get it wrong.

However, let's assume they all got it wrong. Based on the Oregon numbers, there would be a 90% chance that the misdiagnosed patient would enter hospice care. The philosophy of hospice is "not to hasten death." In this case, the patient is healthy. So there is no pressing need

---

[61] John B. Mitchell, *Understanding Assisted Suicide: Nine Issues to Consider* (University of Michigan Press, 2007).

[62] House of Lords, *Report of the Select Committee on Medical Ehtics* (Vol.1, 1994).

to take the Nembutal. Life will go on. After six months of hospice care, doctors are required to take a second look at the case to request a hospice stay extension from an insurance provider. (For example, Medicare requires it.) At this point, they may notice that the patient was misdiagnosed and do something about it. If they don't, the patient will most probably continue to enjoy life, under hospice care, until the situation gets resolved. The only danger is that the patient may grow weary of waiting for death and then take the Nembutal. Again, a very unlikely situation. Why? Because the patient is being monitored by the hospice people for signs of depression. I don't see a case against the Nembutal here.

Is the Decision Truly Voluntary?

Point:

Terminally ill patients are too sick, medicated, and confused to think clearly. They are not capable of making an autonomous choice. Any decision they make will be influenced by others—such as caregivers, families, and physicians. Consequently, the terminally ill are not capable of making an informed choice.

Professor Kass informs us that "physicians are masters at framing options to guarantee a particular outcome."[63] Because true autonomy is not possible at the end of life, the terminally-ill must not be allowed to request the Nembutal. The Nembutal must not be legalized.

Counterpoint:

In Oregon, patients requesting the Nembutal must be competent. They must be capable of making decisions on medical matters that directly affect them. According to the data, that requirement has been met. If you think about it, the argument the opponents make has implications that go far beyond the Nembutal. The real question is: Do patients ever have true autonomy?

---

[63] Kathleen Foley and Herbert Hendin, Editors, *The Case Against Assisted Suicide: For the Right to End-of-Life Care* (Johns Hopkins University Press, 2002).

Chapter 7: Point and Counterpoint

In 1991, the federal *Patient Self-Determination Act* was passed. It guarantees that unless you are unconscious or mentally incompetent, you must be provided with sufficient information to make a choice as to what is to be done to your body. This means that if you end up in an emergency room, you must provide your *informed consent* for any treatment that affects you—including surgery or life support. You have the right to refuse treatment. If you are terminally ill, you must provide your informed consent to forego more treatments and apply for hospice care.

These are all life-and-death decisions, but are they truly autonomous? Are you deciding under ideal conditions? No. You're in crisis mode. Your decisions will be influenced by your doctors and caregivers. However, only you (or your proxy) can make that decision. This is what medical self-determination is all about.

The alternative is to return to a system of medical paternalism. Our doctors know best. Let them decide for us. They don't need to inform us of our choices; they can do whatever *they* think is best for us. In the United States, we have rejected such a system.

If the opponents of assisted dying want to pursue that line of thinking, they must also be prepared to challenge the capacity for autonomous decision-making of any seriously-ill patient. Anyone can be subtly manipulated in a time of crisis.

In Oregon, the system is designed to ensure that subtle manipulation does not take place. Instead, there is an open conversation about dying; it's part of informed consent. Two doctors provide information and go over all the available options. They are required to recommend hospice. Ultimately, the patient makes the decision. The earlier this conversation takes place, the better it is for the patients. They will have more control over the decision. Their mind will be clearer. And they will have more time to deliberate and do the necessary research. *Note:* Physicians can try to change the calculus by offering the patient more options. It's legitimate as long as they don't try to control the situation.

Is Oregon Too Good to Be True?

Point:

Oregon's data is too good to be true. Surely, there must be a coverup, somewhere.[64] What is the state hiding? What are the doctors not telling us? Opponents frequently cite the following quote from the September 20, 2008, editorial of the *Oregonian*:

> "Oregon's physician-assisted suicide program has not been sufficiently transparent. Essentially a coterie of insiders run the program, with a handful of doctors and others deciding what the public may know."

Professor Dan Callahan does not trust the official data collected from Oregon's prescribing physicians. He calls it a "Potemkin village" obfuscation. In his words: [65]

> "Regulations of that kind, protected from public scrutiny, but with the ring of authority and oversight, are a Potemkin-village form of regulatory obfuscation. They look good, sound good, feel good, but have nothing behind them."

Counterpoint:

We must be reaching the bottom of the heap. Opponents must now resort to conspiracy theories to make their point. In this case, the state, the doctors, and the patients' families are all conspiring to conceal the truth. Terrible things must be happening behind closed doors during those final moments. Sorry to disappoint. Horrible things are not happening behind the scenes. Here's the full context of that famous *Oregonian* quotation: [66]

---

[64] Kirk C. Allison, "Public Health, populations, and lethal ingestion," *Disability and Health Journal* (Vol. 3, 2010).

[65] Daniel Callahan, "Organized Obfuscation: Advocacy for Physician-Assisted Suicide," *Hastings Center Report 38*, (No. 5, 2008).

[66] Editorial Board of the Oregonian, "Washington State's assisted suicide measure: don't go there," *The Oregonian*, September 20, 2008.

"As Washington State voters decide this fall on a physician-assisted suicide law much like Oregon's, we won't be repeating the warnings we raised more than a decade ago when this state was debating the issue. Ten years' experience with Oregon's one-of-a-kind *Death With Dignity Act* has shown that our deepest concerns were unfounded. Safeguards built into the law appear to be working.... It has not targeted the disabled as feared, nor has it steamrollered vulnerable people into taking their lives.... On the negative side, Oregon's physician-assisted suicide program has not been sufficiently transparent. Essentially, a coterie of insiders run the program, with a handful of doctors and others deciding what the public may know. We're aware of no substantiated abuses, but we'd feel more confident with more sunlight on the program."

Think about it. Oregon's main newspaper has always been anti-euthanasia. However, after ten years of scrutiny, all it could report was: "We're aware of no substantiated abuses." So, the press is not aware of abuses in its own backyard. It just wants "more sunlight on the program."

We need transparency. However, we cannot allow the press and television crews to be present at each ingestion of the Nembutal. As I explained in Chapter 5, there is a delicate tradeoff involved here. The safeguards must be enforced without infringing on the privacy of the patients and their families. In addition, the privacy of the physician-patient relationship must be preserved. It's all a fine balancing act. I believe that Oregon has done a stellar job maintaining that balance. As noted, in Chapter 5, academic researchers were able to interview large numbers of patients and their families. They reported that it all works as advertised; there is no foul play. The newspapers can do their own investigative reporting. So far, they haven't been able to dig up any dirt. There are no Potemkin villages in Oregon.

Bottom Line

It's time to close this debate. Otherwise, I'd have to deal with slippery slopes that imply that legalizing the Nembutal will lead to increases in global warming. (*Note:* Legalizing the Nembutal does not affect global warming.) Yes, America faces some serious health-care challenges. Yes, there is a crying need for universal health care, better services for the disabled, and a way to keep Medicare and Medicaid afloat as baby boomers join the end-of-life queue. However, the legalization of the Nembutal is completely orthogonal to these challenges: it does not make them either better or worse. In fact, it has nothing to do with these issues. Legalizing the Nembutal is all about how we die. It's a matter of extreme importance for the likes of Sue Rodriguez, Angelique Flowers, and Jeri. The availability of the Nembutal option would have given them peace of mind at the end of their lives.

In the past, the speculation about potential societal concerns was conducted in an empirical vacuum. The Oregon experience allowed me to rely on solid data to put these alarmist fears to rest. There were no slippery slopes: the moral center of medicine did not collapse, grandmas did not die en masse, there was no duty to die, the vulnerable were not at risk, and the Nembutal was not used to ration health care. I pointed out new benefits: Oregon set a new bar for palliative care, and patients can now demand zero suffering at the end of their lives. Consequently, the medical and palliative practices have improved—even in states where the Nembutal is not a legal option.

Both the Oregon and Dutch experiences have taken the wind out of the secular case against euthanasia. It's hard to counter reality using hypothetical slippery slopes. And without the slippery slopes, the secular case against the Nembutal simply falls apart. The opponents don't have a leg to stand on.

What happens next? I believe the secular opponents may drop out of this debate. It's really not their fight, and I assume they have more important fish to fry. The pro-life vitalist forces will then come out of the shadows. Without the cover of secular slippery slopes, they will have to resort to moral arguments featuring the sanctity of life. As you read in the previous chapter, the vitalists have a totally different end-of-life paradigm; it is both consistent and cohesive from top to bottom.

Unfortunately, it deals in moral absolutes. Their paradigm does not allow individuals to make their own choices, and it provides no room for coexistence.

I believe that the consistency of their paradigm will lead the vitalists to attack the entire palliative care movement. They may attempt to set back the clock on *all* the palliative advances of the last thirty years—including patients' rights, advance directives, palliative sedation, and hospice. It's all "euthanasia" and "death panels" to them. There is little room for give-and-take when dealing with moral absolutes. Typically, there are loud shouting matches instead. By comparison, the debating points and counterpoints presented in this chapter will seem genteel and well-balanced.

The next chapter explores the murky world of underground euthanasia. I will turn the tables around and tell you how the prohibition against the Nembutal has created its own slippery slopes.

Chapter 8

Leave It to the Market:
The Exit Pill

"He searched for his accustomed fear of death and could not find it"

—Leo Tolstoy[1]

The Oregon *Death with Dignity Act* is an American success story. The dreaded slippery slopes did not materialize. The safeguards worked as advertised. The hypothetical societal concerns turned out to be non-issues. I argued, throughout this book, that legalizing the Nembutal greatly improves our palliative care system. It provides insurance for the dying. Most importantly, it facilitates that missing palliative conversation on death and dying. I also argued that for some it provides a better way to die than the palliative sedation alternative. Given that death remains the "great untamed," we need all the choices we can get. So, where does this leave us?

Those states that maintain the *prohibition* against physician-assisted dying are faced with one of two options. The first is to leave the existing laws unchanged and continue to tolerate the practice of "underground euthanasia." In practice, this means providing leniency for mercy killers. It's the "wink, wink; nod, nod" approach. The second option is to legalize the practice and make it part of the modern palliative care system. In practice, this would mean following Oregon's lead.

---

[1] Leo Tolstoy, *The Death of Ivan Ilyich* (CreateSpace, 2010).

Enforcing the prohibition against euthanasia will not stop the terminally ill from trying to kill themselves. Instead, it only leads to more "botched" suicides which result in more pain and grief for the patients and their families. As a society, our choice is not between having euthanasia and not having it. Our choice is between allowing it to remain underground and seeking to make it legal with safeguards.

In this final chapter, I will be making the case that maintaining the current prohibition can lead to some extremely negative slippery slopes. Yes, slippery slope arguments can work both ways. I'll be using them here to make the case for legalization.

First, I'll argue that maintaining the prohibition hurts the integrity of the medical profession. Every day, doctors perform underground euthanasia in an environment that is shrouded in deceit. This underground practice is marked by a lack of safeguards, norms, guidelines, and accountability. The prohibition forces doctors to use "not-so-lethal" drugs which result in "botched" attempts. In some cases, doctors must complete the act using other methods such as suffocation and strangulation. This underground culture of lawlessness and secrecy is the polar opposite of Oregon's transparent practice.

Next, I will argue that the prohibition provides a strong incentive for the development of an "exit pill," available to anyone with an Internet connection. Should this happen, the game is over. In my view, this scenario could lead us down a very dangerous slippery slope.

I end the book with an appeal for the legalization of physician-assisted dying, Oregon style. Yes, it's a win-win proposition for society, the patients, and the doctors. I also conduct an interview with Hawaii's house majority leader to understand what it will take to end this cruel prohibition in our state. I can't think of a more fitting tribute to Jeri than to see Hawaii become the fourth state in the U.S. to pass a *Death with Dignity Act*. For me, it would be *Jeri's Bill*. I also hope that, one day, *Angelique's Bill* passes in Australia, and *Sue's Bill* passes in Canada. These three extraordinary women were my inspiration for writing this book.

Euthanasia Underground: When Patients Fail

Earlier in this book, I recounted some of the problems Jeri faced when trying to acquire the self-deliverance pills over the Internet. You may recall that she discovered the "do-it-yourself" approach to be fraught with problems. The clandestine pills were crude and "not-so-lethal." They required the use of a plastic bag for backup.

Luckily, Jeri did her homework and decided to abandon the idea. Most people won't be that thorough. Research shows that many use the wrong drugs and fail to die. In many cases, the families must do whatever is necessary to complete the task. This situation can be fraught with fear and confusion. For those families, "experiencing relief" may come only after the cremation or burial of their loved ones (i.e., when they perceive that they can no longer be implicated in the death).

Here is how Daryl, an AIDS patient, committed self-euthanasia using clandestine drugs. The story was related by his partner Allen to Stephen Jamison, PhD, a researcher in social psychology:

"The saga began on a Sunday afternoon. At 2:30 p.m., Daryl took four sleeping pills and then injected himself with one dose of heroin. He then asked Allen to help him get to bed. He soon became unconscious and Allen immediately gave him a second injection followed with four shots of liquid morphine. Over the next several hours, Allen gave him two more shots of heroin, more than sixty shots of liquid oral morphine, and even ten injections of vodka. None of this worked.

Allen went on to explain: 'At ten he was still alive so I slipped a trash bag over his head and held it around his neck with my hands. It only seemed to take about four minutes before he finally stopped breathing.' Allen then called 911 and told them he thought Daryl was dead, but they arrived in full force. He hopped into the ambulance, and a medic began working on Daryl and thought he got a pulse. That did it. Allen began to cry, and said: 'Please, just let him die.' The medic looked at him, stopped working on Daryl, and slowed down all the way to the hospital."[2]

It's a very sad story. Euthanasia is not about dying with a trash bag over the head. That's not my idea of a "good death." It's hard to tell how many of these clandestine, self-deliverance attempts fail and require assistance to complete. According to Dr. Stephen Jamison:

"Both self-enacted and assisted deaths by the terminally ill are often masked by the nature of their medical condition...the official label of 'suicide' is seldom applied. Partners, family members, and friends often cover up the actual cause of death to eliminate the 'stigma' of suicide for religious, familial, or social purposes, or to protect themselves or physicians from any suspicions of involvement.... For example, in the 140 cases of assisted deaths that comprised my research, only 15 were designated as suicides. None were considered assisted deaths, though all were aided in some fashion."

Information on euthanasia drugs is widely available on the Internet or through self-deliverance books, like Derek Humphry's *Final Exit, Third Edition*.[3] Warning: The drugs commonly available are both inferior and "not-so-lethal." So, buyer beware.

Note: As noted in the previous chapter, Nembutal may be found on the black market but only at exorbitant prices—over $10,000 for a two-bottle lethal dose. At this price, only the rich can afford it. However, even the rich must have the right connections to procure Nembutal; often, that's not easy. Consequently, most patients can't depend on its availability, so they will resort to inferior drugs.

---

[2] Stephen Jamison, "When Drugs Fail: Assisted Deaths and Not-So-Lethal Drugs," *Pharmaceutical Care in Pain & Symptom Control* (Vol. 4, 1996).

[3] Derek Humphry, *Final Exit, Third Edition* (Delta Publishing, 2010).

According to researchers, patients and their families are frequently ill-prepared to perform euthanasia on their own.[4] Errors can and do occur, even with the best of plans. The AIDS Council of New South Wales estimated failure rates of 50% (i.e., half of all attempts were botched). Those who do best, consult advocacy organizations who guide them through the process. Of course, no one wants to die alone. Friends and family are typically present to provide moral support. But, this also puts them in a precarious situation: they could be called upon to assist with the death in the case of a botched attempt. As a result, they worry about the legal ramifications of their involvement; it makes them secretive and anxious.

The underground practice of self-euthanasia creates an environment fraught with fear and deceit. Like I said, it's certainly not my idea of a good death. Nevertheless, clandestine drugs, even when not-so-lethal, may still provide the most peaceful self-deliverance technique. It appears that there are much worse ways to commit self-euthanasia. For example, the self-deliverance methods of patients with AIDS are well documented. Most use clandestine drugs. However, the literature also reports the following methods as being quite prevalent: jumping from buildings and bridges, crashing through hospital windows, hanging by the neck, getting run over by trains, shooting oneself in the head, and slashing one's wrists.[5] Most of these practices result in a violent death. Clearly, the prohibition causes a lot of unnecessary suffering.

Euthanasia Underground: When Doctors Fail

The other time-honored approach to underground euthanasia is to seek the help of a friendly doctor or veterinarian—that is, someone with access to the better drugs and techniques. Many in the medical profession know that euthanasia is practiced, and may believe the issue is best left to the discretion of doctors. How widespread is this

---

[4] Margaret Battin and Arthur Lipman, Editors, *Drug Use in Assisted Suicide and Euthanasia* (Pharmaceutical Press, 1996).

[5] K. Pugh et al., "Suicide and HIV Disease," *AIDS Care* (Vol. 5, 1993).

practice? In the United States, 18-24% of primary care physicians and 46-57% of oncologists report having been asked for their assistance in a patient's hastened death, and about one-quarter of them complied.[6]

How successful is the physician-assisted underground practice? Apparently, it's messy and error-prone. Most physicians are not well versed in the practice of "euthanasia." They have a limited understanding of the required prep work, the effective drug dosages, or which drugs work best. Studies have shown that "botched attempts" involving doctors are common. Think about it, euthanasia is not taught in medical schools. It took much trial-and-error for Dutch physicians to develop a solid knowledge-base.

Note: *We know Nembutal works and the protocols for its administration are well understood. This raises the question: Why don't doctors who perform underground euthanasia simply prescribe Nembutal? It turns out that physicians do not have easy access to Nembutal. It was recently classified as a euthanasia drug and is, therefore, a tightly-controlled substance. Doctors no longer prescribe it for insomnia. At this point, any such prescription will certainly draw the attention of law enforcement; it raises a red flag. Of course, veterinarians still have wide access to Nembutal, which they use to euthanize pets. Bottom line: The patient must either have access to a friendly vet or procure the Nembutal on the black market. If the patient has Nembutal, the doctors will know what to do.*

Professor Roger Magnusson collected detailed, first-person accounts of physician involvement in underground euthanasia. He did not like what he found. He reports:

"The ideals of *medical professionalism* frequently become corrupted in the *euthanasia underground*. Perhaps the most striking feature of covert euthanasia is the complete absence of

---

[6] Helene Starks et al., "Family Member Involvement in Hastened Death," *Death Studies* (Vol. 31, 2007).

norms, guidelines or stable criteria for deciding when it is appropriate to become involved. Accountability is absent. Participation is shrouded in secrecy, triggered by highly idiosyncratic factors, with evidence of casual and precipitative involvements. Participants lack the training required to achieve a gentle death, and 'botched attempts' are common. In place of a tradition of disinterested service to patients, there is evidence of conflicts of interest and examples of euthanasia without consent."[7]

Not good! This has all the elements of a slippery slope. Doctors performing underground euthanasia are constrained by the drugs available to them, the risk of detection, as well as by the patient's clinical condition. Many prescribe a drug and then try to protect themselves by giving input from a distance. In many cases, they underestimate the dose required to achieve death. Some are called to assist when there is a "botch." The doctors then try to induce "death by overdose" by injecting whatever drugs are available. A common reaction is to "empty the doctor's bag" into the patient. Magnusson and others provide numerous, detailed examples of episodes where doctors had to strangle comatose patients, suffocate them with pillows, or inject air into their veins. In his book *Angels of Death*, Magnusson reports the following first-person account by Gary, a general practitioner:

"I've only had one real botch...it was horrible—it took four or five hours...it was like Rasputin, we just couldn't...finish him off.... I tried insulin, I tried just about everything else that I had around and it just took forever.... It was very hard for his lover. So um I sort of shooed the lover out of the room at one stage and put a pillow over his head, that seemed to work in the end.... That was one of the most horrible things I've ever done."[8]

---

[7] Roger S. Magnusson, "Underground Euthanasia and the Harm Minimization Debate," *Journal of Law, Medicine, and Ethics*, (Vol. 32, 2004).

[8] Roger S. Magnusson, *Angels of Death: Exploring the Euthanasia Underground* (Yale University Press, 2002).

Again, the problem is that these underground doctors operate within a code of silence. Their actions are clandestine and discretionary. Despite their noble intentions, they are operating outside of the established medical practice with no safeguards and drug protocols. They lack models, experience, and training. In addition, law enforcement exacerbated an already bad situation by making it almost impossible for these doctors to prescribe Nembutal.

Distilled, the prohibition against euthanasia is not working in favor of either the doctors or their patients. Patients needlessly suffer and doctors must operate in a culture of secrecy and deceit. Neither has access to Nembutal, the most effective euthanasia drug. The prohibition has created an underground nightmare. It puts the practice of medicine on a slippery slope. Doctors are killing clandestinely. The underground practice is crude, unruly, and totally unregulated. There are no safeguards; and, hence, there are "botches."

This prohibition also works against the general good. The underground nightmare it helped create is the direct opposite of what is currently happening in Oregon. By bringing the practice of euthanasia into the open, Oregon's *Death with Dignity Act* was able to achieve enormous palliative benefits. Here's a question for the opponents: Who is undermining the integrity of medicine? For the rest of my readers, I think we can agree that this prohibition is not working. If you're still not convinced, read the next section.

Ending the Prohibition: The Exit Pill Way

If necessity is the mother of invention, then prohibition is the great incubator of black-market solutions—especially, when the price is right. The Holy Grail of euthanasia has been called the *exit pill*. A worldwide search is on to create a little red pill that is deadly, fast, and easily available without a prescription. Dr. Philip Nitschke has been working on this for years; he calls it the *peaceful pill*. He's been trying to reverse-engineer the Nembutal and make it legally available. In his best-selling book, *The Peaceful Pill Handbook,* he devotes an entire chapter on how to synthesize such a pill using off-the-shelf chemicals.

However, he is not there yet. At this stage, it's a bit like assembling a personal computer from a bag of parts. Nitschke does not provide an off-the-shelf finished product.

In all probability, the Dutch will be the first to create such a pill. They have the scientists, the labs, and the incentive. You may have heard of the *Drion pill*: it's a hypothetical suicide pill proposed by former Dutch Supreme Court judge Huib Drion. It consists of two pills. The first is ingested to enable the process. The second is taken a day later, when the person is ready to end life. The idea is to provide a waiting period that ensures that the person is not acting on an impulse. Currently, no such pills exist in the Netherlands or anywhere else.

In the meantime, the hunt for the deadly elixir continues. With a lethal dose of Nembutal selling for over $10,000 on the black market, it's only a matter of time before a close substitute is developed. If the substitute can be packaged in a single pill, it will become widely available over the Internet and on the street. Underground labs will be able to clone the pill and distribute it through various channels. If and when this happens, the game will be over. There will be no need to discuss the legalization of euthanasia. The little red pill will become unstoppable; it will be accessible to just about everyone.

Personally, I believe that this would be a terrible outcome. Why? For one thing, it would also put an end to the safeguards and the palliative conversation at the end. Additionally, the "peaceful pill" would be available to anyone who wants to commit suicide, including teenagers. Yes, it would be more peaceful than putting a bullet into one's head, but it's also a lot more impulsive. Now you understand why Drion wanted a two-phase solution. My hope is that, by lifting the prohibition against the Nembutal, we will stop the peaceful pill in its tracks.

Ending the Prohibition: The Legalization Route

The current prohibition against the Nembutal is a losing proposition. It neither inhibits the practice of "underground euthanasia" nor adequately protects the terminally-ill patients who most desire it. It also stands in the way of providing better palliative care. Some believe that the police should work harder to prosecute offenders. They are wrong. Policing the use of Nembutal has already created a huge problem by making the underground practice more error-prone—even physicians can't get it right. The next step would be to police morphine and other lethal drugs. This would have a devastating impact on the quality of care received by those in pain and those who are dying. Introducing more constraints is not the answer.

Professor Magnusson argues that the euthanasia underground is a "public health and safety issue which should be addressed in pragmatic terms." I agree. The answer is to end the legal prohibition. The practice must be brought aboveground where it can be monitored. Legalization makes it possible to introduce safeguards that protect both the patients and their doctors. It allows doctors to use the best euthanasia practices. Instead of underground morphine, they can use Nembutal.

Besides being a medical issue, the prohibition is a political one that must be resolved in political terms. According to the U.S. Supreme Court, the legalization must be done at the state level. Every state must have this discussion and then put it to a vote. The issues must be openly debated and resolved at the local level. No top-down solution can be imposed. In the words of U.S. Supreme Court Justice Sandra Day O'Connor: [9]

> "Every one of us at some point may be affected by our own or a family member's terminal illness. There is no reason to think the democratic process will not strike the proper balance between the interests of terminally ill, mentally competent individuals who would seek to end their suffering, and the state's interests in protecting those who might seek to end life mistakenly or under pressure.... States are presently undertaking extensive and serious re-evaluation of physician-assisted suicide and other related issues.

---

[9] U.S. Supreme Court, Washington v. Glucksberg (1997).

The challenging task of crafting appropriate procedures for safeguarding the liberty interest is entrusted to the laboratory of the States."

The public must be informed about the palliative benefits of the Nembutal. Instead of dealing with hypothetical slippery slopes, we now have solid data from Oregon on which to base the arguments. If the public, the patients, and the doctors agree that there are benefits, then the legal prohibition will be lifted one state at a time. Oregon provides a working model that can easily be cloned in the United States. The Europeans may want to replicate the Netherlands' model.

The Legislative Work Ahead

The Nembutal will be legalized, state by state, either by legislatures or through ballot initiatives. The issue of "how to die" affects every single one of us. We need to have this open debate and put the issues on the table. The voters must be informed about the important consequences. As noted earlier, doing nothing only perpetuates the prohibition and the suffering. The time for change is now. We must do it for people like Angelique, Sue, and Jeri, as well as for ourselves when we end up in their situation. Think about it: If not us, who? If not now, when?

I am a resident of Hawaii. My first focus is on lifting the prohibition in the state where I live. You must do the same in your state. Here is my conversation, on how to bring about this change, with Blake Oshiro, Hawaii's House majority leader:

Robert: Thank you for championing this cause over the years. You're a young man in your prime. What motivates you to do this work on behalf of the dying? It takes a lot of vision to see that far ahead.

Blake: Thank you for saying I am in my "prime"! I have been extremely fortunate that I've not experienced nor had to watch a loved one pass through the inextricable pain of terminal illness. However, when I hear the stories of those who have had to bear witness, when I look at the hard data and facts from the Oregon State experience for over a decade, and when I think about the fallacy and fear mongering used by the opposition, I see a much needed change in our laws and policies to allow Hawaii to become a more compassionate and caring place for those facing end-of-life choices.

Robert: How many times have you tried to pass this legislation in Hawaii?

Blake: Governor Cayetano first introduced a bill in 2001 based on the recommendations of a blue-ribbon panel. It was my first term in office and I became passionate about doing what I thought was "right" regardless of the mounting opposition. Every year since then, I have been the primary sponsor and advocate for the bill.

Robert: Is your bill an exact clone of the Oregon Act?

Blake: The bill is based on the Oregon Act—the language, process, safeguards and reporting are all similar. There are technical and structural changes since states have different ways of drafting their laws; but, essentially, the two are the same.

Robert: Given that the people in Hawaii are over 71% in favor, why does this legislation keep failing in the state Senate?

Blake: The bill nearly gained passage back in 2002 but was just two votes shy in the Senate. Since then, neither the House nor the Senate has been able to effectively take up the bill again, as it fails to gain passage through public testimony before a committee. We've seen a slow decline in the level of support at the public hearings. The opposition is well organized and able to effectively mobilize people to come out in full force at the hearings. They do show up and testify. Thus, regardless of what polls may say, it often comes down to this: those who participate in the process, who show up at the fight, end up winning.

Robert: Why not put it on a state ballot initiative and let the people decide?

Blake: Hawaii's Constitution does not permit laws to be enacted via initiative. All laws must come from the Legislature. The only exception is when we want to change our Constitution.

Robert: Who is spearheading the opposition? Why are they opposed?

Blake: Primarily, the conservative churches and associated religious organizations. They are fighting this bill tooth and nail. Their primary opposition is faith-based, as they see this as an infringement on what should be a theocratic society. Rarely does their opposition turn on the data, the issues regarding patient choice, or any other evidence-based or reasonable position. In the end, when you boil it all down to the core, their opposition is due to the fact that it is against their religious beliefs about the sanctity of life.

Robert: Who are your supporters? What are they doing to help?

Blake: There are a few small organizations that are helping, like the Hawaii *Death with Dignity Society* and others. However, these are small groups that do not have the same level of membership and outreach ability as the opposition.

Robert: What are the next steps?

Blake: A bill is being drafted and I will then seek other legislators to co-sponsor the measure with me. The bill then gets referred to a committee, where there is a public hearing; it must get committee approval before then going to the entire House for debate. If it gets a majority vote, it then passes and goes to the Senate. There the process is repeated. A majority vote in the Senate means it can then go to Governor Abercrombie for consideration. There are a lot of other, more complicated, legislative procedures and hurdles, but that is the basic framework.

Robert: What will be different this time?

Blake: I remain hopeful, but have no assurances that there will be anything different this time around. Optimistically, we have a new governor who is likely to be more favorable to this bill and that helps change the dynamics and the playing field. In addition, the legislators that were elected did not change too much in the last election, despite a direct frontal attack by the conservative religious right to take out legislators who voted in favor of civil unions. Thus, legislators need not continue to harbor any fear of retribution and can, instead, look at the data and evidence to make a reasoned rational decision. Pessimistically, the fact remains that the opposition is much better funded, organized, and able to voice its objections. The only way that will be overcome is for the silent majority—the 71%—to start voicing their support to drown out what is usually the vocal minority.

Robert: What can my Hawaii readers do to help?

Blake: Contact your legislator and voice your support. Whether it is via phone, a letter or an e-mail, take just the few minutes out of your day to contact your elected senator and representative. Look at the www.capitol.hawaii.gov website to find your legislators and contact information. In addition, talk about this issue with your friends, your family, your co-workers. When this bill comes on the news or when it hits the newspapers, talk about it. The more public discussion and discourse on this issue, the more people will come to understand that Oregon's experience demonstrates that the myths and criticisms being conjured up by the opposition are nothing but unjustified fears.

Robert: I plan to make the e-book versions of this book free on Kindle, iPad, Nook, Android, and so on. Will this help? How do I put these free versions in the hands of the decision makers?

Blake: I am a firm believer that the best way for democracy to work, for the people to be empowered through participation in their government, is by knowledge. Thus, I highly commend you for making this book readily available to anyone, so that we can start to dispel the unfounded attacks on what is a simple, compassionate and much needed law. I think that having your e-books go "viral" is a good way to create a buzz, to generate a true groundswell of support, so that it is the everyday person who becomes the biggest supporter and advocate. And by that, decision-makers are forced to read the book for themselves, to deal with and understand the issue. That is my hope.

Robert: Thank you for taking time to answer these questions. Let's get this bill passed.

Note: Typically, it's a much bigger challenge to pass a bill through legislation, instead of taking it directly to the voters. Why? Because the legislators are much more susceptible to pressure by special-interest groups. Some of these groups even employ full-time lobbyists to counter these types of bills. In contrast, the proponents of the Nembutal are not very organized. They will only show up at the hearings if they are truly motivated. As I said, we live in a death-denying culture, and we only die once. So it takes a lot of motivation to attend these legislative hearings. However, doing nothing is not an option. It seems that the best strategy is to educate, make the facts known, attend the relevant committee meetings, and keep trying year after year. Eventually, the bill will pass.

In the Name of Mercy, End This Cruel Prohibition

Knowledge is power. My original intent was to write a short book in support of "my life, my death, my choice." I wanted to present a tight case for why the Nembutal must be made an option for the terminally ill. I'm quite pleased with the final product. I believe it clearly makes the case that there is absolutely no reason to deny this choice to people like Sue, Angelique, and Jeri. I hope to have provided a ton of fresh, new ammunition to help end this cruel prohibition.

This book is now a bit longer than anticipated. What happened? The answer is that the more I dug into the issues the more fascinating they became. For a topic that has been hotly debated ever since antiquity, there was an incredible amount of new material to draw from. There were many new angles to cover. Much to my surprise, I now believe that I was able to make a fresh contribution to this ancient debate. In addition to making the case for the Nembutal, here are some of the firsts that appear in this book:

• An in-depth look at how we die in America.

• An in-depth analysis of the shortcomings of the modern end-of-life system.

- A critical examination of hospice's strengths and weaknesses.
- A critique of the shortcomings of palliative sedation.
- An in-depth review of the Oregon experience based on 12 years of data.
- A reappraisal of the Dutch experience based on the latest data.
- A fresh look at "sanctity of life" based on new data.
- A rebuttal of "slippery slopes" based on new data.
- A fresh look at the "integrity of medicine" based on new data.
- A fresh analysis of how the Nembutal complements hospice.
- A fresh look at the dilemma of "underground euthanasia" based on Jeri's experience.
- A review of key milestones in America, Europe, Australia, and Canada.

The beauty of these firsts is that together they make a very compelling and "fresh" case for the Nembutal. The goal now is to end the prohibition. If you agree with what I have presented, please help spread the word by making this book go viral. Send e-mails to friends and your state representatives. Point them to the free e-book versions. Post the link on blogs that debate the issue. Pointing to the free e-book is far easier than spending hundreds of hours online debating the slippery slopes.

Because of the originality of the material in this book, the opponents will need to come up with "fresh" new rebuttals. It won't be easy! In the past, the computer books I coauthored were pretty airtight. I tried to do the same thing here. As much as possible, my arguments are based on empirical data, solid facts, and primary sources. I've done my homework.

Finally, just reading this book may help you or someone you care about "die better." I wish I had had all this information when I was helping Jeri navigate through her dying process. Instead, we had to grope our way across this strange landscape we call "end of life." Hopefully, I cleared enough of the brush to help you find your way through this unfamiliar terrain. With some luck, you may even find a traveled path to an "easy and gentle death" in this age of high-tech medical interventions. Until then, may you enjoy a long and healthy life!

Find Out More

"You want to live as long as you enjoy life. That's the real truth."

—Dr. Robert Butler[1]

Here, I organize the resources sprinkled throughout this book into lists to make them more accessible to readers who like lists. I sorted the resources by date and put them in categories. The material covers both sides of the euthanasia debate. Again, these are just the resources that I referred to throughout the book. I don't recommend that you read them all, but most make interesting reads.

Euthanasia: Books

- Derek Humphry, *Final Exit, Third Edition* (Delta Publishing, 2010).
- Frances Norwood, *The Maintenance of Life* (Carolina Academic Press, 2009).
- Philip Nitschke and Fiona Stewart, *The Peaceful Pill Handbook* (Exit International US, 2009).
- John Griffith et al., *Euthanasia and Law in Europe* (Hart Publishing, 2008).
- Shai Lavi, *The Modern Art of Dying: A History of Euthanasia in the United States* (Princeton University Press, 2008).
- John B. Mitchell, *Understanding Assisted Suicide: Nine Issues to Consider* (University of Michigan Press, 2007).
- Sidney Wanzer and Joseph Glenmullen, *To Die Well* (Da Capo Press, 2007).

---

[1] Joshua Tapper, "A Last Conversation with Dr. Robert Butler," *New York Times*, July 7, 2010.

- Robert P. Jones, *Liberalism's Troubled Search for Equality: Religion and Cultural Bias in the Oregon Physician-Assisted Suicide Debates* (University of Notre Dame Press, 2007).

- Robert Young, *Medically Assisted Death* (Cambridge University Press, 2007).

- Tom Preston, *Patient-Directed Dying* (iUniverse Press, 2006).

- Carrie L. Snyder, Editor, *Euthanasia: Opposing Viewpoints* (Thomson Gale Press, 2006).

- Timothy Quill and Margaret Battin, Editors, *Physician-Assisted Dying: The Case for Palliative Care and Patient Choice* (Johns Hopkins University Press, 2004).

- Jocelyn Downie, *Dying Justice: A Case for Decriminalizing Euthanasia in Canada* (University of Toronto Press, 2004).

- Steven H. Miles, *The Hippocratic Oath and the Ethics of Medicine* (Oxford University Press, 2004).

- Daniel E. Lee, *Navigating Right and Wrong: Ethical Decision Making in a Pluralistic Age* (Rowman and Littlefield Publishers, 2003).

- Kathleen Foley and Herbert Hendin, Editors, *The Case Against Assisted Suicide: For the Right to End-of-Life Care* (Johns Hopkins University Press, 2002).

- Constance E. Putnam, *Hospice or Hemlock?* (Praeger, 2002).

- Roger S. Magnusson, *Angels of Death: Exploring the Euthanasia Underground* (Yale University Press, 2002).

- John. S. Keown, *Euthanasia, Ethics, and Public Policy: An Argument Against Legalisation* (Cambridge University Press, 2002).

- Raphael Cohen-Almagor, *The Right to Die with Dignity: An Argument in Ethics, Medicine, and Law* (Rutgers University Press, 2001).

- Paul Carrick, *Medical Ethics in The Ancient World* (Georgetown University Press, 2001).

- Georges Minois, *History of Suicide: Voluntary Death In Western Culture* (Johns Hopkins University Press, 1999).

- Sue Woodman, *Last Rights: The Struggle Over The Right To Die* (Perseus Publishing, 1998).

- John Griffiths et al., *Euthanasia and Law in the Netherlands* (Amsterdam University Press, 1998).

- Michael Manning, *Euthanasia and Physician-Assisted Suicide* (Paulist Press, 1998).

- Margaret Battin and Arthur Lipman, Editors, *Drug Use in Assisted Suicide and Euthanasia* (Pharmaceutical Press, 1996).

- Jonathan D. Moreno, Editor, *Arguing Euthanasia* (Simon and Schuster, 1995).

- Ron Hamel, Editor, *Choosing Death: Active Euthanasia, Religion and the Public Debate* (Trinity Press, 1991).

- Ludwig Edelstein, *Ancient Medicine* (Johns Hopkins University Press, 1987).

- Paul Carrick, *Medical Ethics in Antiquity: Philosophical Perspectives on Abortion and Euthanasia* (Reidel Press, 1985).

Euthanasia: Articles

- Oregon Department of Human Services, *Twelfth Annual Report on Oregon's Death with Dignity Act* (March, 2010).

- Harris Meyer, "First Year Complications with Assisted-Suicide," *Crosscut*, March 23, 2010.

- Gloria L. Krahn, "Reflections on the debate on disability and aid in dying," *Disability and Health Journal* (Vol. 3, 2010).

- Suzanne McDermott, "Assisted suicide: Why this is an important issue," *Disability and Health Journal* (Vol. 3, 2010).

- Marilyn Golden and Tyler Zoanni, "Killing us softly: the dangers of legalizing assisted suicide," *Disability and Health Journal* (Vol. 3, 2010).

- Kirk C. Allison, "Public health, populations, and lethal ingestion," *Disability and Health Journal* (Vol. 3, 2010).

- Anemona Hartocollis, "Hard Choice for a Comfortable Death: Sedation," *New York Times*, December 28, 2009.

- Tim Sakahara, "Husband's Suicide Resurrects Right to Die Debate," *KGMB HawaiiNewsNow*, December 14, 2009.

- Ganzini et al., "Mental Health Outcomes of Family Members of Oregonians Who Request Physician Aid in Dying," *Journal of Pain and Symptom Management* (Vol. 38, 2009).

- Kathryn Tucker, "At the Very End of Life: The Emergence of Policy Supporting Aid in Dying Among Mainstream Medical and Health Policy Associations," *Harvard Health Policy Review* (Vol. 10, 2009).

- Margaret Dore, "Death with Dignity: What do we Advise our Clients?" *King County Bar Bulletin*, May 9, 2009.

- Editorial Board of the Oregonian, "Washington State's assisted suicide measure: don't go there," *The Oregonian*, September 20, 2008.

- Sherrill Nixon, "This Is Angelique: She Wanted to Die with Dignity," *The Age*, September 13, 2008.

- Kathryn L. Tucker, "Choice at the End of Life: Lessons from Oregon," *American Constitution Society* (June, 2008).

- Robert Steinbrook, "Physician-Assisted Death—From Oregon to Washington State," *New England Journal of Medicine* (Vol. 359, 2008).

- Ganzini et al., "Prevalence of Depression and Anxiety in Patients Requesting Physicians' Aid in Dying," *British Medical Journal* (Vol. 337, 2008).

- Daniel Callahan, "Organized Obfuscation: Advocacy for Physician-Assisted Suicide," *Hastings Center Report 38*, (No. 5, 2008).

- Timothy E. Quill, "Legal Regulation of Physician-Assisted Death—The Latest Report Cards," *New England Journal of Medicine* (Vol. 356, 2007).

- Helene Starks et al., "Family Member Involvement in Hastened Death," *Death Studies* (Vol. 31, 2007).

- Agnes van der Heide et al, "End-of-Life Practices in the Netherlands Under the Euthanasia Act," *New England Journal of Medicine* (Vol. 356, 2007).

- Margaret Battin et al., "Legal Physician-Assisted Dying in Oregon and the Netherlands: Evidence Concerning the Impact on Patients in Vulnerable Groups," *Journal of Medical Ethics* (Vol. 33, 2007).

- Californians Against Assisted Suicide, *Points to Remember: Opposition to Bill AB 374* (2007).

- Jean-Jacques Georges et al., "Physicians' Opinions on Palliative Care and Euthanasia in The Netherlands," *Journal of Palliative Medicine* (Vol. 9, 2006).

- Amicus brief of AUTONOMY, Inc., et al. to U.S. Supreme Court. Filed in *Gonzales v. Oregon* (2005).

- Roger S. Magnusson, "Underground Euthanasia and the Harm Minimization Debate," *Journal of Law, Medicine, and Ethics*, (Vol. 32, 2004).

- N. Swarte et al., "Effects of Euthanasia on Bereaved Family and Friends: A Cross-Sectional Study," *British Medical Journal* (Vol. 327, 2003).

- Barry Corbet, "Physician-Assisted Death: Are We Asking the Right Questions?," *New Mobility* (May, 2003).

- Wesley J. Smith, "A 'Doctor Death' Runs for President," *National Review Online*, September 4, 2003.

- R. Steinbrook, "Physician-Assisted Suicide in Oregon: An Uncertain Future," *New England Journal of Medicine* (Vol. 346, 2002).

- David J. Mayo and Martin Gunderson, "Vitalism Revitalized: Vulnerable Populations, Prejudice, and Physician-Assisted Death," *Hastings Center Report* (2002).

- Willard Gaylin et al., "Doctors Must Not Kill," *JAMA* (Vol. 259, 1998).

- John Hardwig, "Is There a Duty to Die?," *Hastings Center Report* (Spring, 1997).

- U.S. Supreme Court, *Washington v. Gluksberg* (1997).

- Herbert Hendin, *Seduced By Death: Doctors, Patients, and the Dutch Cure* (Norton, 1997).

- B. Corbet, "Assisted Suicide: Death Do Us Part," *New Mobility* (Vol. 8, 1997).

- D. Callahan, "Controlling the Costs of Health Care for the Elderly: Fair Means Foul," *New England Journal of Medicine* (Vol. 333, 1996).

- Amicus brief of Not Dead Yet et al. to U.S. Supreme Court. Filed in *Washington v. Glucksberg* (1996).

- Stephen Jamison, "When Drugs Fail: Assisted Deaths and Not-So-Lethal Drugs," *Pharmaceutical Care in Pain & Symptom Control* (Vol. 4, 1996).

- Margaret A. Somerville, "Death Talk in Canada: The Rodriguez Case," *McGill Law Journal* (Vol. 39, 1994).

- House of Lords, *Report of the Select Committee on Medical Ehtics* (Vol.1, 1994).

- Ronald Dworkin, "Life Is Sacred. That's the Easy Part," *New York Times Magazine*, May 16, 1993.

- K. Pugh et al., "Suicide and HIV Disease," *AIDS Care* (Vol. 5, 1993).

- Dan. W. Brock, "Euthanasia," *The Yale Journal of Biology and Medicine* (Vol. 65, 1992).

- Nat Hentoff, "The Slippery Slope of Euthanasia," *Washington Post*, October 3, 1992.

- Leon Kass, "Neither for Love nor Money: Why Doctors Must Not Kill," *National Affairs* (No. 94, 1989).

- Kenneth L. Vaux, "Debbie's Dying: Mercy Killing and the Good Death," *JAMA* (Vol. 259, 1988).

- Yale Kamisar, "Some Non-Religious Views Against Proposed Mercy Killing Legislation," *Minnesota Law Review* (Vol. 42, 1958).

Euthanasia: Websites

- ERGO (www.finalexit.org).
- Death with Dignity (www.deathwithdignity.org/).
- Dignity in Dying, United Kingdom (www.dignityindying.org.uk).
- Not Dead Yet (www.notdeadyet.org).
- The World Federation of Right to Die Societies (www.worldrtd.net).
- Dignitas Switzerland (www.dignitas.ch).
- Dying with Dignity Canada (www.dyingwithdignity.ca).
- Right to Die Society of Canada (www.righttodie.ca).
- AQDMD Quebec (www.aqdmd.qc.ca).
- ADMD France (www.admd.net).
- Anti-euthanasia coalition (http://www.religioustolerance.org/euthca5.htm).
- *Death with Dignity* book (http://www.DeathwithDignityBook.com).

End-of-Life: Books

- Robert Orfali, *Grieving a Soulmate: The Love Story Behind "Till Death Do Us Part"* (Mill City Press, 2011).

- Lewis Cohen, *No Good Deed: A Story of Medicine, Murder Accusations, and the Debate over How We Die* (Harper, 2010).
- Stephen P. Kiernan, *Last Rights: Rescuing the End of Life System From the Medical System* (St. Martin's Press, 2007).
- David Feldman and Andrew Lasher, *The End-of-Life Handbook* (New Harbinger, 2007).
- David Kessler, *The Needs of the Dying* (Harper, 2007).
- William H. Colby, *Unplugged: Reclaiming Our Right to Die in America* (Amacom, 2006).
- Virginia Morris, *Talking About Death* (Algonquin Books, 2004).
- Timothy Quill, *Caring for Patients at the End of Life* (Oxford University Press, 2001).
- George D. Lundberg, *Severed Trust: Why American Medicine Hasn't Been Fixed* (Basic Books, 2000).
- Joanne Lynn and Joan Harrold, *Handbook for Mortals* (Oxford University Press, 1999).
- Marilyn Webb, *The Good Death* (Bantam Books, 1997).
- Sherwin Nuland, *How We Die* (Vintage Books, 1995).
- Susan Sontag, *Illness as Metaphor* (Picador Press, 1978).
- Elizabeth Kübler-Ross, *On Death and Dying* (MacMillan, 1969).
- Ernest Becker, *The Denial of Death* (Free Press, 1973).

End-of-Life: Articles

- Atul Gawande, "Letting Go: What Should Medicine Do When It Can't Save Your Life?," *The New Yorker*, August 2, 2010.
- Timothy W. Kirk et al., "NHPCO Position Statement and Commentary on the Use of Palliative Sedation in Imminently Dying Terminally Ill Patients," *Journal of Pain and Symptom Management* (May, 2010).

- Jennifer S. Temel et al., "Early Palliative Care for Patients with Metastatic Non–Small-Cell Lung Cancer," *New England Journal of Medicine* (Vol. 363, 2010).

- Amy S. Kelley, et al., "Palliative Care—A Shifting Paradigm," *New England Journal of Medicine* (Vol. 363, 2010).

- Social Security and Medicare Board of Trustees, *Status of the Social Security and Medicare Programs* (2010).

- Charles Stanley, "Do No Harm: Catholic Clergy, Hospitals Torn Over New Church Directives," *The SundayPaper,* December 20, 2009.

- National Hospice and Palliative Care Organization, *Facts and Figures: Hospice Care in America* (October, 2009).

- Mellar P. Davis, "Does Palliative Sedation Always Relieve Symptoms?," *Journal of Palliative Medicine* (October, 2009).

- Anemona Hartocollis, "At the End, Offering Not a Cure but Comfort," *New York Times*, August 20, 2009.

- Suresh K. Reddy et al., "Characteristics and Correlates of Dyspnea in Patients with Advanced Cancer," *Journal of Palliative Medicine* (Vol. 12, 2009).

- Peter Singer, "Why We Must Ration Health Care," *New York Times*, July 15, 2009.

- Goldsmith et al. "Variability in Access to Hospital Palliative Care in the United States," *Journal of Palliative Medicine* (Vol. 11, 2008).

- S. Connor et al., "Comparing Hospice and Non-Hospice Patient Survival," *Journal of Pain Symptom Management* (Vol. 33, 2007).

- J. Dasta et al., "Daily Cost of an Intensive Care Unit Day: The Contribution of Mechanical Ventilation," *Critical Care Medicine* (Vol. 33, 2005).

- U. Hobohm, "Fever Therapy Revisited," *British Journal of Cancer* (Vol. 92, 2005).

- D. C. Angus et al., "Use of Intensive Care at the End of Life in the United States: An Epidemiologic Study," *Critical Care Medicine* (Vol. 32, 2004).

- P. Miller et al., "End-of-Life Caring in Intensive Care Unit: A Challenge for Nurses," *American Journal of Critical Care* (Vol. 10, 2001).

- G. M. Rocker et al., "End-of-life issues in the ICU: A Need for Acute Palliative Care," *Journal of Palliative Care Supplement* (October, 2000).

- The SUPPORT principal investigators, "A controlled trial to improve care for seriously ill hospitalized patients: the Study to Understand Prognoses and Preferences for Outcomes and Risks of Treatments (SUPPORT)," *JAMA* (Vol. 274, 1995).

- Vittorio Ventafridda et al., "Symptom Preference and Control During Cancer Patients' Last Days of Life," *Journal of Palliative Care* (Vol. 6, 1990).

End-of-Life: Websites

- Compassion & Choices (www.compassionandchoices.org).

- Hospice Patients Alliance (www.hospicepatients.org).

- The National Hospice and Palliative Care Organization (www.careinfo.org and www.nhpco.org).

- Hospice Net (www.hospicenet.org).

- Hospice Foundation of America (www.hospicefoundation.org).

- Growth House End-of-Life Planning (www.growthhouse.org).

- AARP Grief and Loss Program (http://www.aarp.org/family/caregiving/).

- National Alliance for Caregiving (www.caregiving.org).

- PalliativeDoctors (www.palliativedoctors.org).

- GriefNet Internet Support Group (www.griefnet.org).

Find Out More

- *How to Die in Oregon* movie (www.imdb.com/title/tt1715802/).
- Jeri's memorial website (www.JeriOrfali.com).
- *Grieving a Soulmate* book (www.GrievingaSoulmate.com).

Acknowledgments

It takes a village to create a great book and multiple e-books. Luckily, I was able to enlist a small support group of friends who read the manuscript and helped channel my thinking. It's hard to remain coherent when writing about death. My support group kept me on track by providing constant and helpful feedback. My professional editors, on the other hand, provided the less gentle feedback; they made sure the book was perfect.

I want to thank my friends who read the manuscript from cover to cover and commented on the chapters. They include Ronald H., Norah T., Brian H., Kathy H., Maureen D., Mike M., Deborah S., Mitch B., Dan H., and Denise G. I was very lucky to have your comments and suggestions.

I thank my three professional editors for improving the manuscript and making it flawless. Thank you Norah Thomas (editor-in-chief), Nadine Newlight, and Kimberly Fujioka. I thank the good people at Mill City Press for producing a superb book and then publishing it. I thank the folks at Publish Green for exquisitely handcrafting and customizing each e-book to take full advantage of the unique features of iPad, Kindle, iPhone, Sony, Nook, Palm, Nokia, Android, and many more. I was lucky to work with all of you.

Finally, I want to thank Jeri, my soulmate and late coauthor, for being a constant source of inspiration and support. As always, Jeri kept me honest at all times. In a sense this makes her the coauthor of this book, in absentia. Our latest collaborative effort is a concrete demonstration of the power of *continuing bonds* which I described in *Grieving a Soulmate*. Jeri taught me about the right to die in dignity. In addition, I was inspired by the heroic end-of-life struggle of two very brave women: Sue Rodriguez of Canada, and Angelique Flowers of Australia.

CPSIA information can be obtained at www.ICGtesting.com
Printed in the USA
LVOW071726130412

277542LV00003B/25/P